AT WAR WITH CHINA?

AT WAR WITH CHINA?

WASHINGTON'S PUSH FOR
A U.S.-CHINA COLD WAR

Wouter Hoenderdaal

Algora Publishing
New York

Library of Congress Cataloging-in-Publication Data

Names: Hoenderdaal, Wouter, 1985- author.
Title: At war with China? : Washington's push for a U.S.-China Cold War /
    Wouter Hoenderdaal.
Description: New York : Algora Publishing, 2023. | Includes bibliographical
    references. | Summary: "Rising tension between the United
    States and China is leading in a dangerous direction towards escalation
    and conflict. Yet the fact that Western leaders are largely responsible
    for this new Cold War is ignored by the mainstream. This book, a
    critique of Western policies, shows exactly how Western actions are
    adding fuel to the fire"— Provided by publisher.
Identifiers: LCCN 2023026196 (print) | LCCN 2023026197 (ebook) | ISBN
    9781628945157 (trade paperback) | ISBN 9781628945164 (hardcover) | ISBN
    9781628945171 (pdf)
Subjects: LCSH: United States—Foreign relations—China. | China—Foreign
    relations—United States.
Classification: LCC E183.8.C6 H646 2023 (print) | LCC E183.8.C6 (ebook) |
    DDC 327.51073—dc23/eng/20230707
LC record available at https://lccn.loc.gov/2023026196
LC ebook record available at https://lccn.loc.gov/2023026197

Printed in the United States

For Yue and Lieke

TABLE OF CONTENTS

INTRODUCTION

Underneath a scorching sun, three hundred Chinese soldiers stand at attention. With their chins up and backs straight, they have already conquered the African desert heat. Despite having just set foot in unfamiliar territory thousands of miles away from home, these men and women from the People's Liberation Army and Navy are not afraid. On the contrary, they look confident, determined, and eager to carry out their mission.

A few meters in front of them, in the middle of the square, two flagpoles rise. One flies the familiar Five-Star Red Flag of the People's Republic of China, the other the light-blue and light-green colors of Djibouti — a small West African country located next to one of the world's most important shipping lanes. An impressive display of a dozen modern armored fighting vehicles completes the opening ceremony of China's first foreign military base. Its mission? To protect Chinese overseas political and business interests, and, perhaps, to expand them too.[1]

Located only twelve miles away sits Camp Lemonnier, a United States military base. It is home to the Combined Joint Task Force Horn of Africa of the U.S. Africa Command. From Lemonnier, U.S. bombers, fighter planes, and special forces took off to attack Iraq in 2003. Nowadays, however, American soldiers stationed at the base are less concerned with fighting the war on terror. Instead, they look at their Chinese neighbors and wonder for how long they will remain at peace.

You can find this uneasy relationship in many other places. The vast tropical waters of the Pacific Ocean also hide a darkening and dangerous standoff between the world's two superpowers. Beijing is busy militarizing

---

[1] Wang Xuejing. China's first overseas military base opens in Djibouti. CGTN. August 1, 2017. See https://news.cgtn.com/news/3d6b7a4e3241544e/share_p.html

islands in the South China Sea to expand its influence. The Chinese government is also eyeing Taiwan, and for years has been practicing all kinds of military maneuvers, including all-out invasions, to bring the island under its control.

But in these same waters and the airspace above them, the United States Navy and Air Force are practicing too. These forces operate from the hundreds of U.S. military bases located in the Indo–Pacific theater, stretching from South Korea and Japan in the north all the way down to the Philippines, Australia, Singapore, Thailand, and many other places. U.S. officials like to refer to this military system as a "noose," which they are tying around China's neck.

What all this military hardware is supposed to achieve is to "contain" China, which means keeping the country isolated, vulnerable, and at the mercy of Washington. In military exercises that leave no room for doubt, the U.S. is practicing cutting off China's economic lifelines, setting up military "island chains" to box China in, and testing how to best intimidate Beijing into submission.

Yet the superpower confrontation does not limit itself to these flash points in East Asia. China's Belt and Road Initiative has moved Chinese businesses and investments to Central Asia, the Middle East, Africa, and beyond. Following in their wake are Chinese security forces tasked to protect these interests. Indeed, what the presence of the People's Liberation Army in Djibouti illustrates, is that China is going global. In the process, the Chinese government is ending the so-called unipolar world order characterized by the overwhelming dominance of the United States of America.

It comes as no surprise that U.S. officials in Washington are not taking this very well. In fact, they are terribly angry. In response, they are planning how to effectively undermine or even roll back China's global economic and military rise. Hybrid War, Western-backed Color Revolutions, and covert CIA operations are among the methods they will bring to bear. Their effect? The overthrow of governments, civil wars, and devastating Vietnam and Ukraine-style military conflicts raging all around the Global South with the United States and China backing opposite sides in an endless competition over resources, markets, and strategic locations.

Meanwhile, back in the offices of the U.S. Treasury and China's Ministry of Finance, elegantly dressed gentlemen wearing black and white suits are sharpening their financial blades. They are laying the groundwork for an economic war that will dwarf anything the world has ever seen.

U.S. officials do not shy away from saying exactly what they want to achieve. They would like to starve the Chinese economy of vital components and resources, such as oil, metals, semiconductors, and other advanced technology. They wish to bankrupt important Chinese corporations like Huawei and ZTE and do the same to any other organization that might replace them. Meanwhile, Chinese officials are thinking about how to retaliate. They know that their country is an important producer of machinery, electronics, medicine, medical equipment, and other vital supplies. As such, they realize they have a strong hand to play in case relations turn sour and conflict begins. Although both sides understand that an economic war can easily escalate into full-blown military conflict, they show no signs of backing down.

Finally, the emerging U.S.–China Cold War will not only be waged militarily, economically, and technologically. The entire conflict will be shrouded in intense information warfare. In fact, the information war has already begun. It has become routine for the New York Times, Washington Post, BCC, CNN, and others to portray China as aggressive, expansionist, and a threat to the West and the Western way of life. In this one-sided presentation, it is democracy versus dictatorship, freedom versus authoritarianism, good versus evil. Indeed, the Western media are already preparing their people for war.

Beijing too has directed its media organizations to spread a similar message, only with the roles reversed. In their one-sided take on events, the Chinese are the good guys, and the U.S. government is the bad actor. China is trying to create a fair and just world order, one that does not only benefit Western countries, whose history remains tainted by colonization and military aggression that has harmed so many nations all around the world, including China itself.

As always, the goal of this information war is to mask and justify a ruthless geopolitical game played by both sides. Consequently, this makes it very hard to understand who is doing what and for which reasons. Yet if we want to prevent another Cold War, we must know exactly what our leaders are doing, and how their policies are pushing us ever closer towards escalation and war. If we allow them to continue playing their geopolitical games, given the many different places where the United States and China can come to blows, conflict seems very likely. It may indeed be only a matter of time.

The Abysmal State of Western Diplomacy and Foreign Policy

With war looming on the horizon, what we need now more than ever are competent diplomats who are dedicated to avoiding World War III.

Unfortunately, in leading Western capitals such as Washington, London, and Brussels, rational and responsible diplomacy is nowhere to be found. Indeed, the caliber of Western politicians and diplomats has never been this poor. In fact, as is recognized throughout the non-Western world, American and European leaders are arrogant, aggressive, and out of touch with reality.

For many decades, Western diplomats traveled the world lecturing foreign leaders on how they should run their countries. Without any sense of hypocrisy, the former colonial powers felt it was upon them to impose on the rest of the world the Western view on economic development, political institutions, and human rights. Hundreds of years of colonial domination has given Western governments the idea that they not only own the world but that they are entitled to it. In their minds, Western dominance is simply the natural order of things.

They felt further emboldened and justified in their beliefs when the Soviet Union — the West's main challenger — collapsed and the West won the Cold War. Today's Western diplomats including the U.S. Secretary of State Anthony Blinken lived through that period, and it took their belief in Western superiority to religious levels, if it wasn't there already.

This then had a profound effect on Western diplomacy. In fact, it has come to the point where people like Blinken, the top U.S. diplomat, don't do diplomacy. They never try to understand the other side or listen to their concerns. Instead, Western leaders and diplomats simply dictate terms — they tell foreign leaders what to do, and they expect to be obeyed. And when a foreign government is not subordinate and obedient enough, U.S. and other Western leaders use intimidation, threats, and further escalation to get their way. This is, in fact, the only trick they know. More pressure, more sanctions, and more regime change, until the other side submits or gets crushed.

Meanwhile, with the United States and its European allies having been the world's sole dominant power until only very recently, few skilled diplomats staff Western governments. Without a challenger for several decades, there was no need to reward competence. Instead, mediocre officials who happened to have the right political connections dominate the ministries and other government agencies. They climbed the ranks by saying what their bosses wanted to hear. Although they religiously believe in their own superiority and infallibility, they lack vision, courage, and elementary morality. Above all else, they are amateurs clinging on to irrational and outdated doctrines while sitting on top of the world's most powerful and deadly militaries. All in all, the current generation of Western leaders is utterly unprepared and incapable for today's world — a world in which the West, with the United States in the lead, is no longer the only game in town.

Towards a New Cold War

With the rise of China, accompanied by a whole range of projects and institutions like BRICS and the Belt and Road Initiative, we have arrived in a multipolar world. China has become a superpower too, one that, most importantly, has its own independent foreign policy. What this means is that Western diplomacy and foreign policy should adapt to this new reality. Refusal to do so is misguided and dangerous, probably catastrophic. Yet this is exactly what is happening.

Confronted with another superpower, U.S. and other Western leaders feel frustrated and angry. How dare China challenge Western dominance? How dare the Chinese come up with their own economic model, how dare they set up financial institutions alternative to those of the West, and how dare they follow a foreign policy independent of Western interests? Why don't the Chinese simply accept their subordinate place in a U.S.-dominated world system?

With emotions slipping out of control, U.S. leaders have decided to deny China its place in the world. Washington, like a spoiled child who no longer can get everything his way, has resorted to what it does best, namely threats, intimidation, and escalation. Again, this is the only thing Western officials know how to do. They are unwilling and incapable of negotiating a peaceful coexistence. In fact, they say so straight out. "There is no real prospect of building fundamental trust, 'peaceful coexistence', 'mutual understanding', a strategic partnership, or a 'new type of major country relations' between the United States and China," concludes an important U.S. document from Washington's most important think tank, the Council on Foreign Relations. Although building trust, peace, and understanding should be the hallmark of diplomacy, the West wants nothing to do with it. "Intense U.S.-China strategic competition becomes the new normal," the document continues, and that will be the sole aim of U.S. 'diplomacy'.[2]

China, however, is not a small and much weaker nation that can be bullied into submission. As such, the result of Western policies has been disastrous because it has moved the world to the brink of war.

To more fully understand how utterly amateurish, irrational, and dangerous the state of Western diplomacy and foreign policy is, let's look at one of the most important developments of the past decade: the emerging China–Russia alliance. It is a perfect example to showcase how ill-suited Western leaders are for dealing with today's reality, and how their aggressive and misguided policies are setting us up for the next World War.

---

[2] Blackwill, R. D. & Tellis, A. J. *Revising U.S. Grand Strategy Toward China.* Council on Foreign Relations, Council Special Report No. 72. March 2015.

The possibility of a China–Russia alliance has been a long-time concern for Washington, because it seriously challenges and jeopardizes U.S. global dominance. But U.S. strategists like Zbigniew Brzezinski, who wrote the book on how Washington should play the geopolitical chess game, concluded that only U.S. hostility towards both countries could drive the two together. This, he wrote, should be avoided at all times. Interestingly, Brzezinski, who waged the Cold War against the Soviet Union throughout the 1960s and 1970s, believed future U.S. diplomats would not be so "shortsighted" as to mess this up. In this, as in many other things, he was wrong.

The main achievement of U.S. diplomacy in the past decade has been to unite China and Russia against their common enemy — the United States. It is the outcome of Washington threatening Moscow and Beijing with military force and regime change together with the West waging economic warfare and information warfare against both countries.

Furthermore, U.S. leaders have never bothered listening to the concerns and wishes of the Chinese and Russian governments who were, in fact, open to amicable relations with the West. Instead, in their meetings, U.S. leaders simply dictated demands and lectured their Chinese and Russian counterparts on how to be obedient and subordinate players in a U.S.-dominated world system.

Then, when Western governments realized that China and Russia were moving closer to each other, they did not draw the obvious conclusion that it was their own anti-China and anti-Russia policies that drove these two together.

Consequently, they committed themselves to a disastrous attempt to break up the developing alliance. Instead of trying to change their approach, for example by making friends with one of the two in order to drive a wedge between them, U.S. leaders simply told the Chinese and the Russians that the U.S. government does not approve of their alliance and that, consequently, it needs to be broken up. It's the Emperor telling its subjects what to do. In the process, U.S. diplomats also insulted their Chinese and Russian colleagues, and threatened both countries with more economic warfare and more regime change.

Then, when that only strengthened China–Russia relations — who would have thought? — Washington, in an ultimate attempt, decided to use the conflict over Ukraine to wage a full-blown economic and military war against the weaker party of the two, namely Russia. They hope to overthrow the Russian government, replace it with a pro-Western one, and then use a Western-controlled Russia to combat China. To the amateurs in charge of Western foreign policy, who fancy themselves in thinking they are masters in four-dimensional geopolitical chess, this seemed like a brilliant move. But to anyone who possesses a shred of common sense, it is insane. It means a nuclear superpower waging war against another nuclear superpower with the expectation that victory would allow it to wage war against yet another nuclear superpower.

Naturally, the only thing this dangerous and misguided policy has achieved is a further deepening of China–Russia relations, together with a hostile and dangerous relationship between these two superpowers and the United States.

The Western war against Russia has also failed in every respect. Contrary to the expectation of the amateurs in charge of Western foreign policy, the Russian economy did not collapse. Instead, the economic sanctions backfired and are harming the Western countries themselves. Russia is also not isolated internationally. It shocked Western leaders that the non-western world did not obey orders coming from Washington and Brussels to break off relations with Russia. They failed to grasp that the world has become multipolar and that other nations now have a choice whether to align with one or the other side or to remain neutral. Finally, all the Western 'wonder weapons', from Javelin anti-tank missiles to Leopard 2 tanks, have not defeated the Russian army. Amazingly, however, despite all these failures, Western leaders continue with these policies and block all attempts at negotiating an end to the war.

The above examples also illustrate a fundamental flaw in Western diplomacy. When something does not work, Western diplomats do not change their behavior or adjust their way of thinking. They simply conclude they have to do more of the same. Consequently, they double down and triple down on the same misguided policies. They come up with more threats, more economic sanctions, and more military escalation in the hopes that that will do it. In other words, Western leaders show an inability to learn and adapt. Instead, they can only escalate.

Meanwhile, trust between the U.S. and Chinese government is at an all-time low. In their meetings, U.S. leaders, besides lecturing their Chinese counterparts, also made all kinds of lofty promises. At the G20 summit in Bali in December 2022 in a private meeting, Biden told Xi Jinping to his face that the U.S. government wants to avoid a conflict with China, that they respect the one-China policy regarding Taiwan, and that they do not intend to prevent China's economic development. Xi, who already did not trust Biden, responded by saying that although these words sound promising, they must be met with action, otherwise these are just empty words and false promises. Biden reassured Xi that he meant what he said. Then, in the following months, Biden announced that the U.S. government would send weapons and military advisors to Taiwan, open four military bases in the Philippines that are aimed at China, and impose more economic sanctions intended to harm China's economic development and bankrupt its technology sector.

This was not an isolated incident. In fact, it is the pattern of Western diplomacy. They believe they can get away with anything and that, unlike everyone else, they do not have to keep their word. In the minds of Western leaders, rules do not apply to those who own the world. It reflects the prevailing mindset: "You are going to do whatever we say, and we do whatever we want."

It is this combination of arrogance, a loss of touch with reality, a fanatical compulsion to escalate, and anger and frustration towards the rise of a non-Western superpower that makes Western policy towards China so dangerous. And the fact that the people in charge in the White House, the State Department, and the Pentagon control the largest military in the world makes it extremely concerning.

We need people in the West to wake up. Although our media obediently echoes the anti-China statements coming from Western governments, our own governments in the West are the problem. Behind elegant suits, practiced speeches, and catchy slogans lies a class of irrational, irresponsible, and dangerous leaders who are completely incapable of navigating us through these dangerous times. In fact, the only thing they do is move us closer towards war. It is our responsibility to stop them before it is too late.

Taking Responsibility

A search on Amazon or a look in your local bookstore will show you that there are many books written about the U.S.–China rivalry. Yet these tend to ignore the most vital point. What Western authors like to do is to describe in detail what China is up to, why that is threatening to the West, and what Western governments, with the United States in the lead, should do about it. As such, the focus is on Chinese aggression and expansion, and on Beijing's authoritarian style of government and its alleged human rights abuses. But what these authors do not tell you is how Western actions are increasing the likelihood of a new Cold War. Yes, Western governments can be aggressive too. Their policies can be misguided and dangerous. They too are responsible for major crimes. But why is this often ignored? Why don't we discuss these things thoroughly?

The answer is actually quite simple. Psychologists call it the in-group-out-group bias. It means that we favor our own group and show a tendency to dislike others. The sociologist William Sumner provided an excellent description when he wrote how "each group nourishes its own pride and vanity, boasts itself superior, exists in its own divinities, and looks with contempt on outsiders." What this means in practice is that you are not supposed to criticize the group you belong to. As in sports, you are indeed supposed to cheer on the home team. If you do not, you are quickly making yourself unpopular. You may even be expelled from the group as a result. Criticizing the other team, group, or country, however, especially when it is a rival, is very much appreciated and will earn you much praise and respect. Politicians are experts in playing this game, even if it is only to hide their own mistakes and shortcomings. But you find this in-group-out-group bias everywhere, including in the media and in the way history is written. Interestingly, there is another side to this phenomenon as well, which reveals something particularly important.[3]

If you are an American or European, you are trained to admire those people in China, Russia, and other Western rival nations who protest against their government and point out the things that are wrong in their own societies. We consider these so-called dissenters to be brave, honorable, and deserving of our respect and support. We may even give them a Nobel peace prize. Yet when Americans or Europeans strongly criticize Western policies, they are not treated in this same way. On the contrary, they tend to be smeared, vilified, and labeled as anti-American and anti-Western. They may even be labeled as Chinese or Russian agents. It is fascinating to see how we understand the value of criticism when it is directed at others, while at the same time, we have elaborate defense mechanisms to crush all criticism aimed towards ourselves.

So, what this means is that Western authors tend to cheer on the West, boast about their own country's superiority, and focus all their criticism on the Chinese. But why should we care about this? Why spoil these very self-serving stories with self-criticism?

As every professional athlete will tell you, the answer is that if you want to improve, you must be able to look at yourself in the mirror and search for mistakes and other shortcomings. That is what elite level athletes do every single day. They may even hire professional coaches and trainers to help them identify what they are doing wrong. Unfortunately, in the realm of politics, this critical approach to oneself is rarely taken. Politicians tend to confuse opportunities to learn with perceived weakness. That is one of the

---

[3] Sumner, W. G. (2014). *Folkways: a study of the sociological importance of usages, manners, customs, mores, and morals*. CreateSpace Independent Publishing Platform, p. 13.

reasons why history tends to repeat itself. We fail to learn. Yet if we wish to prevent an escalating U.S.–China conflict, we should do exactly this.

There are many policies pursued by Western leaders that are increasing the likelihood of war. And it does not need to be this way. The easiest way to think about this is the following: imagine a politician sitting at his desk in his office in the U.S. State Department or the Pentagon. Leaning backward a little bit in a comfortable chair, he stares intently at a large map hanging on the wall. On the map, which displays the entire globe, colors separate the world into different camps. The United States and its allies are blue, and China and its allies are red. Like a strategy game, the task is simple: turn as much of the world blue and remove everything red. Shifting his gaze away from the map and to the papers on his desk, the politician goes to work, day in and day out, to make it so. While papers are being drafted and circulated inside U.S. bureaucracies, orders reach carrier strike groups operating in the Indo–Pacific to begin their naval maneuvers. Fighter squadrons are moved into position, and U.S. marines load their guns. Financial experts start imposing strangulating economic sanctions, and the Western media beat the drums of war. Meanwhile, the population is supposed to cheer all of this on, support the war effort, and eagerly join the fight. What we are not supposed to do, however, is to ask critical questions that expose how our leaders and their dangerous and misguided policies are responsible for the emerging U.S.–China Cold War.

It is therefore crucial to critically examine our own actions. Let us, for a moment, leave criticizing the Chinese government up to the Chinese people. That is their responsibility, not ours. Instead, let us focus all our attention on what Western leaders are doing, and investigate whether and how these policies are increasing the likelihood of war. Let us be like elite athletes who want to improve themselves. If we do that, we may be able to avoid war. This then, is the ultimate goal of this book.

Content of this book

In the chapters that follow, the different types of conflict between the United States and China are discussed. This includes military conflict, covert (secret) operations, economic war, and information warfare. Actions from both sides are described, but with an emphasis on how Western acts will result in escalation and war, and how, in some cases, they already are.

But before getting into the action, chapter 1 lays out how we got there. It describes how, not that long ago, American expansion brought the U.S. military into the streets of Shanghai and Beijing. For over a hundred years,

China was weak and colonized by the Western powers. But, in a long and brutal struggle, the Chinese managed to win back their independence in 1949. They went on to prevent several attempts by Washington to overthrow their newly formed Communist government. And then, to make matters worse from a U.S. point of view, the Chinese set on a course of developing their economy and military power.

Today, China is getting closer and closer to catching up with, and even overtaking, the West. For U.S. and European leaders, who have been so used to dominating world affairs, this is a very bitter pill to swallow. In fact, they are unwilling to accept China's rise and intent to undo it. They prefer a China that is weak and vulnerable. Chinese leaders, however, want nothing more than to leave behind their country's history of humiliation and weakness. It is what drives them forward toward the great rejuvenation of the Chinese nation. As such, it becomes easy to understand why Western actions intended to undermine this effort are increasing the chances of escalation and war.

Chapter 2 focuses on the U.S. military approach towards China and Taiwan. An important theme is Washington's attempt to surround and "contain" China with hundreds of military bases. Confronted with all this military might, Beijing has responded with a military buildup of its own. It has led to a dangerous standoff between the two superpowers, one that can easily escalate. With both sides constantly crossing each other's red lines, war over Taiwan seems only a matter of time. But what will such a conflict look like? In what ways would Washington be responsible for this outcome? And what lessons can we learn from history, including the recent war in Ukraine, in our efforts to prevent it from happening?

Chapter 3 dives into the realm of economic and technological warfare. The South China Sea is at the center of China's trade, which is why Beijing is busy building up military installations on a series of artificially created islands. Meanwhile, American strategists are thinking of sending in the U.S. Navy to blockade key waterways to choke off China's economic lifelines. Back in Washington, U.S. economic and financial experts are designing a whole barrage of economic, financial, and technological sanctions to strangle the Chinese economy, bankrupt its businesses, and starve the country of key resources and technology. Interestingly, even U.S. officials are expecting that Beijing will consider these as acts of war, and that they may respond accordingly, setting into motion Pearl Harbor-like scenarios.

In Chapter 4, the global nature of the emerging U.S.–China Cold War is explored in detail. The United States is a global power with military bases and economic interests all around the world. China too, through its Belt and

Road Initiative, is sending its corporations and investments into Central Asia, the Middle East, Africa, and beyond. To safeguard these interests, the Chinese military is following in their footsteps. It has led to a global struggle for resources, markets, and strategic locations between the two super-powers—one that is only intensifying as both countries seek to gain the upper hand. As a result, in many countries in the Global South, the United States and China are hoping to install governments obedient and loyal to their cause and to overthrow those that oppose them. As in the U.S.–Soviet Cold War, the likely outcome will be brutal civil wars, covert (secret) regime change operations, and devastating Vietnam-like military conflicts with the U.S. and China supporting opposite sides.

Chapter 5 deals with the last dimension of the U.S.–China Cold War, which is information warfare. Both superpowers have elaborate media and information systems. Yes, they are different in character, one state-owned, the other private. Yet they both produce remarkably similar news. All of them tend to produce and spread information that supports their government's actions. In fact, Western news organizations have a long history of working together with their governments. In doing so, they have helped justify and support Western wars. But what would happen if you were to step outside of this media bubble? Would you see the world and the U.S.–China Cold War differently? And will it help you to understand what is really going on?

Finally, chapter 6 explains Washington's endgame. What do U.S. officials want from China? The answer is surprisingly simple. Beijing needs to subor-dinate itself to Washington, to follow its rules, and to obey its orders. In other words, Washington's endgame is a fantasy that can never be realized, which then makes it extremely dangerous. With U.S. officials angry and increasingly reckless and the Chinese being fed up with U.S. lies and aggres-sion, who is going to break us out of this escalation cycle?

Let us explore these important topics with an open mind, and with a desire for cooperation and peace instead of competition and war. Dangerous and misguided policies can be reversed, and conflict is not inevitable, but only if we decide to do the right thing. We owe it to ourselves, our children, and to those people all around the world who do not want to become a victim of yet another destructive and unnecessary Cold War.

Chapter 1: Towards a New Cold War

Kang Youwei breathed a sigh of relief. He had escaped, and just in time. His friends had not been so lucky. Most likely, the Empress Dowager had them executed by now. She was a vengeful woman. He had been so close, Kang thought, as he stared over the water towards the shore. So close to saving China from the foreign powers. If only the Empress had let him finish his lifelong work.[4]

Kang knew the enemies, these Westerners, that China was facing, and he knew them well. He had studied them for years and relentlessly read all the books he could find. He admired them greatly, Kang had to admit. The British steamship that was now bringing him to safety symbolized everything that Kang desired for his own country. The Western powers possessed sophisticated technology and powerful industry. Kang was convinced that China had to leave its outdated ways behind and modernize too. China must copy these Western technologies and make itself stronger if it wanted to survive. In an age of Western colonialism, there simply was no other way.

With his mind made up, Kang had set out and traveled all around the country, talking to hundreds of officials. Most had not been persuaded. In fact, some thought of him as insane. Thousands of years of tradition were hard to change. But Kang had not given up, and ultimately he found his way to the young Emperor, who had an open mind and was willing to listen. Unfortunately, his mother, the real power behind the throne, had found out. The modern Western ways threatened her position of power, she believed, and so she had put a stop to it. The emperor himself had been imprisoned.

---

[4] Hsu, I. C. Y. (2000). *The Rise of Modern China.* Oxford University Press, p. 360-380.

Kang, however, had fled Beijing before she could get to him. With Kang's failed attempt, any hopes of saving China were now lost.

The China that Kang grew up in was vastly different from what it used to be, and from what it is today. In the early 1900s, taking a walk through China's major cities would have been a strange experience. Take the city of Tianjin, for example. A prosperous trading city during the Ming period, and a multi-million metropolis today. But in Kang's days, a walk through the city would take you through a Japanese, a French, a British, and a German area, and then, after crossing the Hai River, you would walk into a Belgian neighborhood followed by a Russian, Italian and then an Austro-Hungarian district.

In Shanghai, the city to which Kang fled, you could see U.S. marines carrying their rifles parading through the streets, and a U.S. general inspecting his troops. Out in the harbor, foreign warships from Japan, France, Britain, Germany, and the United States were patrolling the waters.

Elsewhere, foreign gunships steamed up the Yangtze River. And in the skies above Beijing, U.S. Douglas military airplanes would fly over, occasionally dropping bombs. A sign outside the doors of public toilets in downtown Shanghai divided people not between men and women but "Gentlemen" and "Chinese." The Chinese refer to this period as the Century of Humiliation, the time when China was overrun and taken by foreign powers.[5]

Words cannot do justice to China's fall. For more than a thousand years, and probably much longer than that, China was the economic superpower of the world.

In this historical sense, China's status as the number one is the normal state of affairs. Like many other civilizations throughout history, the Chinese considered their country to be the center of the civilized world — the Middle Kingdom — to which all other nations should pay tribute. This feeling, China's long reign of economic dominance, a whole series of defeats by the Western powers, and the sight of foreign military forces patrolling its cities — it all is part of China's dramatic fall. How did it come to this?[6]

---

[5] Bickers, R. (2017). *Out of China.* Harvard University Press. p. 15-16; Clark G. B. (2001, p. 15-16). *Treading Softly: U.S. Marines in China, 1819-1949.* Praeger, see photos; Xiaoming, Z. *For China's Internal Stability: U.S. Arms Sales Policy, 1929-1936.* The Journal of American-East Asian Relations, Vol. 2, No. 3, p. 249; Tuchman, B. (2017). *Stilwell and the American Experience in China 1911-45.* Random House Trade Paperbacks, chapter 2; Bickers, R. (2012). *The Scramble for China.* Penguin Books, p. 22 ebook;

[6] Maddison, A. (2007). *Contours of the World Economy, 1-2030 AD.* Oxford University Press. See Statistical Appendix A, Table A.6. on p. 381

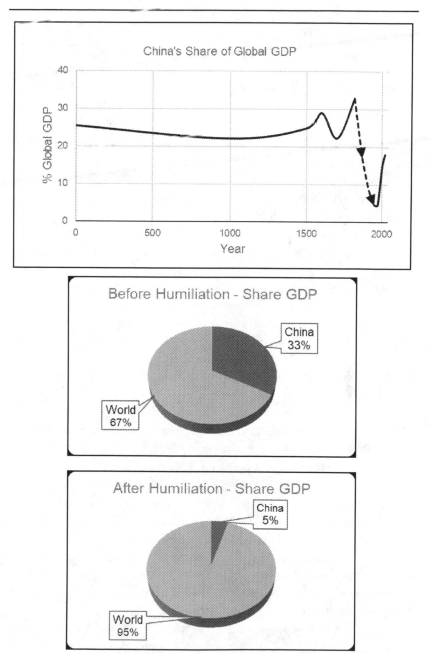

Fig. 1. China's share of global GDP before and after the Century of Humiliation. Data from Maddison, see Fn no. 3.

Manifest Destiny

Dreams of expansion and world domination go back to the beginnings of American history. Already in the early 1600s, British settlers, confined to the small settlement of Jamestown on the East Coast, decided to expand westward. From the mid-19th century, the American settlers were driven by Manifest Destiny — the belief that they were destined to spread out across North America. The Native Americans, who had lived there for centuries, simply had to make way.

Not only the belief in racial and religious superiority spurred the Americans forward. Geopolitical and economic considerations played a major part as well. The settlers knew that the southern states were perfectly suitable for the production of cotton. And control over cotton — the fuel of the Industrial Revolution — would give the United States more power "than millions of armed men," President John Tyler concluded. It "places all other nations at our feet." Before long, American armies started marching west.[7]

Tyler's successor, President James Polk, continued the conquest. He waged war with Mexico to capture the state of California. From its shores on the Pacific Ocean, restless Americans now looked past the horizon towards Asia, especially China, and wondered what treasures they might find there. Polk noted that access to the Pacific enabled the United States "to command the already valuable and rapidly increasing commerce of Asia." And then, Secretary of the Treasury Robert Walker added, they were destined to obtain "the command of the trade of the world." Soon after, American warships started crossing the Pacific Ocean to establish a foothold in Asia.[8]

A few years later in 1853, Commodore Perry sailed his U.S. Navy battleships into Tokyo Bay — violating Japan's customs in the process. After landing ashore, Japanese officials hurriedly came to meet him. Perry handed them a letter from the U.S. President to the Japanese Emperor. Its opening words "GREAT and Good Friend" puzzled the Japanese, since their Emperor and the U.S. President had never met. The letter's intimidating tone worried them, but they relaxed when Perry mentioned the gifts of friendship that he had brought with him. Perhaps all would still be well, the Japanese thought. This sense of relief did not last long.

Among the "tokens of our sincere and respectful friendship," there was a white flag. A curious gift that confused the Japanese. What did it mean, they

---

[7] Hietala, T. R. (1985). *Manifest Design: American Exceptionalism & Empire.* Cornell University Press, p. 68-70.

[8] Hietala, T. R. (1985). *Manifest Design: American Exceptionalism & Empire.* Cornell University Press, p. 87-89

asked Perry. With this white flag, the Commodore explained, you can signal your surrender after your army has been decisively defeated by ours. That is, if you decide to resist my President's demands. To leave no room for doubt, Perry's warships fired a salvo from its special Paixhans shell guns to demonstrate America's military superiority. Terrified of such force, the Japanese gave in. Perry acquired, among other things, U.S. access to Japanese coaling stations. He was preparing the Asian waters for American warships.[9]

Another convenient outpost in the Pacific was Hawaii. These islands were quickly colonized. When Queen Lili'uokalani attempted to resist, a group of U.S. businessmen, with the blessing of Washington, deposed her in 1895. It was the first government overthrown by the United States. Hawaii was officially annexed in 1898, after which it ended up as America's 50th state.[10]

That year, 1898, was momentous in the history of U.S. expansion. Not only did the Americans acquire Hawaii, but Manifest Destiny also led them to the Philippines. These islands gave the Americans a strategic outpost near China's markets, which they so much desired. To justify taking the Philippines from the Filipinos, the colonizers claimed that, just like the Native Americans, the Filipinos were not developed enough to govern themselves. "There was nothing left to do but take them all, and educate the Filipinos, and uplift and civilize them," U.S. President McKinley said. Unfortunately for McKinley, the Filipino population did not see it that way. But there were ways to make them understand how foolish they were to resist American destiny. "I am in my glory," an American soldier wrote in a letter to his parents, "when I can sight my gun on some dark skin and pull the trigger." All in all, at least 200,000 Filipino souls were uplifted — all the way up to heaven — until the island nation and its people were forced to accept U.S. rule.[11]

In 1898, the United States also occupied Cuba and Puerto Rico, followed by Nicaragua (1912), Haiti (1915), the Dominican Republic (1916), and again Cuba (1917). The United States Marine Corps has never been this busy planting the American flag on foreign lands.

From little Jamestown, the United States of America grew into a strong regional power with a firm foothold in East Asia. From there, Americans eyed the Chinese and their markets eagerly. Seeing such wealth and opportunity for profit, the next step for U.S. expansion was the Middle Kingdom itself.

---

[9] Feifer, G. (2006). *Breaking Open Japan*. HarperCollins Publishers, 128-131.

[10] Kinzer, S. (2006). *Overthrow*. Times Books, chapter 1.

[11] Brands, H. W. (1992). *Bound To Empire*. Oxford University Press, p. 25; Miller, S. C. (1982). *Benevolent Assimilation*. Yale University Press, p. 88-89.

From Middle Kingdom to Sliced Melon

China's status as the world's superpower ended abruptly following the arrival of the Western powers. Britain dealt the first major blow, but the United States did not stay far behind.

Two wars, known as the Opium Wars, marked the beginning of China's collapse in 1839. Britain, the military superpower of that time, launched a naval attack and invasion of China. Their motivation was economic gain. For many years, the British had been buying tea from China. Because the Chinese were not interested in any goods coming from Britain, the British paid for tea with gold and silver. In economic terms, this means Britain had a trade deficit with China. The dominant economic doctrine of the day, however, considered trade deficits a grave mistake and therefore unacceptable. Fortunately for the British, they eventually found a product that the Chinese would buy. Opium, a highly addictive and deadly drug (a narcotic), was in high demand. Probably the greatest international drug operation in history quickly took off, with the British government in the lead.

Opium plantations in India — a British colony — produced much of the drug, and specially designed ships transported it to China. Gold and silver now started flowing from China to Britain. The trade deficit was solved. But when the number of drug addicts started to reach dangerous levels, the Chinese government intervened. Special Commissioner Lin, a formidable bureaucrat whose statue today can be found in New York Chinatown, was sent to Canton. Making good use of his authority, he abolished the opium trade. The British were appalled. But they still had three options. They could give up the trade, start trading by Chinese rules, or use their military superiority to forcefully break open China. Naturally, they chose the latter option.

In a series of naval assaults and invasions, the British attacked major coastal cities until the Chinese were forced to accept British terms. More cities were opened to foreign trade and Hong Kong became British property. China also lost some of its economic and territorial independence, and it had to pay a huge fine to Britain. A second war ended in 1860, in which European forces attacked Beijing and burned down the Summer Palace, further opening up China to foreign trade. In this war, several hundred U.S. marines and two navy ships conquered four heavily fortified forts located along the Pearl River near Canton in Southern China, killing around 500 Chinese troops in the process. Overall, it was a great victory for the foreign powers. Opium had become the single most valuable commodity trade in the world. Interestingly, among those merchants who made fabulous profits, there were several noteworthy Americans.[12]

Warren Delano, Franklin Delano Roosevelt's grandfather, not only oversaw the first American incursion into China, but he was also one of the merchants who made huge profits from the illegal opium trade. Warren Delano worked his way up in Russell and Company, the biggest smuggling business of opium into China, until he became the company's senior partner in 1840 amid the First Opium War (1839–1842). As a U.S. consul, he cheered for the British as they forcefully opened China to foreign trade, and he welcomed the arrival of the first American warship to enforce U.S. interests.

The fortunes that Warren Delano and his contemporaries made from opium were invested in the United States — spurring its industrial and technological development. Ironically, given the harmful effects of opium on health, society, and economic development in China, much of the opium money was used to fund hospitals, special clinics, universities, and industry in the United States. Massachusetts General Hospital and Manhattan's hospital for special surgery, for example, were built with profits from opium. Opium money also funded universities such as Yale, Columbia, and Princeton, and aided in the construction of the textile manufacturing city of Lowell, Massachusetts, which played a key role in the industrial development of the United States. These were great times for American expansion. Unfortunately for China, however, the Opium Wars were the beginning. The Century of Humiliation had only just begun.[13]

After the second Opium War, China was forced to grant the foreign powers the right to establish permanent bases on Chinese soil. With so much money to be made, foreign merchants and investors were eager to stay. They built offices, warehouses, and infrastructure to facilitate trade. Then they added spacious compounds, gardens, churches, racetracks and fancy clubs — all for the Western gentlemen of course, not the Chinese.[14]

After the 1894–1895 Sino-Japanese war, in which the Japanese defeated the Chinese military, a 'scramble' for concessions took place. The foreign powers took this opportunity to completely redraw China's map by taking control of more territory. The Chinese were in no position to resist. In the language of Social Darwinism, China was among the dying nations on which

[12] Beeching, J. (1975). *The Chinese Opium Wars*; Waley, A. (1958). *The Opium Wars Through Chinese Eyes*. Stanford University Press; for U.S. military involvement see Clark G. B. (2001). *Treading Softly: U.S. Marines in China, 1819-1949*. Praeger, p. 7-10.
[13] Bradley, J. (2015). *The China Mirage*. Back Bay Books.
[14] Bickers, R. (2012). *The Scramble for China*. Penguin Books, p. 214-220 and 262 ebook.

the living Western countries were feeding. China's extinction, so British officials argued, was in the natural order of things.[15]

Important political thinkers like Kang Youwei understood this as well. Kang presented the Chinese Emperor with the example of 16th and 17th century Poland — one of the largest empires in Europe at that time. It ceased to exist after it was split into three parts by Russia, Austria, and Prussia. A powerful kingdom got carved up like a melon until there was nothing left. Many believed China was awaiting a similar fate. Some, like Kang, were insisting that China had to modernize following the Western example. Unfortunately for them, they ran into a political class that stubbornly held on to the traditional ways and blocked any other alternative. As times grew more desperate, others decided to start fighting back.[16]

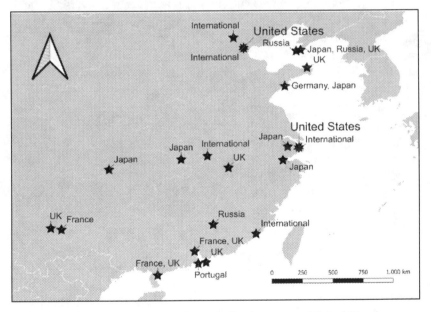

Fig. 2. China's concessions to the major foreign powers (United Kingdom, France, Japan, Russia, and the United States) during the Century of Humiliation. International means these were concessions to all or most of the foreign powers.

One major uprising and sign of resistance was the Boxer rebellion of 1900. It led to something remarkable. In the face of a horde of incredibly angry Chinese, all the foreign powers united in their counterattack. British marines, Japanese infantry, and German, Russian, French, Italian, American,

[15] Bickers, R. (2012). *The Scramble for China.* Penguin Books, p. 471 ebook.
[16] Bickers, R. (2012). *The Scramble for China.* Penguin Books, p. 472 ebook; Teng, S & Fairbank, J. K. (1979). *China's Response to the West.* Harvard University Press.

Belgian, Dutch, and Spanish troops, joined by colonial armies consisting of Sikhs, Bengalis, Black Americans, and Algerians, could be seen fighting side by side. A rare display of unity among nations that have a long history of hostility towards each other.

The United States Marine Corps was the first to arrive. Facing up to 50,000 Chinese protesters near Tientsin, they were joined by Russian forces. There, U.S. Marines and Russian soldiers fought side by side for hours. Chinese resistance had turned longstanding enemies into brothers in arms. An old black and white picture taken at the time tells the whole story. In it, officers from the United States, Britain, France, Italy, Germany, Russia, and Japan can be seen posing in front of the camera. Standing shoulder to shoulder and wearing crisp uniforms, they look strong and proud, although out of place in an ancient land far away from home.

But not everything was as it seems. The cooperation between the foreign powers was real, but it was also fragile and opportunistic. Together, they could take on China, and there was enough money to be made for everyone. Excessive greed, however, could spoil the whole thing. The fact that China did not suffer Poland's fate was because of concern among the foreign powers that if they acted too greedily, they might end up fighting each other. It was a precarious balance, one that ultimately saved China from total dismemberment. Nonetheless, when greed finally did prevail, war broke out. Events were heading to a climax.[17]

The final decades of the Century of Humiliation were even more destructive than the period before had been. Two things happened simultaneously. Japan began invading China. In a brutal war, Japanese forces started conquering more and more territory. Meanwhile, China itself was torn apart by a brutal civil war between two Chinese groups: the Nationalists and Communists. Washington, afraid of losing China, decided to throw its lot with the Nationalists. Together, they hoped to defeat Japan and simultaneously eliminate the communist threat. It was yet another example of the United States being on the wrong side of Chinese history.

Eager to boost the Nationalists' strength, up to thirty of its army divisions were armed and trained by the United States. Yet with all this military might, they were unable to defeat Japan and Mao's Communists. Although Washington could use the help, serious gestures by Mao to fight Japan together were ignored by the White House. In the minds of U.S. officials, suspicion and fear of anything remotely communist remained strong — the

---

[17] Bickers, R. (2012). *The Scramble for China*. Penguin Books, p. 474 ebook; Clark G. B. (2001). *Treading Softly: U.S. Marines in China, 1819-1949*. Praeger, p. 27-28 and 477; Langellier, J. (2009). *US Armed Forces in China 1856-1941*. Osprey Publishing, see the photo in the section "Garrisons, 1900-1941

product of decades of anti-communist hysteria following the Russian 1917 Revolution. It drove the Americans to yet another invasion of China.[18]

Following the surrender of Japan in 1945, within 48 hours Washington ordered the III Marine Amphibious Corps to land in China. With Japan's defeat, a power vacuum existed in China. The Nationalists and Communists were the only two powerful groups left to take advantage of this. Therefore, the goal of the Marines was to deny Mao's forces from gaining control over important cities and strategic locations formerly controlled by Japan. Washington also wanted to make sure the Japanese did not surrender to the communist forces, and in doing so hand them over their weapons. The U.S. Marines were to control northern China until the Nationalists were able to take over.[19]

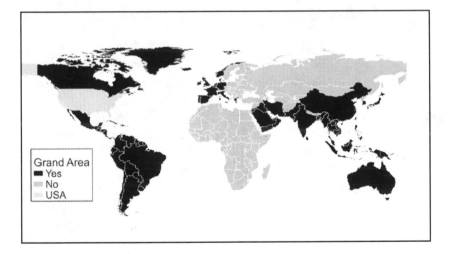

Fig. 3. Countries that made up the Grand Area. Reconstruction by the author.[20]

[18] Bernstein, R. (2014). *China 1945: Mao's Revolution and America's Fateful Choice.* Alfred A. Knopf; Tuchman, B. (2017). *Stilwell and the American Experience in China 1911-45.* Random House Trade Paperbacks

[19] Clark G. B. (2001). *Treading Softly: U.S. Marines in China, 1819-1949.* Praeger; Blum, W. (2004). Killing Hope. Zed Books. Chapter 1.

[20] The Grand Area has been determined by the author and is based on descriptions from Shoup & Minter (1977) and the author's interpretation of which countries (especially in Asia) should belong to the Grand Area. All Asian countries included are those that are either an important part of the British Empire or that have a history of U.S. involvement in the period 1940-1960. Africa is excluded due to George Kennan's statement on 'granting' Africa to Europe. For a description of the Grand Area, see: Shoup, L. H. & Minter, W. (1977). Imperial Brain Trust: The Council on Foreign Relations & United States Foreign Policy. Authors Choice Press.

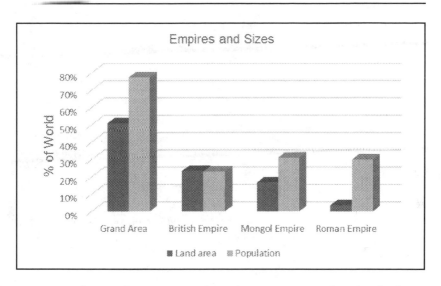

Fig. 4. The Grand Area compared to other major empires based on land area and population.[21]

To speed things up, the U.S. 14th Air Force flew the 92nd and 94th Nationalist armies from south and central China all the way to Beijing. U.S. General Albert Wedemeyer, in a letter to Dwight Eisenhower, described it as "the largest troop movement by air in the world's history." U.S. ships also transported the 13th Nationalist army to the northeast. In total this amounted to about 400,000 to 500,000 troops. Meanwhile, 50,000 U.S. Marines occupied important railways, coal stations, and supply trains to prevent them from falling into Communists hands. But despite its massive scale, the whole military operation failed. The Nationalists were corrupt and unpopular in the eyes of the Chinese people. In 1949, they were beaten by Mao's forces. With U.S. assistance, the Nationalists fled to Taiwan. By this time, the U.S. military forces had left China as well. Finally, the Chinese had shaken off domination by the foreign powers. Or so it seemed. Washington had big plans for China and was not yet ready to admit its loss.[22]

---

[21] Data on the British, Mongol, and Roman Empire come from Bang, P. F. et al. (2021). *The Oxford World History of Empire: Volume One The Imperial Experience.* Oxford University Press. See table 2.1 and 2.2; Population statistics come from United Nations Population Division. World Population Prospects: The 2010 Revision. POP/DB/WPP/Rev.2010/04/F01A. Retrieved 22-4-2022; Area sizes come from World Bank. Land area (sq. km). AG.LND.TOTL.K2. Accessed 22-4-2022.

[22] Clark G. B. (2001). *Treading Softly: U.S. Marines in China, 1819-1949.* Praeger; Bernstein, R. (2014). *China 1945: Mao's Revolution and America's Fateful Choice.* Alfred A. Knopf, p. 343 ebook for Wedemeyer's statement.

The Grand Area

In the fall of 1940, a secretive group of well-dressed gentlemen met in New York, Manhattan. They were all members of the Council on Foreign Relations — America's most influential think tank. Inside a six-story mansion, just one block away from Central Park, the Council worked out the details of the "Grand Area." This was a region in which the United States would hold "unquestioned power." It consisted of North and South America, East Asia, the Middle East, Western Europe, and much of the British Empire. While all eyes in the world were focused on Hitler's conquest of Europe, these men were preparing for the ultimate expansion. America was about to rule the world.[23]

Where do you begin if you want to understand power systems like the Grand Area? The best place to start is to identify the designers, because the system will be designed to benefit them. From there, it is not difficult to determine how the system works.

Another important rule is to pay only the slightest attention to what the designers are claiming the system is for. They will tell you that the system is to the benefit of all or the greater good. Sometimes, they even believe in that themselves. The human brain has all sorts of ways of twisting wrong into right and to defend the indefensible, as George Orwell famously stated. Therefore, before going into detail about what the Grand Area was, it is helpful to discuss briefly who its designers were. At the same time, it is best to put aside, for now, what politicians and others alike tend to say United States foreign policy is all about.[24]

The wealthy members of the Council on Foreign Relations — most of them coming from big business and elite universities — played a key role working on the Grand Area, but they did not do it alone. U.S. officials working in the State Department were also heavily involved. Together, they had regular meetings in which they planned and designed the post-WWII world order. One group in particular stood out.[25]

The Policy Planning Staff (PPS) of the State Department was created in 1947 to come up with analysis and long-term strategic planning. Its director, George F. Kennan, liked the Council's idea, and quickly started implementing it. The fact that the Grand Area was incredibly ambitious did not deter him, because who would be able to stop them? The United States had come out

---

[23] Shoup, L. H. & Minter, W. (1977). *Imperial Brain Trust: The Council on Foreign Relations & United States Foreign Policy.* Authors Choice Press; Wala, M. (1994). The Council on Foreign Relations and American Foreign Policy in the Early Cold War. Berghahn Books, chapter 1 and 2.

[24] George Orwell (1946). *Politics and the English Language.*

[25] Parmer, I. (2004). *Think Tanks and Power in Foreign Policy.* Palgrave Macmillan. Chapter 2.

of WWII as the most powerful nation on Earth by far. All its competitors such as Japan, Germany, Russia, France, and England, were either heavily damaged or destroyed. The United States also greatly outmatched the Soviet Union — its closest competitor — in industrial production, key strategic materials, and energy. Besides, Washington alone possessed the atomic bomb, the most powerful weapon ever created. As a result, with this much power and advantage, they went for nothing less than world domination.[26]

The Grand Area consisted of two parts. First, there were the economically lesser developed countries in Latin America, the Middle East, and Asia. Their "function," as George F. Kennan called it, was to provide raw materials and foodstuffs, and to be markets for the industrialized nations. To ordinary people, it may seem odd to talk about nations and entire peoples as having a function, but that is how the designers of great power systems think. Asia, in their eyes, was a "cheap source of vital raw materials," an "economic and strategic prize." The resources of Latin America were simply described by Kennan as "ours." Although these resources were located outside of the United States, they did, in fact, belong to the U.S. The oil reserves of the Middle East were regarded as "one of the greatest material prizes in world history," and, if under U.S. control, a "stupendous source of strategic power." For Africa, which was missing from the Grand Area, George F. Kennan had another function in mind.[27]

The continent was handed over to Europe. Africa's "exploitation" by the Europeans, Kennan wrote, something Europe already had experience with, would help pay for Europe's reconstruction. It would also give the ravaged and war-shaken European nations some much-needed confidence. The United States, for reasons soon to be discussed, wanted Europe to rebuild itself quickly. Africa's exploitation would do wonders in setting the Europeans on their way.[28]

---

[26] Kennan, G. PPS/23, February 24 1948; NSC 68: United States Objectives and Programs for National Security, April 7, 1950. See table 2; Maddison, A. (2007). *Contours of the World Economy, 1-2030 AD.* Oxford University Press. See Statistical Appendix A, Table A.6. on p. 381 for a current estimate of U.S. share of global GDP.

[27] On Asia, see Schaller, M. (1985). *The American Occupation of Japan: The Origins of The Cold War in Asia.* Oxford University Press, p. 78, 83, 88, 160; Shoup, L. H. & Minter, W. (1977). *Imperial Brain Trust: The Council on Foreign Relations & United States Foreign Policy.* Authors Choice Press, see p. 138-139 for the division between industrial areas and regions producing raw materials, 225 for Asia being a cheap source of raw materials, 227 for Asia being an economic and strategic prize; On the Middle East, see Miller, A. D. (1980). *Search for Security: Saudi Arabian Oil and American Foreign Policy, 1939-1949.* The University of North Carolina Press, see p. 144.

[28] Kennan, G. PPS/23, February 24 1948.

Inequality 1945

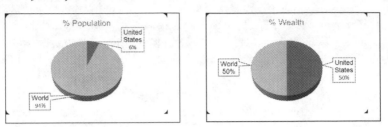

Fig. 5. "[W]e have about 50% of the world's wealth but only 6.3% of its population... Our real task in the coming period is to... maintain this position of disparity..." — George F. Kennan, PPS/2.

One major problem had to be dealt with though. U.S. officials realized that the people living in the Third World most likely would disagree with the subordinate function assigned to them by Washington. Kennan, who was later fired from the Policy Planning Staff because his superiors considered him too soft, recommended setting up authoritarian regimes capable of suppressing the population: "harsh governmental measures of police suppression may be the only answer." This might be "unpleasant," he continued, but "not shameful." Having decided the fate of the Third World, plans for the other part of the Grand Area, namely Western Europe and Japan, were laid out as well.[29]

Western Europe and Japan were allowed to develop and industrialize. The reason was simple. U.S. businesses not only needed raw materials and other resources, but also several wealthier regions to sell the more expensive products that they were producing. Poor people in the Third World do not buy cars, refrigerators, radios, and televisions, so the Grand Area also needed some more developed economies. The function of Europe and Japan, therefore, was to be lucrative markets for U.S. businesses. They would also host U.S. military bases on their soil, giving them a strategic function as well. One problem, however, had yet to be solved.[30]

---

[29] Acheson, D. Perimeter speech on Asia. 1950; Kennan, G. PPS/23, February 24 1948; Schaller, M. (1985). *The American Occupation of Japan: The Origins of The Cold War in Asia.* Oxford University Press, see p. 170-171 for George Kennan being replaced; Rabe, S. G. (2012). *The Killing Zone: The United States Wages Cold War in Latin America.* Oxford University Press. See p. 24; Lafeber, W. *Inevitable Revolutions.* (1993). *The United States in Central America.* W.W. Norton & Company. See p. 108-112.

[30] Schaller, M. (1985). *The American Occupation of Japan: The Origins of The Cold War in Asia.* Oxford University Press; Shoup, L. H. & Minter, W. (1977). *Imperial Brain Trust: The Council on Foreign Relations & United States Foreign Policy.* Authors Choice Press.

How do you ensure that U.S. control over a reconstructed Western Europe and Japan would continue? Surely, as the wealth and power of these countries increases, they would be less motivated to operate within a U.S.-dominated framework. Therefore, several mechanisms were set up to integrate Europe and Japan within an American system in a manner so they could not escape.

One particularly important method had to do with energy supplies. Highly industrialized economies require vast supplies of energy. Making Japan and Western Europe heavily dependent on Middle Eastern oil — a region under U.S. control — gives the U.S. enormous power over them. In the case of Japan even "veto power," according to Kennan, because the country has very little energy resources of its own. For Europe, part of the Marshall aid, about which the designers tell us it was generously and unselfishly given, was used to shift Europe's mostly coal-based energy system to one based on Middle Eastern oil. This dependency was exactly what U.S. planners wanted. For Washington, the Middle East has always been about control over oil, not so much access, because the U.S. has plenty of energy reserves itself. Today, this mechanism remains important in controlling new emerging economies, such as India and China.[31]

Meanwhile, to bring further benefits to the designers, complex triangular trade systems were set up to move resources, industrial goods, and money around the globe in ways primarily beneficial to the U.S. economy — which means large U.S. corporations. It also gave U.S. politicians tremendous power. This is not surprising, considering that it was they, in organizations such as the Council and the Government, who designed this system. But not everything went according to plan. In fact, in its initial stages, the Grand Area suffered an enormous setback. One of its major components broke away. In 1949, the United States "lost" China.[32]

The Loss of China

The Grand Area was the next big step in America's expansion. There can be no doubt that it was, for the United States would dominate much of the world in the decades following 1945. It is difficult to say why exactly people in Washington freaked out when China announced its independence and

---

[31] Bromley, S. (2005). *The United States and Control of World Oil*; Bromley, S. (1991).*American Hegemony and World Oil*. The Pennsylvania State University Press. See p. 117 and 183-184; Stivers, W. (1986). *America's Confrontation with Revolutionary Change in the Middle East, 1948-83*. Macmillan Press. See p. 3; Painter, D. S. *The Marshall Plan and Oil*. Cold War History, Volume 9 (2009), p. 159-175.
[32] Borden, W. Si. (1984). *The Pacific Alliance*. The University of Wisconsin Press.

broke away from the Grand Area. Maybe U.S. elites were so used to ever further expansion that a loss of control shocked them. Perhaps it was a difficult pill to swallow because the size of China's markets and its wealth had always fascinated Americans. Whatever the reasons, one thing was clear. U.S. leaders would not sit idly by and let Mao and his followers take away what was theirs. China might be lost for now, but perhaps Washington could get it back.

In the fall of 1949, two gentlemen were sent on a secret mission by the CIA's covert arm, the Office of Policy Coordination (OPC) — a benign name for a not-so-innocent organization. Using planes from the Civil Air Transport (CAT) — the CIA's secret Asian airline — they flew across China and visited important non-Communist military Generals. They tried to convince them to keep on fighting against Mao's forces and offered them money if they would do so. With the Nationalists defeated, Washington still hoped to prevent an inevitable communist victory.

Before the end of the year, however, the Chinese Generals that had received CIA money were either defeated or simply stopped fighting. Most of them then fled to Taiwan. Still unwilling to give up, the U.S. government ordered the CIA to carry out another, even more ambitious, covert operation to win back China.

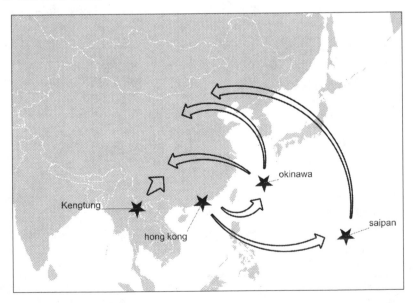

Fig. 6. U.S. Third Force movements aimed to overthrow the government of the newly established People's Republic of China.

In the early 1950s, the CIA had begun setting up secret bases in Hong Kong, Saipan, and Japan. In Hong Kong, former Nationalists were recruited and then sent to Saipan and Japan for training in the art of guerilla warfare, psychological operations, sabotage, and espionage. The CIA then parachuted these men into mainland China. Their mission was to collect information and organize rebellions. The CIA hoped, perhaps even expected, that hundreds of thousands of Chinese would sign up, creating what they called a Third Force. The CIA intended that this Third Force would overthrow Mao's government.[33]

In the meantime, the CIA also built up an army of former Nationalists in Burma (now Myanmar) on China's southwestern border. Weapons were delivered through Thailand, a U.S. ally, and several invasions into China were launched in the 1950s. These were supervised by a 'Major' or 'Captain' James Steward and a 'Lieutenant' Marks, if those were their real names. Both said they were civilians yet used military ranks. They accompanied the invading forces to coordinate weapon deliveries by CIA airplanes. As with the Third Force, the CIA anticipated that many Chinese would join the invading forces in bringing down the Communists. Unfortunately for the CIA, they were wrong once again. There existed no such support. The Third Force and the invasions from Burma all failed. The Century of Humiliation had finally ended.[34]

You can only lose something that you own. China was owned by foreign powers for over a century. In 1949, Mao declared China's independence. A few years later, despite U.S. attempts, the Communists were still in power. The United States had "lost" China for good. China would set out on a journey to restore its former glory as the Middle Kingdom. At the same time, the United States, still driven by its Manifest Destiny, tried to hold on to as much of the Grand Area as it could. One era of confrontation between China and the West might have ended. Another was shaping itself into something far more dangerous.

Towards a New Cold War

It was very difficult for U.S. leaders to accept the loss of China. It meant that in its early years, the Grand Area, which was so carefully planned, lost an important component. But it also dealt a blow to the Americans on a much deeper level. Since its conception, the United States had been a nation of expansion. Manifest Destiny kept on pushing the Americans further until

---

[33] Jeans, R. B. (2018). *The CIA and Third Force Movements in China during the Early Cold War.* Lexington Books

[34] Gibson, R. M. & Chen, W. H. (2011). *The Secret Army.* Wiley.

they had crossed Earth's biggest ocean, moving from Hawaii, Japan, and the Philippines all the way into the heart of China. Then the U.S. had successfully fought off Japan in WWII in a battle for control over the Pacific. Despite all that, however, China became independent, or from the U.S. point of view, lost. It ended a process of expansion. And then it got worse.

China's economic and military rise in the past few decades has demonstrated that the United States may not be the exceptional and indispensable nation. Yes, the rise of the United States as a superpower has been spectacular. But so is China's.

Kang Youwei and others like him failed to get China to modernize. The political class they needed to convince was still stuck in their traditional ways. The Chinese government, however, especially after Mao's death, has embraced industrial and technological development. It is where they draw much of their legitimacy to rule. And after decades of growth, China has become a superpower once again.

Meanwhile, many in the West believed that their victory over the Soviet Union ended history, because no other people or nation would ever be able to challenge the superiority of the American-led system. But China's rise is threatening to shatter all of this. It makes the White House, the Pentagon, and people working for the Council and other think tanks very uncomfortable. Many are now devoting their careers to prevent this from happening.

Some welcome the fact that the United States has started to confront China in what they call the second Cold War. The famous political realist John Mearsheimer writes that it is about time the United States has begun flexing its muscles. The U.S. should have weakened China much earlier, he argues. From a pure power politics point of view and putting all moral values aside, he is correct.[35]

From 1949 until 1972, that is for 23 years, Washington did impose an embargo on China to prevent certain raw materials, machinery, and other products from entering the country. The goal was not only to prevent China from building up its military. It was also to prevent China's economic development. Having failed to prevent China's independence, Washington tried to take away its chances of getting stronger.[36]

Then, however, Washington and Beijing became friends because both saw the Soviet Union as a threat. After the Soviet Union collapsed in 1991, this friendly relationship continued. Politicians and businesspeople in the United States looked at China as a weak nation that, with its hundreds of

[35] Mearsheimer, J. *The Inevitable Rivalry*. Foreign Affairs, Volume 100, Number 6, November/December 2021.

[36] Cain, F. America's trade embargo against China and the East in the Cold War Years. Journal of Transatlantic Studies (2020) 18:19–35.

millions of consumers and cheap laborers, could make them rich. Instead of trying to limit China's rise, as Mearsheimer liked to see, the United States and other Western countries increasingly invested in and traded with China. They were not afraid of sharing technology, believing that the Chinese would not be able to develop a high-tech economy anyway. A fair assumption, because how many Third World nations manage to make that transition?

But now that China has risen right in front of their eyes, U.S. leaders, starting with President Trump and continuing under President Biden, have begun to do what people like Mearsheimer wanted the United States to do all along. Interestingly, Biden has been more "vicious" than Trump, a fact that the Chinese recognize. To U.S. officials, the goal is simple: keep China weak enough so that it must accept its subordinate place in a U.S.-dominated world order. If Beijing does that, then it is a "responsible stake-holder." If it does not, China is a "threat" and an "aggressor" that is "desta-bilizing" the "rules-based international order." In that case, so this Western narrative goes, the only reasonable response is to push back against China, and to push back hard.[37]

The Chinese, on the other hand, know their history. They are aware of China's long standing as the world's Middle Kingdom. But they also remember the Century of Humiliation by the foreign powers. Since the 1990s, this has become a particularly important part of how history is being taught in schools. The Chinese government has deliberately spread this message. They want to tell the Chinese people how well China has done under its leadership, how they have turned a broken nation into the world's next superpower. And now that they have made China rich and strong, the time for 'going out' has begun. This includes building and militarizing islands in the South China Sea, having military bases in foreign countries, and constructing vast infrastructure and energy projects all over the world under the Belt and Road Initiative.

Disguised in benevolent words, as all great powers have done, Chinese leaders are creating their own Grand Area. One that overlaps, and thus conflicts, with Washington's. China is not accepting a subordinate place in a U.S.-dominated world order — a system that is designed to give the United States unique advantages and benefits over other nations. Instead, Beijing

---

[37] Almost every report on China produced by the U.S. government or affiliated think tanks describe it in this way, using words like "responsible stakeholder" for when China accepts U.S. rule, and labeling China as an aggressor and its actions as destabilizing if it does not. For a Chinese opinion on Biden, see Ni Guihua. *The Situation and Dilemmas of the Biden Administration's Strategic Competition with China*. Asia-Pacific Security and Maritime Affairs. January 26, 2022. English translation made available by CSIS, Interpret: China, p. 12.

likes to use its newly acquired power to change the international system so that it benefits China.

Another confrontation is thus taking shape. The designers on both sides are very busy planning the next great power competition. From military buildups to secret operations, from economic sanctions to information warfare, and from the Taiwan Strait to Africa, all options are on the table and no region in the world is overlooked. It is up to us to stop it from escalating, which we can only do when we understand exactly what is happening. This then is the focus for the remainder of this book.

Chapter 2: China, Taiwan, and the Dangers of Containment

It is 2027, and the Pacific Ocean looks like a ticking time bomb ready to explode. In the previous years, the United States has continued its military buildup in the region, until a vast array of U.S. military installations stretches all along China's borders. The Chinese people and their leaders, feeling alarmed by these developments, also know that Washington has its eyes set on Taiwan. The U.S., under the guise of supporting the island's independence, is hoping to turn the island, only 80 miles from the Chinese coast, into yet another military base. If that were to happen, there would be no escape. China's containment by the United States would be complete.

Xi Jinping, still the General Secretary and China's supreme leader, realizes that Washington is about to recognize Taiwan as an independent state, and to use that opportunity to station large numbers of U.S. troops on the island. Xi, in an attempt to prevent this from happening, decides to step up China's so-called "Gray Zone" tactics against Taiwan. This includes acts of political infiltration, espionage, economic pressure, and demonstrations of military power. The Chinese President hopes to intimidate the Taiwanese into abandoning their relationship with the United States. This provocative behavior, however, backfires spectacularly.

Following a call for help by the Taiwanese government, a large U.S. cargo ship sets sail for Taiwan to deliver hundreds of advanced long-range missiles that can carry nuclear warheads. The purpose of these weapons is to enable Taiwan to sink Chinese ships, shoot down airplanes, kill PLA soldiers, and destroy China's coastal cities in case of an attack on the island. Several U.S. military advisors secretly accompany this shipment of arms. Their mission is not only to show how to use these weapons, but also to lay the groundwork for the integration of the Taiwanese armed forces into the U.S. military. The ultimate aim is to turn Taiwan's forces into an extension of the U.S. Indo–Pacific command. Although this is supposed to be a secret, the Chinese leadership knows what Washington is up to.

Xi, ambitious and determined to deliver on his promise of reunification with Taiwan, decides to act quickly. On his orders, Chinese marines and special forces carry out amphibious and airborne landings on several small islands located between China and Taiwan. The Taiwanese forces stationed there realize they are completely outnumbered and outgunned. They surrender, except for a small unit that fights back, resulting in two dead soldiers and three wounded.

Next, these islands are turned into Chinese military bases from which the People's Liberation Army (PLA) can launch further operations. Meanwhile, the PLA Navy moves into Taiwanese waters and its warships surround the island. At the same time, the PLA Air Force sends large numbers of fighter aircraft into Taiwanese airspace. Together, they take control of the air and sea borders and put the island under effective quarantine. No ship or airplane goes in or out without Beijing's permission. It is not a blockade. Many ships, after being screened by Chinese security forces, can still proceed to Taiwan's ports to deliver food, medicines, and other vital supplies. But the U.S. cargo ship that is carrying missiles is now forced to turn back.

China's leadership in Beijing says that their actions are purely defensive. They want to keep destabilizing U.S. missiles and military forces out of Taiwan, just like the United States did not want Soviet missiles stationed in Cuba. Xi emphasizes the peaceful nature of the operation. He claims that no-one got killed. China is simply protecting itself against growing U.S. aggression, including an attempt to put nuclear missiles and U.S. forces on Taiwan.

Washington, on the contrary, states that China has carried out a brutal and unprovoked attack on Taiwan. The U.S. media claims that Chinese forces have killed up to a hundred Taiwanese soldiers and civilians – actions amounting to war crimes. No mention is made of Washington's attempt to ship missiles and military advisors to Taiwan. Instead, the story put out by the Western media is about an unprovoked act by China to block all ships and airplanes trying to enter Taiwan, including those carrying food and medicines. According to Washington, the Taiwanese people are running out of vital supplies and a humanitarian crisis is imminent.

With such wild stories going viral, the White House feels it can act aggressively. Besides, the 2028 presidential election is only one year away and the sitting President does not want to appear weak. Therefore, Washington decides to challenge China's quarantine. They organize a convoy of ships. A reluctant Korea, Japan, and several small Pacific islands are pressured by the White House to participate in order to give it the appearance of an international operation instead of solely an act by the United States.

Several large container ships are loaded with food, medicines, and other supplies in what is described as a humanitarian rescue operation to save the Taiwanese from starvation and death. Having created a cover, Washington secretly orders the CIA to place advanced communication equipment on board one of the ships. A handful of CIA operators, traveling undercover, accompany the ship as well. The idea is that if Beijing is too scared to stop this convoy, these CIA agents will get into Taiwan, from where they can start coordinating secret weapon deliveries by U.S. submarines and airplanes to the Taiwanese military. With these weapons, Taiwan can then challenge China's quarantine and force Beijing to back down.

As the convoy sails closer and closer to Taiwan, tensions rise to new heights. Xi Jinping must make a decision on what to do, and he decides to take a gamble. Backing down now will only make him look weak. He sends in several heavily armed warships to intercept. In a tense situation, they manage to blockade the convoy. Then they begin boarding the ships, because Beijing again suspects that besides food and medicine, they may also find U.S. weapons. But before that can happen, the CIA agents decide to blow up their secret cargo with several controlled explosions. Any damage to the ship can be put on the Chinese anyway. Unfortunately, four U.S. and Japanese sailors fail to move away in time, and together with two Chinese marines, are killed. The explosion creates a fire, and thick black clouds of smoke begin to rise into the air.

Images of a U.S. civilian cargo ship on fire surrounded by Chinese warships go viral all over the internet. CNN, MSNBC, the BBC, and other Western media outlets scream that the Chinese have deliberately attacked and fired upon a civilian convoy that was transporting food and medicine, killing dozens of innocent sailors in the process. Xi Jinping has gone insane, they conclude, and is intent on conquering the entire Pacific, starting with Taiwan. The U.S. military must move in now to stop China from carrying out other barbaric and unprovoked acts of violence.

Meanwhile, the Chinese media puts up a completely different story. Several CIA agents have been captured and are displayed on Chinese television. Although they appear unharmed, they have in fact been tortured and forced to confess that their mission was to weaponize Taiwan and attack China.

With tensions close to reaching boiling point, the United States and China begin a dramatic military buildup. As U.S. aircraft carrier groups move in closer, China puts its Rocket Forces, naval, and air force units on high alert. The media on both sides beat the drums of war. The top leaderships in Washington and Beijing feel they cannot back down now.[38]

Will this be the start of a new World War? And if so, could it have been avoided? Are the Chinese paranoid about fearing being encircled by U.S. military bases? Was the United States sending weapons to help the Taiwanese people and protect their freedom? Or is the island simply a pawn in a geopolitical and military chess game played by Washington to keep China down?

Such questions need answers. And as the above example shows, getting to the truth is very difficult once the conflict has started. But understanding why Taiwan is at the heart of a most explosive setting, and how Western governments are making matters more dangerous, is crucial if we wish to avoid war. We in the West are responsible for our own actions, so let us look at them critically and try to understand how they impact China's people and its leadership.

A "Noose" of Bases

Why are the Chinese so afraid of being surrounded by U.S. military bases? Is it not China that is destabilizing the region with its construction of military installations on artificial islands in the South China Sea?

In the West, everyone is familiar with China's military expansion in the Pacific. But the other side of the story — that of a vast network of U.S. military bases aimed at China — tends to be ignored. But to understand Beijing's actions, especially China's military buildup, we should put ourselves in the shoes of the Chinese. To see what they see. And to fear what they fear.

Imagine walking along the banks of the Huangpu River in Shanghai, enjoying the beautiful view of the city's famous skyline. It is a perfect example of Xi Jinping's 'China Dream'. During the day, the numerous and wonderfully designed skyscrapers demonstrate China's growing strength and prosperity.

---

[38] This fictitious war scenario is partly based on documents discussing war games and potential future conflicts. See for instance Military and Security Developments Involving the People's Republic of China. A Report to Congress Pursuant to the National Defense Authorization Act for Fiscal Year 2000; Easton, I. China's Top Five War Plans. Project 2049 Institute; Blackwill, R.D. & Zelikow, p. .(2021). *The United States, China, and Taiwan: A Strategy to Prevent War*. Council on Foreign Relations; Blackwill, R. D. (2020). Implementing Grand Strategy Toward China. Council on Foreign Relations, Council Special Report No. 85; Dougherty, C. et al. (2021). *The Poison Frog Strategy*. Center for a New American Security.

At night, after the sun has set, the amazing light show and rocket-shaped Oriental Pearl Tower seem to come right out of a science fiction movie — symbolizing a modern high-tech nation. Amid all this wealth and power, surely Chinese citizens must enjoy a feeling of safety. Or so it seems.

Although foreign gunboats no longer patrol the river that curves around Shanghai's city center, and no U.S. marines can be seen marching through the streets, it does not mean that the foreign powers have truly left this part of the world. They are still there.

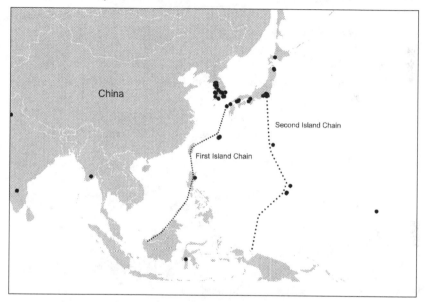

Fig. 7. U.S. military bases and the first and second island chain. Their goal is to contain China.39

Imagine going up the 2,073 ft (632 meters) tall Shanghai Tower, all the way up to the observation deck. From this high up, you see the sparkling blue waters of the Yellow Sea. Now imagine you can look even further, past the horizon. What do you see?

One thing that will be hard to miss are the 28,500 U.S. military forces stationed in South Korea. These are spread out over 76 U.S. military bases, many of which are only several hundred miles away from where you are standing. A Tomahawk cruise missile block V can hit Shanghai within 40 minutes after launch. The U.S. Air Force's new hypersonic missile, fired from a B-52 heavy bomber, only needs 7 minutes. Imagine for a second that the people of New York and Washington would go to bed at night knowing that

39 David Vine, "Lists of U.S. Military Bases Abroad, 1776-2021," American University Digital Research Archive, 2021, https://doi.org/10.17606/7em4-hb13.

7 minutes from now their house could be blown up by a Chinese missile. What a shock would this be for Americans! Yet for the people of Shanghai, and for many other Chinese living in coastal cities, this is a reality. Unfortunately for them, it is not the end of their worries but only the beginning.[40]

If, from the Shanghai Tower, you were to shift your gaze away from the Yellow Sea and a little bit more to the Southeast, you would look upon Okinawa. The beautiful landscape of this small Japanese island is dotted with over 30 U.S. military bases. From Okinawa, U.S. military forces were deployed to the Korean War, Vietnam, and later Afghanistan and the 2003 Iraq war. Heavy B-52 bombers flew countless missions to carpet bomb Vietnam, Laos, and Cambodia. Okinawa was home to the notorious chemical Agent Orange, which was stored at Kadena Air Base, where it was loaded on planes that sprayed the Vietnamese countryside — poisoning plants, food crops, animals, and up to three million people. The island also stored large numbers of nuclear weapons, as formerly secret documents show.[41]

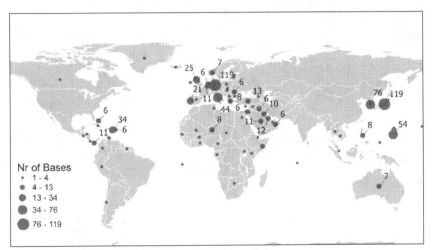

Fig. 8. Location of U.S. military bases abroad.[42]

[40] See datasets on military bases by David Vine (author of Base Nation) and Patterson Deppen, which can be found here https://dra.american.edu/islandora/object/auislandora%3A94927 and here https://quincyinst.org/report/drawdown-improving-u-s-and-global-security-through-military-base-closures-abroad/

[41] Wilcox, F. A. (2011). Scorched Earth: Legacies of Chemical Warfare in Vietnam. Seven Stories Press, p. 35; Kirk, D. (2013). Okinawa and Jeju. Palgrave Macmillan, p. 7; Japan Times. July 24, 2014. Japan agreed to hide Okinawa's role in U.S. bombing of Vietnam. See https://www.japantimes.co.jp/news/2014/07/24/national/japan-agreed-hide-okinawas-role-u-s-bombing-vietnam/

[42] David Vine, "Lists of U.S. Military Bases Abroad, 1776-2021," American University Digital Research Archive, 2021, https://doi.org/10.17606/7em4-hb13.

Besides the 30+ bases on Okinawa, Japan itself hosts dozens more, bringing the total number of U.S. military bases in Japan to a whopping 119. These range from small communication centers and weapon depots to enormous U.S. Marine Corps camps, the largest U.S. airfield in the Pacific, and Yokosuka naval base in the Tokyo region — home to the aircraft carrier the U.S.S. Ronald Reagan.

If you continued to scan the Pacific Ocean, you would find U.S. military bases everywhere. The island of Guam is a perfect example. One analyst jokingly stated that this beautiful tropical island is about to sink because of all the military hardware the United States has placed on it. Around forty percent of the land has been turned into a giant military base.[43]

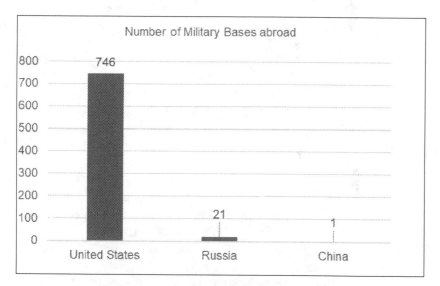

Fig. 9. Estimated number of U.S. military bases abroad

This global network of U.S. military bases goes back to WWII. During the war, the U.S. military designed a system for worldwide military dominance. The Joint Planning Staff proposed a plan for a global system of air bases. Heavy bombers would be stationed at 50 strategically located sites to control the world's energy resources. Meanwhile, the Navy wanted extensive basing sites in the Pacific, including in the Philippines, Guam, Okinawa, Japan, Korea, Taiwan, Thailand, and China, which at the time was still under the control of the foreign powers.[44]

[43] See John Pilger's documentary "The Coming War on China". Comment comes from James Bradley, the author of The China Mirage.
[44] Converse, E. V. (2005). Circling the Earth. Air University Press, p. 3, 9, 24, 73

This expansion of U.S. military power all over the globe was justified to the people of the United States by saying that it was necessary to preserve world peace. The real reason, however, was to "effectively smash any threat" to U.S. dominance, as U.S. planners described it in internal documents.[45]

Although Nazi Germany and the Soviet Union no longer exist, this global system of military bases remains. Today, some 300 to 400 of them, depending on how you count, are aimed at China. U.S. military strategists refer to this as a "noose," which they are tying around China's neck. The goal of all this military might is to "contain" China, to keep it locked up in a as small a region as possible, behind a wall of U.S. bases, missiles, bombers, and battle groups. To Washington, China is the threat now, one that may need to be smashed.

Containing China

If you want to understand what is happening in the U.S.–China standoff in the Pacific, and why it is so dangerous, then the strategy of containment is key. In fact, containment is one of the most important ideas in Cold War history. It was the strategy the United States used to combat the Soviet Union.

Its creator, George F. Kennan, introduced it in 1947. To Kennan, containment was a subtle strategy that was all about psychology. He wanted the United States to win the hearts and minds of people all over the world so they would never support a communist party. Meanwhile, Washington should use "behavior modification" to punish 'bad' and reward 'good' Soviet behavior. Ultimately, so Kennan reasoned, Moscow would realize that it had no chance of defeating the United States, leaving a negotiated agreement with Washington as their only option. With this nuanced strategy of psychology and negotiations in mind, Kennan made it also very clear to U.S. leaders what they should not do. They should not surround the Soviet Union with a ring of U.S. military bases.[46]

Unfortunately for Kennan, most politicians in Washington were thinking exactly this. To them, strength and power were all that mattered. Therefore, instead of a combination of reward and punishment, as Kennan advised, they used only punishment. Even worse, whereas Kennan considered containment as a means to an end, politicians saw containment as an end in itself. They set out to encircle Russia with U.S. military forces stationed in Europe and Asia. They also created an anti-Soviet military alliance (NATO), and developed the hydrogen bomb — all of which Kennan opposed. The fact

---

[45] Converse, E. V. (2005). *Circling the Earth*. Air University Press, p. 111
[46] Gaddis, J. L. (2005). *Strategies of Containment*. Routledge. Oxford University Press.

that this military buildup increased suspicion and fear in Moscow and thus undermined the chances of a negotiated agreement between the two super-powers — Kennan's ultimate goal — was simply brushed aside.

NSC-68, one of the Cold War's most important documents, embodied this new containment strategy. It was all about creating positions of strength from which the United States could keep the Soviet Union down. A negoti-ated peace was out of the question. The Soviet Union had to be completely isolated and surrounded. Only then would the world be safe. Naturally, the Soviet Union responded with a military buildup of its own, and before long, both superpowers were involved in the most dangerous arms race the world had ever seen.[47]

Today, nothing has changed. The type of containment that is being pursued by Washington is to surround China with as much military hardware as possible. In medicine, containment means "the confining or prevention of further dissemination of a potentially hazardous – e.g., biologic, radioactive or toxic–agent." In other words, in the eyes of U.S. strategists, China is a disease or a poison that needs to be contained so it cannot spread anywhere else.[48]

Many U.S. foreign policy experts prescribe a 'recipe' of a military buildup in the Pacific, fortification, expansion of military bases, and the creation of NATO-like military alliances with Asian countries. Those military planners who possess a little bit more imagination like to see cargo ships loaded with munitions and weapons all across the Pacific to serve as mobile floating munitions platforms. Others want the U.S. coast guard to patrol not American waters, but China's coast instead, as if the U.S. coastline begins at China's shores, and America owns the entire Pacific.[49]

In these discussions, the concept of "island rings" or "island chains" is often mentioned. They, more than anything else, show what Washington wants. Several lines of 'defense' are key to containing China. Of course, from the Chinese point of view, this has nothing to do with defense, but instead is about intimidation, threats, and U.S. aggression. Imagine if China had the United States surrounded with military bases. Would U.S. citizens sleep

---

[47] NSC 68: United States Objectives and Programs for National Security, April 7, 1950

[48] https://medical-dictionary.thefreedictionary.com/containment#:~:text=Public%20health%20The%20confining%20or,%2C%20radioactive%20or%20toxic%E2%80%93agent.

[49] Anonymous. (2021). *The Longer Telegram*. Atlantic Council; Paul, C. et al. (2021). *A Guide to Extreme Competition with China*. RAND Corporation; Collins, G. & Erickson, A. S. (2020). *Hold The Line Through 2035*. Baker Institute; Blackwill, R. D. (2020). Implementing Grand Strategy Toward China. Council on Foreign Relations, Council Special Report No. 85.; Collins, G. & Erickson, A. S. (2021). *U.S.-China Competition Enters The Decade Of Maximum Danger*. Baker Institute.

better at night after Xi Jinping reassured them that these were all purely defensive? Wouldn't U.S. presidents feel pressured into a military buildup of their own to counter all this Chinese military might that is amassed near their country's borders?

With the U.S. military's "noose" around China, one thing stands out that has everything to do with the war scenario that opened this chapter. It is the position of Taiwan. Taiwan sits in the middle of the first island chain. If it falls into Beijing's hands, the first line is broken, and containment of China may no longer be possible. But if Washington gets the island, then China is in mortal danger. Taiwan is thus key to both superpowers, and that makes it extremely dangerous.

Red Lines

The most fundamental factor in anything that the Chinese Communist Party (CCP) does is holding on to power. It affects everything. For example, the main reason the CCP is so serious about successful economic development is to have the Chinese people accept its rule. The same holds true for Taiwan. As long as the CCP is making steps to reunify Taiwan with mainland China, the Chinese people feel that the party leadership is doing a good job. But the moment Taiwan becomes independent, they will question the CCP's competence and its right to rule. To Beijing, the question of Taiwan is thus one of survival. Losing Taiwan comes close to losing power — the ultimate threat to Xi Jinping and his associates.[50]

But there are other important reasons why the island matters so much. The loss of Taiwan can threaten the integrity of China as a whole. Territorial integrity, like economic growth and reunification, is another major promise on which the CCP has to deliver if it wants people to accept its rule. As matters stand, the Taiwanese are not alone in China when it comes to having ideas about independence. In Tibet and Xinjiang, there are groups that want the exact same thing. If Taiwan is allowed to be independent, it can greatly encourage those people to press, or perhaps fight, for independence as well. This could then lead to a breakup of large parts of China, and with it, maybe end the party's dominance.

Taiwan, of course, is also important to Beijing in its plans to expand into the Pacific region. Without it, it will be very hard to escape the bounds of the first island chain.

For the United States, Taiwan is of great interest as well, but for different reasons. Of course, there is the desire of turning Taiwan into a U.S. military

---

[50] Dickson, B. J. (2021). *The Party and the People.* Princeton University Press.

base, but besides that, there is more at stake. In the eyes of Washington, if China manages to reunify with Taiwan, it can start a dangerous domino effect. The domino theory goes back to the Cold War with the Soviet Union and was one of the major drivers of U.S. foreign policy. The idea is that if Taiwan falls into Beijing's hands, the whole East Asian region will see that the United States has failed. Many countries might decide to throw their lot with Beijing, because they feel Washington is not strong or determined enough to contain the Chinese. In this sense, Taiwan is an important domino that if it falls the wrong way, can shift the whole region away from the U.S. and into China's orbit

Taiwan is also a particularly important player in the production of advanced semiconductors. China's high-tech ambitions depend to a large extent on access to such technology. A Chinese-controlled Taiwan will boost Beijing's technological development plans. But a Taiwan in U.S. hands will give Washington some level of control over the pace and extent of China's economic ambitions.[51]

But what about the Taiwanese people themselves? What do they want? Research shows that the people of Taiwan prefer independence and feel more strongly about their Taiwanese identity than their Chinese roots. But the Taiwanese also do not want war. In fact, they consider peace to be more important than independence.[52]

Western leaders are always very happy to point out the desire among Taiwanese to be independent. They praise themselves for standing up for principles of freedom and independence. But this is only to mask their geopolitical Cold War plans. If the West cares so much about giving people their independence, then the United States would not have waged numerous wars to prevent people from doing so. The Philippines, a former U.S. colony, and Vietnam, for example, are cases where Washington has been firmly against independence, and used military force to prevent it.[53]

Western European countries have a similar bad record, and not only because of their history of colonization. In 2017, for example, the people of Catalonia Spain (where Barcelona is located) wanted to have a vote on their

---

[51] Collins, G. & Erickson, A. S. (2020). *Hold the Line Through 2035*. Baker Institute.

[52] See Taiwan National Security Survey by Duke University. See also these graphs on independence/unification attitudes https://esc.nccu.edu.tw/PageDoc/Detail?fid=7801&id=6963 and identity https://esc.nccu.edu.tw/PageDoc/Detail?fid=7800&id=6961. See also research by Pew Research Center, e.g. here https://www.pewresearch.org/global/2020/05/12/in-taiwan-views-of-mainland-china-mostly-negative/

[53] For Vietnam see for example Kahin, G, McT. (1986). Intervention: How America Became Involved in Vietnam. Alfred A. Knopf. Inc. For the Philippines see Miller, S. C. (1982). Benevolent Assimilation. Yale University Press and Brands, H. W. (1992). Bound To Empire. Oxford University Press.

region's independence. This resulted in panic in Madrid, the Spanish capital. There, the government, encouraged and supported by the European Union, sent police forces to Catalonia to prevent people from voting. Although the violence used by the police was widely condemned by human rights organizations, EU Vice-President Frans Timmermans praised it as a "proportionate use of force." The Spanish government also used media censorship to block pro-referendum messages. Catalan leader Carles Puigdemont was forced to flee Spain to escape imprisonment. But despite facing arrest and police violence, 41% of the people still came out and voted, 90% of them in favor of independence. If China would carry out something remotely similar in Taiwan, the U.S. would be ready to declare World War III. Yet in the case of Spain, Washington, like the EU, sided with the Madrid government and supported its crackdown against the independence movement.[54]

Another example is Ukraine, where two provinces in the East wanted to be independent. The United States reacted by encouraging the Ukrainian government in Kiev to use military force to prevent this from happening. Washington provided them with weapons and other aid to accomplish this.

What these examples show is that there are no principles involved. If independence undermines Western geopolitical goals, the United States and Europe move against it, often in force. But when independence benefits the Western powers, they support it and proudly proclaim their dedication to freedom and democracy.

So, what does Washington gain if it helps or pushes Taiwan into declaring its independence? The answer is that if Taiwan becomes an independent state, not only will it terminate any chances for peaceful reunification with China, but the U.S. can then also propose a military alliance and may gain rights to place military bases on the island. That would solidify the first island chain and China's containment. But as if this is not dangerous enough, there may be an even a more cynical motivation at play here.

Although it is always extremely difficult to make accurate predictions, we should not at all be surprised if in the next few years the U.S. will have rallied enough of its allies to its side, especially those in Europe and countries like Australia and maybe even Japan, to recognize Taiwan as an independent state *hoping* that it will spark a military confrontation between the two superpowers which many people in Washington believe they can win and utilize to take out China in the process. And if that turns Taiwan into another Ukraine, then that is the price they are more than happy to pay.

---

[54] McRoberts, K. (2022). *Catalonia the Struggle over Independence.* Oxford University Press; Weiss, B. '*Catalonia is an integral part of Spain': The US sides with Spain's government in Catalonia independence dispute.* Business Insider, October 27, 2017.

The United States' claim to Taiwan has thus everything to do with under-mining China and has very little to do with the well-being of the Taiwanese. As formerly secret documents show, in 1958, the United States preferred to have Taiwan completely destroyed in a nuclear war rather than letting the island fall under Beijing's control. So much for standing up for the Taiwanese people and their wish for independence.[55]

Given the island's importance to both superpowers, China and the United States hold on to red lines. These are actions that the other side will not tolerate. When China or the U.S. makes a serious move toward Taiwan, and if in doing so cross a red line, war becomes very likely. The unfortunate reality, however, is that both sides are constantly making moves. Similar to how the West and Russia are competing over Ukraine, Washington and Beijing are pulling hard on Taiwan to try and claim it for themselves, so they can then use it against the other side. Many of those moves are secret, or 'gray', and are highly dangerous indeed.

Into the Gray Zone

Wang Ping-chung was on a secret mission. As a member of the New Party, a Taiwanese political party that wants unification with China, he was on his way to Beijing. His Communist Party contact, someone from China's Taiwan Affairs Office, told Wang where to pick up a large sum of money. If anyone asked questions, Wang was supposed to say that the money was a generous donation to a charity organization. The real purpose, however, was to fund a secret operation named the Star Fire T Project.[56]

Besides Wang, at least one other member of the New Party was involved. Hou Han-ting, a celebrity on Taiwanese television, also played a key role. With Beijing's money, Wang and Hou created Fire News, a Taiwanese news outlet on Facebook. Hou's pro-unification and pro-China articles were published there. But publishing news was not the operation's true purpose. This was the trick that Wang and Hou used: If a Taiwanese person read one of these articles and gave it a 'like', it marked this individual as having sympathy for Beijing. Wang and Hou were encouraged by the Chinese government to connect to those people and get them to talk about their

---

[55] Savage, C. Risk of Nuclear War Over Taiwan in 1958 Said to Be Greater Than Publicly Known. The New York Times, May 22, 2021.

[56] Barss, E. J. (2022). Chinese Election Interference in Taiwan. Routledge, p. 144-148 ebook. See also the references used for additional information, especially https://www.mirrormedia.mg/story/20180102inv014/ and https://www.taipeitimes.com/News/front/archives/2018/01/04/2003685148

political views, their personal lives, and their friends and relatives, especially those who serve in the Taiwanese military.

Fire News was not so much about news per se. It was about recruitment. The ultimate goal of the Star Fire T Project was to build an underground group of Taiwanese military officials who are sympathetic to China. During peacetime, they would serve as spies and provide the Chinese government with information on Taiwan's military. In the event of a Chinese invasion of Taiwan, this group would spring into action to carry out acts of sabotage in coordination with the PLA to aid Beijing.

Unfortunately for Wang and Hou, the operation was revealed after the capture of a CCP spy, Zhou Hongxu, who had been working closely with the New Party for several years. Wang and Hou were captured and prosecuted on charges of espionage.

The Star Fire T Project appears to be just one example of many secret operations that China is carrying out in Taiwan. They belong to the general category of so-called 'gray zone' activities. These are aggressive actions that, at least in theory, are not serious enough to cause a war. In practice, however, China is conducting so many of them that when you add them all up, they might do just that.

Gray zone activities involve infiltration, espionage, and preparation for war, as in the example above. Other gray zone operations have to do with fake news, misinformation, and propaganda. For example, the Chinese government has been secretly buying Taiwanese news organizations, while hiding themselves behind assets in the British Virgin Islands. News coverage by these companies then changed to being more pro-China, pro-unification, and against independence. News that discredits Taiwan's political system while at the same time praises the accomplishments of the Chinese government also became much more prominent. The idea is to signal to Taiwanese listeners that unification with mainland China is in their best interests.[57]

Beijing's biggest success involves a wealthy Taiwanese businessman, Tsai Eng-meng. Tsai owns the famous 'Want Want' rice crackers brand yet decided to expand his crackers empire by buying up the China Times Media Group. This gave him ownership over several Taiwanese newspapers and a cable channel. Tsai's connections and sympathy to the CCP are well known, and his new Want Want Media Group received funding from the Chinese government. Next, pro-independence news was suppressed, and news became more pro-China and stronger in favor of unification. With a

---

[57] Barss, E. J. (2022). Chinese Election Interference in Taiwan. Routledge, p. 100 ebook. For other examples of information warfare see Hornung, J. W. (2021). Chinese Disinformation Efforts on Social Media. Rand Corporation.

foothold in Taiwan, the Chinese government tried to use the Want Want Media Group to buy other giant Taiwanese media organizations to give Beijing a dominant position in Taiwan's media market. This, however, failed, but not because of the lack of trying.[58]

The Chinese government has also tried to influence Taiwan's elections to prevent pro-independence politicians from rising to power. In a case of great irony, Beijing's gray zone actions have actually promoted democratic participation in Taiwan, although not for the right reasons. Many Taiwanese live and work in China, and when it is election time, they need to travel to Taiwan to cast their vote. The Chinese authorities have been giving them large discounts on airline tickets, accompanied with a small note, of course, advising them to vote for "cross-strait peace," which is a slogan of the KMT, a Taiwanese political party more in favor of unification.[59]

The Chinese government has also been funding several Taiwanese political parties, like the New Party, which are against independence. Some of them are linked to organized crime. Chang An-Lo, for example, is not only a gangster, but also the founder of CUPP, a pro-unification party whose members have used violence against pro-independence protesters.[60]

Other gray zone operations include cyber warfare, such as hacking government institutions, the financial system, and high-tech semiconductor companies. The number of cyber attacks against Taiwan coming from China is staggering, up to many millions a month. Each one of them may be below the threshold for war, as gray zone actions are supposed to be, but they do add up to dangerous levels.[61]

Last but certainly not least, gray zone actions also include military shows of force. Beijing has been demonstrating to Taiwan that it can take the island if it wants to. Examples are large-scale military exercises that mimic actual invasions, sending hundreds of aircraft and battleships into Taiwan's space, live fire drills, and simulated assaults by PLA army units against a building that looks surprisingly similar to Taiwan's presidential office.[62]

---

[58] Barss, E. J. (2022). Chinese Election Interference in Taiwan. Routledge, p. 102-106 ebook.

[59] Barss, E. J. (2022). Chinese Election Interference in Taiwan. Routledge, p. 120-122 ebook.

[60] Collins, G. & Erickson, A. S. (2021). *U.S.-China Competition Enters The Decade Of Maximum Danger.* Baker Institute

[61] Lin, B. et al. (2022). Competition in the Gray Zone. RAND Corporation, p. 59-63; Lakshmanan, R. *Chinese Hackers Target Taiwanese Financial Institutions with a new Stealthy Backdoor,* February 6, 2022. https://thehackernews.com/2022/02/chinese-hackers-target-taiwanese.html ; Greenbert, A. *Chinese Hackers Have Pillaged Taiwan's Semiconductor Industry.* August 6, 2020. https://web.archive.org/web/20200813041037/https://www.wired.com/story/chinese-hackers-taiwan-semiconductor-industry-skeleton-key/; Lee, Y. *Taiwan says China behind cyberattacks on government agencies, emails,* August 19, 2020. https://www.reuters.com/article/us-taiwan-cyber-china-idUSKCN25F0JK

[62] Lin, B. et al. (2022). Competition in the Gray Zone. RAND Corporation.

The United States is also heavily involved in gray zone operations. The U.S. Navy practices cutting off China's trade routes. U.S. warships enter waters claimed by China, just to show that they can. Washington has also been selling large amounts of sophisticated weapons to Taiwan worth tens of billions of dollars, including Apache attack helicopters, high-tech F–16 fighter jets, tanks, and a wide variety of modern missiles and rocket launchers.[63]

The National Endowment for Democracy (NED), an organization linked to the U.S. government that, according to its founder Allen Weinstein, carries out operations that the CIA used to do, is also active in Taiwan. Washington has a variety of organizations like the NED that operate in other countries supposedly to 'promote democracy'. In reality, however, they build up opposition movements to overthrow governments that the U.S. does not like, or in the case of Taiwan, to train people in resisting Beijing and moving towards independence. Projects from the NED are like the Star Fire T Project. Both superpowers are thus playing the same game. And sometimes their plans cross a red line that can start a war.[64]

Washington officials have no problem producing dangerous ideas that may start an all-out war with China. For example, some want Taiwan to join the United Nations as a demonstration of Taiwan's independence. Others are thinking about launching surprise attacks with cruise missiles against China, hiring pirates to attack Chinese shipping lines, secretly arming separatists in Xinjiang to start a breakup of China, and even putting nuclear weapons on Taiwan. These are all examples of irrational and irresponsible policies that, unfortunately, have come to dominate U.S. government thinking.[65]

Meanwhile, only a handful of sober U.S. analysts remain who understand that U.S. provocations have led to an increase in Chinese gray zone operations and vice versa. They also understand that the confidence that politi-

---

[63] Glaser, B.S. et al. (2020). *Toward a Stronger U.S.-Taiwan Relationship*. CSIS, see appendix II; Military and Security Developments Involving the People's Republic of China. A Report to Congress Pursuant to the National Defense Authorization Act for Fiscal Year 2000, p. 98-99

[64] Ignatius, D. *Innocence Abroad: The New World of Spyless Coups.*. September 22, 1991. Washington Post, https://www.washingtonpost.com/archive/opinions/1991/09/22/innocence-abroad-the-new-world-of-spyless-coups/92bb989a-de6e-4bb8-99b9-462c76b59a16/; See the National Endowment Website for examples of NED support for Taiwan. See for instance a $40,000 and $38,811 grant in 2017, a $123,677 grant in 2018, and a $159,297, $375,000 and $700,000 grant in 2020 to "build alliances and stronger partnerships among youth leaders and democrats from Tibet, Hong Kong, Taiwan, and China"

[65] Blackwill, R.D. & Zelikow, p. .(2021). *The United States, China, and Taiwan: A Strategy to Prevent War*. Council on Foreign Relations; Cancian, M. F. (2021). *Inflicting Surprise*. CSIS; Mazza, M. & Schmitt, G. (2021). *Righting a Wrong: Taiwan, the United Nations and United States Policy*. Project 2049 Institute; Codevilla, A. M. *Put Nukes on Taiwan*. June 30, 2021. Hoover Institution. https://www.hoover.org/research/put-nukes-taiwan

cians have in their ability to control the extent of escalation is largely fiction. The truth is, they realize, that when things go wrong, they will quickly spiral out of anyone's control. But with anti-China sentiment dominating in Washington, these people find themselves marginalized. The White House, State Department, and the Pentagon do not want to hear such opinions. Therefore, the vicious circle of intimidation and threat continues unabated. Both Washington and Beijing are pulling hard on Taiwan from opposite directions. There is a very recent case that shows how extremely dangerous and destructive the outcome will be. Indeed, Ukraine is a perfect example of how reckless and irrational Western containment policies and gray zone operations have plunged the West into a war with another superpower.[66]

Lessons From Ukraine: Blunder of Epic Proportions

Learning from our mistakes is how we improve. The famous phrase "history repeats itself" is often used when people have failed to do so. If we fail to learn from the 2022-23 war in Ukraine, then a war over Taiwan becomes much more likely. Unfortunately, politicians are afraid of recognizing their mistakes because they confuse an opportunity to learn with perceived weakness. The Western mainstream news media, who tend to serve those in power, is not that much different.

Putin invaded Ukraine because he is insane, they said. Or maybe Putin is ill, and before his death, he wants to restore the old Soviet Empire. The West, the Western media maintains, is totally innocent and bears no responsibility. The Russian invasion was completely unprovoked. Now, if this seems simpleminded, what did cause the war in Ukraine? In what ways is the West responsible? And most important, could the war have been avoided?

The answer to the last question is a clear 'yes'. In fact, the Ukraine war could have been avoided very easily if Western leaders had acted differently. This is not the wisdom of hindsight. Respected Western geopolitical analysts like John Mearsheimer were saying this for years before the war started. Others, like George F. Kennan, understood this since at least the 1990s, decades before any Russian tanks entered Ukraine.[67]

The roots of the Ukraine conflict go back to the end of the Cold War. The Soviet Union collapsed in 1991. Russia, however, remained a powerful

---

[66] Lin, B. et al. (2022). Competition in the Gray Zone. RAND Corporation, [p. 52-55]; Paul, C. et al. (2021). A Guide to Extreme Competition with China. RAND Corporation, p. 33-34.

[67] Mearsheimer, J. J. Why the Ukraine Crisis Is the West's Fault. Foreign Affairs, September/October 2014; For George Kennan, see Eichler, J. (2021). NATO's Expansion After the Cold War. Springer, p. 42 and Kennan's earlier opposition to NATO as explained in Gaddis, J. L. (2005). Strategies of Containment. Routledge. Oxford University Press.

country with a fervent desire for security. This makes sense, given the fact that European countries had invaded Russia several times in recent history and the U.S. had a strong military presence in several European countries. The last time, in WWII, Russia barely survived and suffered up to 27 million deaths.

Russian leaders from Gorbachev to Yeltsin and Putin had two ideas on how to reorganize European security after the Cold War. According to one model, the former Soviet states in Eastern Europe would be neutral. They would be free to interact with the European Union and Russia, but they would not join sides. In this way, Russia could feel secure in the post-Cold War world. The other option was to create a unified Europe in which the West, the former Soviet states, and Russia were all integrated in some way to improve economic, political, and military cooperation and security. Up until the Ukraine war in 2022, Russian leaders were in favor of these solutions.

From Moscow's point of view, the worst-case scenario would be a politically, economically, and militarily integrated Europe that included all the former Soviet states but excluded Russia. In this case, Russia would be alone and isolated, facing a strong and unified hostile power right on its borders.

Western leaders, however, with Washington in the lead, were seeking exactly this. They wanted to weaken Russia by isolating it from the rest of Europe, so that Moscow could never again be a serious competitor to Western power. Containing Russia with NATO troops, missiles, and military bases all the way up to the Russian border was their dream, or "end game," as some called it.[68]

Many protested. George F. Kennan, for example, warned that expanding NATO toward Russia's borders would be recognized by Moscow as a direct threat and would risk setting off a new Cold War. Expanding NATO into the former Soviet space, according to Kennan, would be a "strategic blunder of potentially epic proportions." Western leaders, however, ignored his advice. The stage was set for NATO expansion.

It is important to remember that NATO was ostensibly the anti-Soviet military alliance. But, instead of dissolving NATO after the Soviet Union disappeared, Western leaders insisted on enlarging it. Although the United States and the European countries had made promises to Moscow that NATO would not expand towards Russia, the first official invitations to join NATO were given in 1997 to Poland, the Czech Republic, and Hungary, three former Soviet satellites. They joined the Alliance in 1999. The second wave of NATO expansion came in 2004 when the Baltic states (Estonia, Latvia,

---

[68] Bilinsky, Y. (1999). *Endgame in NATO's Enlargement*. Praeger Publishers.

Lithuania), Romania, Bulgaria, Slovakia, and Slovenia became new NATO members.[69]

Whereas the first wave of expansion caused bitterness and a feeling of betrayal among Russian elites, the second wave delivered a blow to Russia's sense of security. You only have to look at a map to get a sense of how threatening NATO expansion has become to Russia.

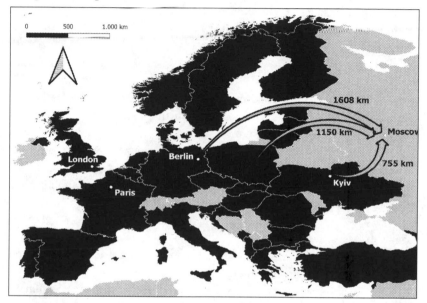

Fig. 10. Intended and realized NATO expansion.

What happened next was entirely predictable. Russia responded to NATO expansion with a military buildup, especially its defensive capabilities, the so-called Anti-Access (A2) and Area-Denial (AD) system. Western leaders interpreted this as Russian aggression and responded with a military buildup of their own. It was the Cold War all over again. And to make matters worse, Western leaders were now eyeing Ukraine as well.[70]

In 2008, NATO announced that it wanted Ukraine to join the alliance in the third wave of expansion. This was extremely disturbing news for the Russian government. They have always considered Ukraine as a vitally important buffer zone, a no-go zone for NATO. This was understood in the West. George Friedman, a well-known geopolitical analyst, wrote in 2009

---

[69] Eichler, J. (2021). *NATO's Expansion After the Cold War.* Springer, p. 34-42; Sakwa, R. (2016). *Frontline Ukraine.* I. B. Tauris, p. 45.
[70] Eichler, J. (2021). *NATO's Expansion After the Cold War.* Springer, p. 52-56

that "Ukraine and Belarus are everything to the Russians. If they were to fall in an enemy's hands — for example, join NATO — Russia would be in mortal danger." Other Western military strategists had also made it clear that if Ukraine were to join NATO, Russia would be unable to defend itself, and for that reason, Moscow would never allow it. In 2008, William J. Burns, then the American ambassador to Moscow, wrote to the U.S. Secretary of State Condoleezza Rice: "Ukrainian entry into NATO is the brightest of all red lines for the Russian elite (not just Putin). In more than two and a half years of conversations with key Russian players, from knuckle-draggers in the dark recesses of the Kremlin to Putin's sharpest liberal critics, I have yet to find anyone who views Ukraine in NATO as anything other than a direct challenge to Russian interests." Ambassador Burns knew what he was talking about. In a personal meeting with Putin, the Russian President had said that every Russian leader would see NATO membership to Ukraine as "a hostile act toward Russia... We would do all in our power to prevent it." But again, European and American politicians ignored all these warnings. Unwilling to change their policies, the EU and U.S. continued pulling hard on Ukraine. And as predicted, Russia responded in the same way.[71]

Both sides tried to influence Ukrainian politics to get someone in power loyal to their cause. Ukraine became a place for front-work operations, propaganda, infiltration, intimidation, and other gray zone tactics conducted by the United States, Europe, and Russia.[72]

Then, in 2014, Ukrainian President Yanukovych was overthrown in a Western-backed coup. Indeed, Western gray zone tactics had played a crucial part in this Color Revolution. EU officials had begun visiting the famous Maidan square to spur protesters to overthrow Yanukovych. In the meantime, U.S. officials were selecting candidates for a new Ukrainian government, and Brussels was hinting at financial aid if Ukraine chose its side. Russian leaders were aware of this, and when Yanukovych was replaced with a far more pro-Western and anti-Russian government — one that was intent on moving Ukraine into NATO — Putin decided to act.[73]

Until this time Putin had been open to the idea of a neutral Ukraine, or even of a fully integrated Europe that included Russia. But his openness was met by the complete refusal by Western leaders to even discuss such

[71] Friedman, G. (2010) *The Next 100 Years.* Anchor Books, p. 112; W.J. Burns. (2019). *The Back Channel.* Random House. See chapter 6.

[72] Mitchell, L. A. (2012). *The Color Revolutions.* University of Pennsylvania Press; McFaul, M. (2007). *Ukraine Imports Democracy.* International Security, Fall, 2007, Vol. 32, No. 2, pp. 45-83.

[73] Charap, S. & Colton, T. J. (2017). *Everyone Loses.* Routledge, p. 122-123; Sakwa, R. (2016). *Frontline Ukraine.* I. B. Tauris, p. 86-87.

matters and their continued insistence on getting Ukraine to join NATO in this Western strategy to weaken Russia.

So, in 2014, following the Western-backed coup in Ukraine, Russia took back Crimea. As Putin explained in a lengthy speech at the time, it was essential for Russia to retain control of the Sevastopol Naval Base and Russia's access to the Mediterranean, and to prevent Crimea from becoming a NATO military base. At the same time, it was critically important to reunite the peninsula with Russia in accordance with a public referendum in which a majority of Crimeans had voted to become part of the Russian Federation. Crimea had been part of the Russian Federation for almost 200 years, from 1783 to 1954, when Moscow made an administrative move to transfer Crimea from the Russian Soviet Federation of Socialist Republics (RSFSR) to the Ukrainian Soviet Socialist Republic (UkrSSR). In a study for the Wilson Institute, Mark Kramer concluded that this transfer remains puzzling, as it does not seem to be justified by history, demographics, cultural ties, or geography.[74]

In the same speech, Putin also pointed out that the Western containment policy — aimed to "sweep us into a corner" — was the reason behind this move. Putin also maintained his position that he wanted to work with the West and NATO and to find a peaceful solution satisfactory to both sides. The West, however, with the United States in the lead, were not interested in making any compromises.[75]

Washington pressed on with its agenda of getting Ukraine into NATO, and with Russia and the West pulling on Ukraine from opposite sides, the country descended into civil war. With Europe and the United States supporting western Ukraine in attacking the Russian-speaking regions of Eastern Ukraine, Putin started giving military assistance to the latter. Even though the drama unfolded right before their eyes, U.S. leaders were still intent on having Ukraine, or what was left of it, join NATO.

In fact, from 2014 until the time of this writing, Ukraine was "being treated as a NATO member in all but name," although it was not a formal NATO member. NATO conducted an interoperability program to turn Ukraine into a de facto NATO army "able to operate together with NATO forces according to NATO standards, rules, procedures and using similar equipment." Ukraine also joined NATO war games and military exercises. In

---

[74] Kramer, Mark. Why Did Russia Give Away Crimea Sixty Years Ago? Wilson Center, 2016. He suggests that the initiative in large part had to do with personal politicking by Khrushchev. See https://www.wilsoncenter.org/publication/why-did-russia-give-away-crimea-sixty-years-ago
[75] Address by President of the Russian Federation. March 18, 2014. See http://en.kremlin.ru/events/president/news/20603

2021, Ukraine hosted and led the latest version, Rapid Trident 21. Ukrainian General Vladyslav Klochkov called it "an important step toward Ukraine's European integration. It will strengthen the operational capabilities of our troops, [and] improve the level of interoperability between units and headquarters of the Armed Forces of Ukraine, the United States, and NATO partners." This, of course, confirmed the deepest concerns of the Russian government.[76]

Opportunities for a negotiated solution to the Ukrainian conflict were brushed aside by the West. The Minsk II agreements, signed by Ukraine and Russia (but also by France, Germany, and the OSCE who were expected to help make sure the agreements held) were not implemented by the Ukrainian government. Western leaders never pressured the Ukrainian leaders to do so. They were still planning to have Ukraine join NATO. In fact, the German and French leaders who helped negotiate the deal have come out and said that they never intended to honor the agreement. It was a trick intended to fool Russia, and to buy time so NATO could further arm Ukraine.[77]

With Western military exercises stepping up on Russia's border by the end of 2021, the Russian government made one last attempt to resolve the situation peacefully. On December 15, 2021, the Russian government presented a draft treaty and agreement to the U.S. government. The hope was to get to a new security framework in Europe in which NATO would not strengthen its security interests at the expense of Russia's. The West was to halt its military expansion, including into Ukraine. With these proposals as a starting point for serious negotiations, the Russian Foreign Ministry said "We hope that the United States will enter into serious talks with Russia in the near future regarding this matter."[78]

Western leaders ignored this request for talks, and the Western media presented these proposals as unreasonable. At that point, the Russian government concluded that diplomacy with the West was impossible and

---

[76] Carpenter, T. G. *Making Ukraine a NATO Member in All but Name.* Cato Institute, 2021, September 30; Carpenter, T. G. *NATO Arms Sales to Ukraine: the Spark That Starts a War with Russia?* Cato Institute, 2021, November 21; Charap, S. & Colton, T. J. (2017). *Everyone Loses.* Routledge; Sgt. 1st Class Chad Menegay and Capt. Aimee Valles. *US, NATO, Ukraine enhance interoperability with Rapid Trident exercise.* U.S. Army. September 21, 2021.

[77] Kevin Liffey, Putin says loss of trust in West will make future Ukraine talks harder. Reuters, December 9, 2022. https://www.reuters.com/world/europe/putin-says-loss-trust-west-will-make-future-ukraine-talks-harder-2022-12-09/

[78] Press release on Russian draft documents on legal security guarantees from the United States and NATO. The Ministry of Foreign Affairs of the Russian Federation, December 17, 2021. See also the proposed draft treaty "Treaty between The United States of America and the Russian Federation on security guarantees" and the proposed agreement "Agreement on measures to ensure the security of The Russian Federation and member States of the North Atlantic Treaty Organization".

that military action was the only way to prevent Ukraine from joining NATO and safeguard Russia's security interests.

Crucially, even during the war, there were chances for a negotiated solution. Former Israeli President Naftali Bennett has revealed that in the early weeks of the war, he was in a unique position to help negotiate an end to the conflict. Bennett had good relations with Zelensky and Putin, and had the ears of the American, German, French, and British leaders as well. Fairly soon, according to Bennett, Putin made two concessions on the issues of Ukrainian demilitarization and denazification. Zelensky followed with a "huge concession" of his own: Ukraine would not pursue NATO membership. Next, Bennett updated the leaders in Berlin, Paris, London, and Washington. Whereas Scholz and Macron appeared to be more in favor of a negotiated solution, Boris Johnson took a more aggressive approach — he wanted the war to continue — something that Biden could also appreciate. The aggressive stance prevailed, and the U.S. and its allies blocked further negotiations between Ukraine and Russia. The war would go on, even though it could have been stopped in its initial stages.[79]

In a similar fashion, another negotiation attempt in Istanbul in March and April of 2022, which also could have ended the war, was stopped by the United States and the United Kingdom, when Boris Johnson flew to Kyiv to tell Zelensky personally to end negotiations and continue the war.[80]

These events make it clear that the intention of Washington, London, and Brussels was to use Ukraine against Russia. In fact, this strategy was already established in 2019 by one of America's most important think tanks. The RAND corporation, in a report named "Overextending and Unbalancing Russia," recommended arming Ukraine so that in a war with Russia it would drain Russian men and matériel—not to benefit Ukraine, but simply to bleed and weaken Russia.[81]

For the West, the willingness to fight the war in Ukraine to the last Ukrainian is a tactic that has been used before. In the 1980s, after the Soviet Union invaded Afghanistan, the United States decided to deliver weapons to the Mujahideen to "make Soviet involvement as costly as possible." At the time, Washington and the CIA did not believe the Mujahideen could

---

[79] See Naftali Bennett's Youtube channel where he has uploaded the entire 4 hour interview.
[80] Rahman, A. Ukrainian news outlet suggests UK and US governments are primary obstacles to peace. Peoples dispatch, May 9, 2022.
[81] Dobbins, James, Raphael S. Cohen, Nathan Chandler, Bryan Frederick, Edward Geist, Paul DeLuca, Forrest E. Morgan, Howard J. Shatz, and Brent Williams, *Overextending and Unbalancing Russia: Assessing the Impact of Cost-Imposing Options*. Santa Monica, CA: RAND Corporation, 2019.

win, even with U.S. help, but they started arming them nonetheless. Nobody cared about the morality of "fighting a losing war to the last Afghan." [82]

The lesson we should learn from this whole affair is that containing Russia through a military buildup and NATO expansion did not improve security. In fact, as Kennan, Mearsheimer, and others predicted, it increased tensions, led to military buildups on both sides, and a return of Cold War thoughts and emotions. The refusal of the West to take Russian security interests into account and the failure to use negotiation and diplomacy to come to an agreement led to the Ukraine war in 2022.

Somewhere along the line, there came a moment when Putin and his government lost faith in the West. At that point, all trust and hope in negotiating some sort of security arrangement vanished. If we fail to learn from history and allow Western leaders to continue their reckless and irrational containment policy toward China, there will come a moment when Beijing draws a similar conclusion. Then a war over Taiwan becomes almost inevitable, a war that was easily avoidable, a war whose disastrous consequences will be discussed in the following sections.

Storming Taiwan

For the 10,000 soldiers of the 1st Amphibious Mechanized Infantry Division, the moment had finally come. Packed tightly together in dozens of transport ships, many wondered whether they would ever see home again. Although they had practiced this operation countless times, knowing that this was for real made everything different. The night before, under the cover of darkness, they had left the safety of China's shores. Together with a large armada of ships and hundreds of thousands of other storm troopers, they were making the crossing towards their target areas. In the skies above, the PLA Air Force provided air cover. If the pilots would look down, they would see a giant V shape formation of ships — with the tip pointing towards Taiwan.[83]

The Joint Island Attack Operation, as it is known in Chinese military manuals, had begun two months earlier. To 'soften up' their enemy, the Chinese Rocket Forces had been launching ballistic and other missiles against carefully selected targets. Because of their hyper- and supersonic speeds, the people of Taiwan did not hear or see them coming. On an otherwise ordinary afternoon, buildings and people suddenly started exploding

---

[82] For military analysts see for instance Scott Ritter and former Senior Advisor to the Secretary of Defense Col. Douglas Macgregor; Coll, S. (2004). *Ghost Wars.* Penguin Books, p. 108-109, 119, 136 ebook; Riedel, B. (2014). *What We Won.* Brookings Institution Press, p. 113.
[83] Easton, I. (2017). *The Chinese Invasion Threat.* Project 2049 Institute. Eastbridge Books.

all around them. A terrifying thought. The explosion that obliterated the Taiwan Presidential Office had been especially spectacular. The deaths of many high-level officials, including the President, had pleased Beijing greatly.

As missiles and bombs rained down in the following weeks, destroying everything from army headquarters to bunkers and supply depots, the first wave of Chinese special operation units assaulted the Kinmen, Matsu, and Penghu Islands. Located in between China and Taiwan, these islands needed to be captured first, so that the PLA invasion force could safely cross the Taiwan Strait. Only then had the final stage of the operation begun — the invasion itself.

The plan seems simple yet is extremely complicated to execute successfully. Units like the 1st Amphibious Mechanized Infantry Division would storm the beaches in Northern or Southern Taiwan. These areas were carefully selected, because they must have ports, docks, and airfields to help unload war materials. Unfortunately for the PLA, there are not many beaches that meet all these criteria. The Taiwanese know this, and at the few sites that are suitable for a Chinese invasion, they are waiting in heavily fortified positions.

If Chinese forces manage to break through and establish a beachhead, they will quickly unload more men and heavy equipment such as artillery and main battle tanks. Next, these forces will move inland, and encircle and capture cities until all of Taiwan's military has been defeated and its population subdued. That, at least, seems to be the plan. But there are countless uncertainties, and many different things can happen. Two questions that occupy the minds of many are: What will be the fate of Taiwan? And if the United States gets involved, what will be the fate of the world?

Washington, Taiwan, and Whole of Society Destruction

If you think the war in Ukraine is bad, just wait for what the U.S. government has in store for Taiwan. Over the past few years, several developments have shed light on what kind of war Washington wants to fight in Taiwan. It will be a different type of war than the one being fought in Ukraine. And unfortunately for the Taiwanese, it will be more deadly and destructive.

Washington not only has controversial plans on how Taiwan's military ought to fight against a Chinese invader, but U.S. officials are also planning to mobilize, train, and potentially sacrifice Taiwan's entire population. It seems that the small island, with its urbanized coastline and mountainous center, is ideal for guerilla warfare. As such, the U.S. not only wants Taiwan's military to adopt this style of fighting, but they are also supporting the training of millions of Taiwanese civilians in the use of asymmetrical or guerilla warfare techniques — an operation called Whole of Society Defense.[84]

Let us first have a look at Washington's plans for Taiwan's military, and then shift attention to the Whole of Society Defense, or what more appropriately can be called the Whole of Society Destruction.

For years, U.S. and NATO officials have argued that Taiwan needs a different kind of military. Thirty years ago, it made sense for Taiwan to focus on modern equipment such as F-16s and M1 Abrams tanks. But with the modernization and expansion of the PLA, Taiwan's armed forces are outnumbered and increasingly outclassed.[85]

Therefore, Washington wants Taiwan to shift its military doctrine to the Overall Defense Concept, with a heavy emphasis on asymmetric irregular defense — guerilla warfare in other words.

What Taiwan needs is "large numbers of small things," David F. Helvey, the Assistant Secretary of Defense for Indo–Pacific Security Affairs, told the U.S.-Taiwan Business Council Defense Industry Conference in his keynote address. This refers to weapon systems suitable for long-term guerilla warfare, such as mobile artillery and cruise missile systems, naval mines, small fast-attack crafts, miniature missile assault boats, and mobile anti-armor weapons.[86]

But to the dismay of Washington, Taiwan's leadership is reluctant to embrace this style of war fighting. The island's Defense Ministry seems uninterested. The United States, however, does have a few cards to play to force this kind of military strategy upon the island. It also appears that at least one of them is already being played.

On February 23, 2023, the Wall Street Journal reported that the United States would be sending 100 to 200 troops to Taiwan in the following months to train the island's military. Although initially shrouded in mystery — the White House, the Pentagon, and the U.S. Indo–Pacific Command all refused to comment — all indicators point to an attempt by Washington to resur-

---

[84] Global Taiwan Institute. Biden Administration Unveils New Security Assistance Policy towards Taiwan. March 23, 2022. See https://globaltaiwan.org/2022/03/biden-administration-unveils-new-security-assistance-policy-towards-taiwan/

[85] Lee Hsi-min & Eric Lee. "Taiwan's Overall Defense Concept, Explained." *The Diplomat.* November 3, 2020. See https://thediplomat.com/2020/11/taiwans-overall-defense-concept-explained/

[86] U.S. Taiwan Business Council Defense Industry Conference. Closing Keynote Remarks by David F. Helvey. October 6, 2020. See https://www.us-taiwan.org/wp-content/uploads/2020/02/2020_october06_david_helvey_dod_keynote.pdf

rect a Cold War relic: the Military Assistance Advisory Group (MAAG) in Taiwan, that existed on the island from 1951 until 1978.[87]

In fact, for several years, U.S. think tanks and U.S. military officials have called on Washington to consider this option. The most telling call for resurrecting MAAG Taiwan comes from two U.S. Marine Corps intelligence officers who, in January 2022, wrote a long article titled "Reestablish The U.S. Military Assistance Advisory Group - Taiwan." [88]

The article describes in detail the need for the United States to recreate MAAG-Taiwan. "It should start with 100 to 200 personnel", the two intelligence officers write, and "Rather than hyping it, U.S. officials should only indirectly reveal the new organization's existence." Washington seems to have taken their advice to heart.

The key point to understand about the first MAAG-Taiwan is that unlike what its name might suggest, its function was not to advise. The job of the 116 officers and men that were sent in 1951 was to take charge of Taiwan's military development.[89]

In the words of its commanding officer Maj. Gen. William Chase, "Our job... is to get them the hardware they need — what I say they need, not what they think they need — and then teach them how to use it and take care of it."[90]

With several hundred U.S. military advisors working alongside the Taiwanese military, and perhaps also within Taiwan's Defense Ministry, Washington is in a good position to impose its will upon a reluctant government and military. Taiwan's growing dependency on U.S. weapons and training also gives the United States much leverage. But unfortunately for the Taiwanese, U.S. influence does not end there.

Washington not only wants Taiwan's military to adopt the Overall Defense Concept, but it also wants to use the entire Taiwanese population to fight in a whole-of-society approach. It means that the entire population should be mobilized and utilized to wage a long and exhaustive war against

---

[87] Nancy A. Youssef & Gordon Lubold. U.S. to Expand Troop Presence in Taiwan for Training Against China Threat. The Wall Street Journal. February 23, 2023. See https://www.wsj.com/articles/u-s-to-expand-troop-presence-in-taiwan-for-training-against-china-threat-62198a83

[88] Sean Lin. No guarantees for Taiwan-U.S. military cooperation in NDAA: Academics. Focus Taiwan. December 24, 2022. See https://focustaiwan.tw/politics/202212240012; Jake Yeager & William Gerichten. Reestablish the U.S. Military Assistance Advisory Group-Taiwan. War on the Rocks. January 7, 2022. See https://warontherocks.com/2022/01/reestablish-the-u-s-military-assistance-advisory-group-taiwan/

[89] Setzekorn, E. (2018). *The Rise and Fall of an Officer Corps.* University of Oklahoma press : Norman, see chapter 5.

[90] Setzekorn, E. (2018). *The Rise and Fall of an Officer Corps.* University of Oklahoma press : Norman, p. 131.

a Chinese invader. According to the Global Taiwan Institute, this is one of the pillars of the Biden administration's plan for Taiwan.[91]

In recent years, the Whole of Society Defense idea has been taken up by several Taiwanese non-governmental organizations (NGOs) who receive support or are connected to the United States government and defense establishment.

Enoch Wu, the founder of the NGO Forward Alliance, explains the idea. "Our civil defense vision is [a] community based, localized organization that complements our conventional forces and supports our professional responders, from fire to police". "The idea is that with that kind of civ-mil [civilian-military] cooperation we can actually implement a whole of society defense concept." [92]

With support from the American Institute in Taiwan — the de facto U.S. embassy — and organizations like Spirit of America, Forward Alliance is training civilians in waging guerilla style warfare against a Chinese invader.[93]

Another NGO, the Kuma Academy, is doing the same. It draws much of its inspiration from the United States, and its founders have connections to the U.S. security establishment and related think tanks. Their goal is to create three million "Kuma Warriors" or "Black Bear Warriors," as they are called, in the next three years. The Kuma Academy offers a range of courses, from first aid to modern military science, information warfare, and drone operations. One major aim is to train 300,000 snipers for a civilian militia capable of inflicting great pain on a Chinese invader.[94]

[91] U.S. Taiwan Business Council Defense Industry Conference. Closing Keynote Remarks by David F. Helvey. October 6, 2020. See https://www.us-taiwan.org/wp-content/uploads/2020/02/2020_october06_david_helvey_dod_keynote.pdf; Global Taiwan Institute. Biden Administration Unveils New Security Assistance Policy towards Taiwan. March 23, 2022. See https://globaltaiwan.org/2022/03/biden-administration-unveils-new-security-assistance-policy-towards-taiwan/

[92] Nicola Smith. Taiwan's 'guerilla' home guard gears up for David vs Goliath battle with China. The Telegraph. November 15, 2021. See https://www.telegraph.co.uk/world-news/2021/11/15/chinese-threats-grow-taiwanese-mull-civil-defence-force-protect/

[93] American Institute in Taiwan. Remarks By Ait Deputy Director Raymond Greene At Forward Alliance Workshop. March 20, 2021. See https://www.ait.org.tw/remarks-ait-deputy-dir-greene-at-forward-alliance-workshop/; Spirit of America. Help Prepare Taiwan For An Emergency. See https://spiritofamerica.org/project/help-prepare-taiwan-for-an-emergency#038;swpmtxnonce-6e13159f9b

[94] See the website of the Kuma Academy. Note the reference to the U.S. national anthem on their About page. Also view the lessons they provide here https://kuma-academy.org/lesson/; Kuma Academy founder Dean Shen Boyang is also chairman of Taiwan Democracy lab. On their website you can see a list of contributors, which include a variety of U.S. think tanks. https://china-index.io/about#contributors; Matt Smythe. Billionaire In Taiwan Tells China To F*Ck Off, Starts Own CMP. Free Range American. September 7, 2022. See https://freerangeamerican.us/civilian-marksmanship-program/?__hstc=263703507.0940978347e0e140bb2e241f3d7c4743.1671204326015.1673291692526.1673296468876.45&__hssc=263703507.4.1673296468876&__hsfp=3295102214; Helen Davidson. FEATURE:

Taken together, what the United States wants is to turn Taiwan into a giant "poison frog." The Poison Frog Strategy originally came from the gaming lab of the Center for a New American Security. They simulated a scenario in which China tried to conquer the smaller islands located in the Taiwan Strait. In these war games, the United States was unable to prevent China from capturing them. Therefore, the best strategy, the researchers concluded, was to turn the islands into a military nightmare for the Chinese military — to transform them into "poison frogs." [95]

This is also exactly what the United States and Europe have done in Ukraine. Despite what Western officials and the Western media have been saying throughout the war, Ukraine never stood a chance in a war against Russia. But the United States and Europe gave Ukraine a massive amount of military aid anyway in order to bleed Russia as much as possible. In the process, Ukraine and its people are being sacrificed. Just like in 1958, when U.S. leaders preferred Taiwan to be turned into a nuclear wasteland over Beijing occupying the island, the well-being of ordinary people is of no concern.

By turning Taiwan into a poison frog, Washington hopes the island becomes a death trap for the Chinese army, inflicts maximum casualties, and drags out the conflict for "as long as it takes," to copy the Western slogan for the current war in Ukraine.[96]

If Taiwan adopts, either willingly or unwillingly, this new military doctrine of guerilla warfare, what we will get is a ground war on the island that is far bloodier than what we have seen in Ukraine. China's People's Liberation Army will not only have to defeat Taiwan's military, but they will also have to move over the corpses of millions of poorly trained and equipped Kuma Warriors.

But a long war would serve the United States very well. And as part of its so-called deterrence strategy, a clear cut U.S. victory is not even necessary. The point is to exhaust China, just as the point in Ukraine is to overextend and unbalance Russia. And if that means sacrificing the Taiwanese people and their entire society, then so be it. To U.S. strategists, that is a perfectly acceptable outcome.[97]

Taiwan's citizen warriors prepare to confront China. Taipei Times. October 10, 2022. See https://www.taipeitimes.com/News/taiwan/archives/2022/10/10/2003786762

[95] Dougherty, C. et al. (2021). *The Poison Frog Strategy*. Center for a New American Security. See https://www.cnas.org/publications/reports/the-poison-frog-strategy

[96] Dougherty, C. et al. (2021). *The Poison Frog Strategy*. Center for a New American Security. See https://www.cnas.org/publications/reports/the-poison-frog-strategy

[97] Dobbins, James, Raphael S. Cohen, Nathan Chandler, Bryan Frederick, Edward Geist, Paul DeLuca, Forrest E. Morgan, Howard J. Shatz, and Brent Williams, *Overextending and*

Towards World War III

Among the many uncertainties that an invasion of Taiwan brings, the one thing that you ought to be most worried about is in what ways the United States gets involved. The reason is simple. Once U.S. forces begin engaging the Chinese, things can get out of hand very quickly.

China considers Taiwan an internal issue, not an international affair. It is therefore highly unlikely that China will launch first strikes on U.S. military bases or U.S. Navy ships in the region. No, it will be Washington that decides to strike Chinese targets first. And the question then becomes, given the many options U.S. officials have, how far will they go?

There are, in fact, many things Washington can do to intervene. For example, in the weeks before the actual invasion, the U.S. Air Force might try to intimidate and chase away PLA fighter planes. The U.S. Navy could try to block Chinese warships from coming near Taiwan. But if such gray zone tactics lead to real fighting and casualties, the situation will escalate.

Several studies give important clues to what can happen. A war game simulation carried out by the Center for Strategic and International Studies (CSIS) comes to a surprising and terrifying conclusion. The scenario they played was a U.S.–China stand-off over the Kinmen Islands, the conquest of which is part of the PLA's invasion plan of Taiwan.

The war game showed that when U.S. leaders feel they have no viable long-term options to counter China, they will respond impulsively and aggressively, most likely to the point of escalation and war. If, however, U.S. leaders feel they do have some long-term options and decide to tread carefully, a so-called shadow risk lurks nearby.[98]

When the stand-off over the Kinmen Islands continues despite initial U.S. restraint, Washington will quickly lose its patience, the war game study shows. In fact, at this point, U.S. leaders who initially showed restraint will now be even more aggressive than their more impulsive colleagues would have been, and escalation to war is again highly likely.

Another CSIS war game study reinforces the evidence that the United States military will intervene. After analyzing the results, the researchers concluded that the "Ukraine model" cannot work in the case of Taiwan. The U.S. approach to the war in Ukraine is to supply the country with weapons and money, to train Ukrainian forces, and to provide intelligence and other services that help the Ukrainian army in their fight against the Russian military. In the case of Taiwan, however, this cannot work, CSIS

Unbalancing Russia: Assessing the Impact of Cost-Imposing Options. Santa Monica, CA: RAND Corporation, 2019. See https://www.rand.org/pubs/research_briefs/RB10014.html
[98] Jensen, B. et al. (2022). *Shadow Risk.* CSIS Briefs.

concludes. The reason is simple. One of the first things that China will do is to have its navy and air force surround the island to prevent any ships and airplanes from entering Taiwan. It will be highly costly, if not impossible, for the United States to try and bring in men and material. For example, in one simulation in which the U.S. tried to move an army brigade into Taiwan by air, two thirds of the force, approximately two thousand men, died because their airplanes were shot down. Therefore, the CSIS recommends another approach.[99]

What they say the United States should do to counter a Chinese invasion is to have its military, especially its air, missile, and naval forces, participate directly in the war. They should join the fight quickly, CSIS argues, because the longer the U.S. waits, the more forces and material China will have shipped to Taiwan and the more difficult and costly it will be to prevent a PLA victory. And, importantly, the U.S. military should go in with full force and hit the Chinese hard. Japan should be dragged into the war as well, given the major advantages of U.S. bases on Japanese soil. The Chinese mainland should also not be neglected, and air and missile strikes against Chinese ports, bases, airfields, and other facilities is part of U.S. strategy as well. Last but not least, the people of the United States will have to be prepared for a rate of casualties on the U.S. side not seen since the Second World War.

The issue of striking the Chinese mainland is an extremely dangerous one. In yet another study, U.S. strategists and national security elites investigated what the risk of escalation would be when the U.S. carries out mainland strikes, which they refer to as attacks by United States forces on targets on the Chinese mainland with non-nuclear weapons.[100]

The first conclusion of this study was that U.S. officials do not feel deterred from ordering mainland strikes despite the fact that China has nuclear weapons. Nuclear weapons may scare U.S. leaders a little, but not so much that they will not attack — another testament to their recklessness and irrationality.

If China launches attacks on U.S. military forces in the Pacific, which becomes more likely when Washington decides to challenge Chinese operations, many U.S. elites are willing to attack targets in mainland China. Interestingly, in these studies even if Taiwan shares responsibility for a conflict with China, the U.S. shows the same willingness to attack mainland China compared to when Beijing is solely responsible. We can only guess what Chinese leaders will do when they see their coastline being bombarded by

[99] Cancian, M.F., Cancian, M., Heginbotham, E. *The First Battle of the Next War – Wargaming a Chinese Invasion of Taiwan.* CSIS. January 2023.

[100] Meyers, J.S. (2019). Mainland Strikes and U.S. Military Strategy Towards China. RAND Pardee RAND Graduate School.

American bombs and missiles. If they return in kind, with attacks on the U.S. mainland, World War III has officially begun.

But is there a way to avoid all of this? Or is a major battle somewhere in the near future inevitable?

The 2020s: The Decade of Maximum Danger?

If the Western powers, located far away, are so concerned about China's rise, then the countries of East Asia surely must feel terrified. Just look at China's increasing military budget compared to that of its neighbors. Countries like Vietnam, the Philippines, South Korea, Japan, and Indonesia, not to mention Taiwan, must have been terribly busy preparing themselves to stop Beijing from devouring them. Or are they?[101]

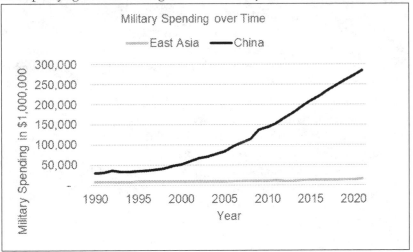

Fig. 11. Military spending over time.[102]

Professor David Kang, an East Asia expert, has come to a radically different conclusion. At first glance, the take-away from the figure above is that China has made a staggering increase in military spending over the past 30 years. A closer look, however, reveals that other major countries in East Asia, including important U.S. allies, have not responded with a military buildup of their own. Western politicians and media outlets may take every opportunity they can get to paint China as a military aggressor, but the rest

---

[101] For data on military spending, see the SIPRI database (accessed May 26, 2022).
[102] SIPRI Military Expenditure Database 2021, https://www.sipri.org/databases/milex

of the region has not been that worried. Several important statistics show this very clearly.[103]

First of all, the figure above is misleading. Why has China increased its military spending so much more than the other countries? Because its economy has grown much faster. Typically, countries spend a certain percentage of their economy on the military. This is called the "defense effort." If you look at China's defense effort, it has not changed over time. Compared to other countries in the region, China is average, and it is much lower than the United States.

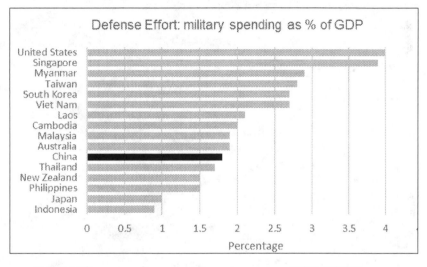

Fig. 12. Military spending per country. Average over 1990-2021.[104]

Furthermore, if you take the average defense effort of many East Asian countries (excluding China), you see that it has not increased. Actually, their combined defense effort has gone down over the years. This shows that on average, East Asia has not reacted militarily to China's rise.

South Korea, however, seems an exception, because since 2017 it has increased its defense effort quite dramatically. From a steady 2.5% for many years, it is now moving towards 3%. Are South Koreans preparing themselves for a Chinese invasion? The answer is no. Many analysts conclude that South Korea's President Moon Jae-in (2017 to 2022) ordered this increase in defense effort to enable his country to take back operational control over its military from the United States. Unknown to many in the West, South Korea does not

---

[103] Kang, D. C. (2017). *American Grand Strategy and East Asian Security.* Cambridge University Press.

[104] SIPRI Military Expenditure Database 2021, https://www.sipri.org/databases/milex

control its own military in times of war. The United States does. This goes back to the Korean War of the 1950s, when U.S. General Douglas MacArthur took command of all military forces in Korea. Since then, Washington has never given this command back. By increasing South Korea's military spending, President Moon Jae-in wanted to signal that South Korea can defend itself, and thus should be given back operational control over its own military. South Korea's Defense White Paper of 2018, for example, repeatedly talks about the need for South Korea to increase its military capabilities to acquire operation control. Ironically, South Korea's increase in defense effort is thus not targeted at China but aimed at the United States.[105]

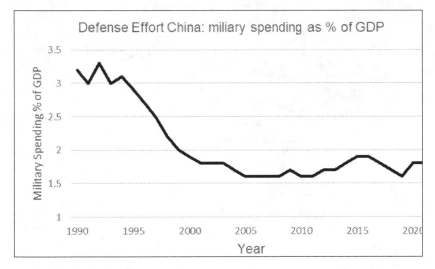

Fig. 13. China's military spending over time.106

Perhaps most surprisingly, at least until 2022 Taiwan had not increased its defense effort. This quite remarkable fact begs the question: "why not?"

The reason is quite simple. The people and governments of East Asia do not want war. They do have real concerns regarding China. Given China's enormous economic and military rise, this is only natural. But instead of looking for a military solution, the people of East Asia are more interested in economic cooperation and more social and cultural exchanges. And in case of a conflict, they use diplomacy to solve it. They do not want to contain China. They do not want to choose sides in a U.S.–China Cold War. They do not even want a U.S.–China contest. And above all, they do not want war.

[105] South Korea's Defense White Paper of 2018.
[106] SIPRI Military Expenditure Database 2021, https://www.sipri.org/databases/milex

For example, a majority of Taiwanese do not want rising tensions with China. They want their government to pursue moderate policies to de-escalate instead of a military buildup.[107]

South Koreans too, despite having real concerns about China, want their government to take a balanced approach to both the United States and China.[108]

In Japan, people believe that the U.S.–China conflict hinders good Japan–China relations. In 2021, the Japanese were more concerned about this than the growth of Chinese military power. According to the Japan–China Public Opinion Survey 2021, the most selected answer by the Japanese was that "Japan and China should build a new relationship based in cooperation in order to stabilize the world economy and bring peace to East Asia." A stunning 70% of Chinese wanted the same.[109]

The Association of Southeast Asian Nations (ASEAN) Studies Centre also concludes that if given a choice, politically informed citizens of Southeast Asia want no part in a U.S.–China contest. They are overly concerned about becoming trapped in the middle of a U.S.–China Cold War. Instead, they want to use diplomacy to solve disputes with China and are not in favor of a U.S. military buildup. What they want is peace and cooperation with China so they too can benefit from China's growing economy.[110]

People in Washington like to refer to the 2020s as the 'decade of maximum danger'. What they fail to mention, however, is that they themselves create this danger. Their attempt to contain and isolate China by threats, intimidation, and a military buildup is causing tensions to rise to dangerous levels. Contrary to the people of East Asia, who desire cooperation and peace, Western leaders are pushing us closer and closer to war.[111]

Unfortunately, in the last few years, Washington has had some success in turning Japan away from a more cooperative and peaceful approach. Washington has encouraged and pushed Japan for decades to expand its military, and the Japanese government is now doing so at an unprecedented rate. It is a sad sight to see a country that has limited the role of its military

---

[107] See Taiwan National Security Survey 2020 Question 22 by Duke University on https://sites.duke.edu/pass/taiwan-national-security-survey/

[108] KINU Unification Survey 2021. *U.S.-China Conflict & South Korean Public Opinion*, p. 37-53.

[109] The Genron NPO. *Japan-China Public Opinion Survey 2022*; The Genron NPO. *Japan-China Public Opinion Survey 2021.*

[110] ASEAN Studies Centre. *The State of Southeast Asia 2020 Survey Report*, see p. 8 and 28; ASEAN Studies Centre. *The State of Southeast Asia 2021 Survey Report*, see Q13 and p. 32 and 38; ASEAN Studies Centre. *The State of Southeast Asia 2022 Survey Report, p. 10-11 and 31.*

[111] Collins, G. & Erickson, A. S. (2021). *U.S.-China Competition Enters the Decade of Maximum Danger.* Baker Institute.

for so many decades (and has been so successfully economically) now throw its defensive military doctrine away and talk about acquiring 'counterstrike capabilities', which refer to offensive strikes at, for example, the Chinese mainland. Although this delights people in Washington, it is setting the scene for an arms race, dangerous escalation, and future war.[112]

We need to realize that Western leaders have not learned anything from the past and are going to march us straight into a war with China. In fact, Taiwan is simply one of many flash points that Washington can use to start a war. Indeed, as discussed in the next chapter, the U.S. government is busy waging an economic and technology war with China to constrain or even roll back its economic rise. This too can easily escalate into a disastrous military confrontation, for example in and around the South China Sea.

---

[112] Smith, S. A. (2019). Japan Rearmed. Harvard University Press; DiFilippo, A. (2015). The Challenges of the U.S.-Japan Military Arrangement. Routledge; Japan's Ministry of Defense. NATIONAL DEFENSE STRATEGY. December 16, 2022; National Security Strategy of Japan. December 2022.

Chapter 3: Economic Warfare and the South China Sea

The island of Subi is a most unusual place. Located in the middle of the South China Sea and surrounded by tropical water, it is not at all what you expect. When we think about islands in the Pacific, we imagine beautiful white sand beaches, coconut palm trees, and pointy green hills covered by an endless jungle of vines, trees, and exotic plants. But on Subi, there are no sandy beaches, nor do palm trees or any other tropical plants grow here naturally. Instead, the shores are stacked with massive concrete structures that prevent the waves from devouring the island. Moving past this man-made blockade, the remainder of the island too displays little of what we call natural.

On Subi, straight roads cut the land into perfect squares. Concrete buildings and other gray structures mark the landscape. There are a few trees, but on closer inspection you will find that these are planted with mathematical precision in symmetrical patterns that you will only find in well-planned urban areas. Contrary to the beautiful mess of the tropical wilderness, Subi conveys a strong feeling of order, control, and planning. And this is, of course, not by coincidence.[113]

Subi Reef, or Subi Island as Beijing likes to call it, is not a natural place. It is one of several artificial islands created by China in the South China Sea. They are built with a purpose. The giant runways on which large cargo and military planes take off and land already give a clue on what that might be. Seen from above, Subi, like its sister islands of Mischief and Fiery Cross,

---

[113] See earth.google.com and search for Subi Reef. Accessed 22-11-2022.

reminds you of an aircraft carrier. An unsinkable one, in fact. One that gives the owner great military potential and control over this part of the globe.

These vast construction projects are carried out over 1,300 kilometers (800+ miles) away from China's shores and take up enormous resources. Why is Beijing doing this? Is this a sign of aggressive expansion by the Chinese government? Or is China merely protecting its economic interests against a potential U.S. economic war?

Turning Rocks into Islands

In the South China Sea (SCS), two superpowers collide. China and the United States each have strong interests in the region. Consequently, both players wish to control and dominate this part of the Pacific. With the stakes being high, it has led to some remarkably interesting developments, a few of them quite bizarre, almost comical, yet all extremely dangerous. In fact, the SCS is one of several flash points that can spark World War III. But before going into detail about what a conflict over the SCS will look like, let us first understand why the region is so important to both China and the United States.

Beijing's concerns are very much economic. Because the SCS connects the Indian and the Pacific Oceans it is a very important shipping route. Hundreds of cargo ships and giant oil tankers pass through every day, many of them coming from or going to the major economies of South Korea, Japan, Taiwan, and China. Chinese leaders know that access to the SCS is crucial for their country's imports and exports, and thus for China's economy in general. Economics aside, they also understand that the SCS is a way to mitigate the militarized island chains that the United States has set up to contain China.

For Washington, the SCS matters because it enables the U.S. Navy to dominate the Indo–Pacific theater. The Indo–Pacific is a term the U.S. military uses to refer to the regions and countries around China, including India, hence the term Indo–Pacific and not Asia–Pacific. U.S. military commanders proudly claim they can dominate an area the size of 52% of the Earth's surface. But without the South China Sea, the Indo and Pacific parts are disconnected, and that makes it much more difficult to dominate this part of the world. And besides, U.S. leaders understand that control over the SCS gives them a wonderful opportunity to not only contain China, but to bring the country and its government to their knees.[114]

---

[114] Department of Defense Press Briefing on U.S. Pacific Command's Area of Responsibility by Admiral Locklear in the Pentagon Briefing Room, comments by U.S. Pacific Command

But how do you gain control over an area as vast as the SCS? In the case of Beijing, the Chinese leadership has opted for a dual approach, one legal, the other military.

With its famous nine-dash line, Beijing has signaled to the world that it considers the SCS as Chinese territory. It is an enormously unreasonable claim. Whereas other countries that border the South China Sea have come up with a much more equal way to divide the region, China simply wants it all.

To justify this, Chinese leaders say that historical evidence proves that ancient Chinese were the first to discover and settle in this area. In a way, this follows Western practices that whoever makes the discovery can claim it. But what Beijing conveniently leaves out is that this is just one of several theories about who discovered the region, and that historians and archeologists are not sure which theory is correct. As you can imagine, this criticism does not sit well with Chinese leaders, who have decided to take the discussion to the next level.

To strengthen its claim and weaken the arguments of its opponents, the Chinese government has responded with a more aggressive approach. In fact, they have sent in Chinese Marine Surveillance ships to chase away foreign archeologists who study the region and its history. They are then replaced by Chinese archeologists who, of course, have no trouble finding 'evidence' of Chinese origins.[115]

This then brings us to China's military approach to the SCS. Just in case the world is not convinced by Beijing's legal and historical arguments, Chinese leaders have been busy increasing their military footprint. In the process, they have come up with some very creative solutions.

Not only is China upgrading its naval forces, but they are also building military installations on several islands in the midst of the SCS. The idea is that from these islands, the Chinese military can project its power and take control of the area. Two groups of islands, the Paracel and Spratly Islands, are key. But there is a complication. These islands are claimed by a whole bunch of countries, not just China. Other contenders include Vietnam, Taiwan, Malaysia, the Philippines, and Brunei. This then has led to a most interesting, somewhat comical, yet very dangerous legal and military cat-and-mouse game between all of them. And if that is not a good enough recipe for escalation, Washington and its mighty navy loom over the area as well.

Commander, Admiral Samuel Locklear, Sept. 25, 2014; Hayton, B. (2014). *The South China Sea: The Struggle for Power in Asia.* Yale University Press, p. 202-203.

[115] Hayton, B. (2014). *The South China Sea: The Struggle for Power in Asia.* Yale University Press, chapter 1

Let us begin with untangling the rather bizarre and comical side of this competition, which is all about ownership and subsequent control. What is happening is the following: International law, specifically the United Nations Convention on the Law of the Sea (UNCLOS), recognizes three types of land structures. There are real islands that are always above sea level, and they can support settlement or economic life. There are 'rocks', which are merely reefs or sandbanks above water level that cannot support either. Finally, there are 'low-tide elevations', which are below water except during low tide. Now, the crucial thing to understand is that each of them gives the owner specific rights and benefits.[116]

An island gives the owner the right to claim the territory surrounding it within 12 nautical miles, plus an exclusive economic zone (EEZ) that stretches 200 nautical miles. Note that the EEZ is important here, because within this zone, many countries claim that they have the right to control which foreign ships are allowed to enter. For China, this is very interesting, because it could deny the U.S. Navy access to large parts of the SCS. An island thus gives the owner great power and control. Contrary to islands, rocks only allow you to claim the 12-nautical-mile sea around it. The low-tide elevations generally give the owner nothing. And this is where the trouble started for Beijing.

Unfortunately for Chinese leaders, they were late to the party. When China attempted to increase its presence in the SCS, all the real islands, as defined under UNCLOS, were already taken by other countries, such as Vietnam and the Philippines. China's leadership thus had to settle for what was left, which were mostly disappointing rocks and low-tide elevations. These, however, do not grant them the benefits that they desired. But instead of accepting this unfavorable reality, Beijing decided to get creative. In fact, they had a very clever trick up their sleeves.[117]

In a series of mind-boggling construction projects, China is turning these rocks and low-tide elevations into islands. Through gigantic reclamation works and the construction of fortified sea walls, these rocks and low-tide elevations are elevated above sea level and expanded in size and surface area. Then, on top of them, Chinese engineers are building airfields, multi-story buildings, radar domes, gun emplacements, docks, and many other structures. Naturally, these are always above sea level, and they are home to settlers and economic activity — the two key requirements to qualify as an

---

[116] Hayton, B. (2014). *The South China Sea: The Struggle for Power in Asia.* Yale University Press; Turcsanyi, R. Q. (2018). *Chinese Assertiveness in the South China Sea.* Springer International Publishing

[117] Turcsanyi, R. Q. (2018). *Chinese Assertiveness in the South China Sea.* Springer International Publishing, p. 37

island. As such, it would grant the owner the right to claim the 12-nautical-mile sea around it plus the 200-nautical-mile exclusive economic zone. Checkmate; or is it?

Although this is a nice trick, probably one of the most expensive ones ever performed, it is not difficult to see through it, question its legitimacy, and to present it to the world as a threat. Unsurprisingly, this is what Western politicians and the Western media have focused on. They have especially emphasized how these Chinese activities in the SCS highlight Beijing's dangerous ambitions for world domination. But as is important to know, what Western reporting on this issue generally ignores is the fact that China is not the only one playing this game. In fact, they were not even the first.[118]

Vietnam, Malaysia, the Philippines, and Taiwan too are in the business of turning rocks into militarized islands. One notable example is Vietnam and the island of Truong Sa Lon, also known as Big Truong Sa. Whatever the name may suggest, the island is everything but big. It is 28 hectares in size, 13 of them natural and 15 man-made. Big Truong Sa's highest point above sea level is a whopping 2.5 meters. This unnatural island's main attraction is a concrete runway, built by the Vietnamese military, which takes up a quarter of the whole place. The remainder of the island displays a weird mix of civilian and military buildings. There is a school, a church, and several homes. There are also radar posts, windmills, bunkers, and battle tanks. Scattered in between are some imported trees that fail to give the island a sense of natural beauty. A high concrete wall surrounds an otherwise beautiful beach to prevent the waves from eating up the island. Meanwhile, the whole purpose of this enterprise by Vietnam is to make it seem that big Truong Sa is home to a vibrant and economically viable community. It is to show that it is a 'normal' island, an island that, under UNCLOS, gives Vietnam the right to establish its territorial and economic zone around it. And the military presence on the island is to signal to others they better respect this claim.[119]

So, to summarize, what you have in the South China Sea is a chain of islands and artificial land structures, many dotted with military installations. The countries who claim these increasingly unnatural structures are all wearily eyeing each other. As a result, the whole region is characterized by pretense, intimidation, and fear. Meanwhile, the United States also wants its

---

[118] Hayton, B. (2014). *The South China Sea: The Struggle for Power in Asia.* Yale University Press, chapter 4; Turcsanyi, R. Q. (2018). *Chinese Assertiveness in the South China Sea.* Springer International Publishing, p. 51-52

[119] Hayton, B. (2014). *The South China Sea: The Struggle for Power in Asia.* Yale University Press, chapter 4; Turcsanyi, R. Q. (2018). *Chinese Assertiveness in the South China Sea.* Springer International Publishing, p. 51-52

military to control this strategic region, and they are seeking military allies to fight against China. Potential candidates are Taiwan, the Philippines, and Vietnam, whose militarized islands are next to China's. It sets the scene for dangerous future confrontations. And, when it comes to confrontation, it is especially one type of conflict that Beijing fears the most. Unsurprisingly, this is the one that Washington is most seriously considering, namely the plan to cut off China's economic lifelines in and around the South China Sea.

Naval Blockades and Economic Lifelines

What would it take to bring the world to the brink of World War III? It could, in fact, happen overnight. For years, U.S. officials have been carefully planning how to cut off what are considered to be China's economic lifelines. The U.S. Navy could do so by blockading strategically located sea lanes in the Indo–Pacific region. All-out war with China may then suddenly become very real. But how would Washington go about this? Will it work? And what would Beijing's response be?

U.S. naval strategists have produced several scenarios. These focus on blockading the very narrow sea lanes in the Indonesian archipelago that connect the Indian Ocean with the South China Sea. The most famous of those is the Malacca Strait, which is a long and narrow stretch of water in between Malaysia and the Indonesian island of Sumatra. It is the main shipping channel between the Indian and Pacific Ocean and is very important for China's economy. Most estimates will tell you that around 70 to 80 percent of China's crude oil imports go through the Malacca Strait. In fact, around 40 percent of China's total trade, worth close to a trillion dollars, may be shipped from the South China Sea through the Malacca Strait towards South Asia, the Middle East, Africa, and Europe. And this makes the strait, and others like it, a very tempting target that Washington can use to thwart its Asian rival.[120]

But how would they do it? This is a much more difficult question to answer than you may think. Although a blockade sounds simple, it is not at all easy. You cannot simply send a fleet of warships into the Malacca Strait and block all cargo ships and oil tankers trying to pass through.

For one, other countries, including important U.S. allies like South Korea and Japan, are also very much dependent on these waters for their overseas trade. They would never tolerate a blockade of their ships. This means that the United States must be selective. Ships carrying Chinese goods must

---

[120] ChinaPower Center for Strategic and International Studies. How Much Trade Transits the South China Sea?; Collins, G. B. & Murray, W.S. (2008). No Oil for the Lamps of China, Naval War College Review, Vol. 61, No. 2.

be turned away or confiscated, while other ships should be cleared to sail through. While identifying to which country a particular ship belongs is comparatively easy, many Chinese goods, including oil, are carried on ships owned by a whole range of countries. How do you know whether an Italian cargo ship carries Chinese goods? You would have to board the ship, investigate papers, and perhaps even carry out a search. This is not only time-consuming, but it also takes up a lot of men and material. You need special teams to conduct these boarding operations. They require ships of their own and even helicopters. Now imagine doing this to every single vessel out of the hundreds of ships that pass through these straits every day. Even if every ship cooperates, which is unlikely, it is an enormous operation.

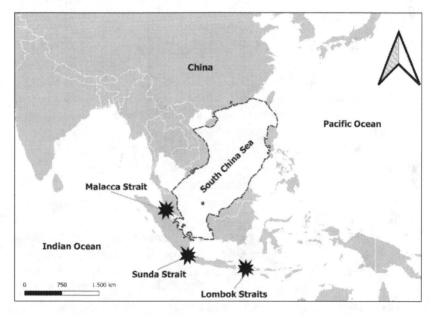

Fig. 14. Key sea lanes that the United States is considering to block to cut off China's economic lifelines.

And what do you do if a cargo ship crew refuses a boarding action by the U.S. military? Do you send in the Navy Seals with the big guns? Do you open fire? And what would be the consequences to international shipping and U.S. relations with the victimized country?

And to make it even more challenging, the U.S. Navy cannot limit itself to the Malacca Strait alone, since several other shipping straits in the Indonesian archipelago need to be blockaded too. Yet despite being faced with such difficulties, U.S. strategists have come up with a comprehensive plan to cut off Chinese overseas trade in the Indo–Pacific. What they believe would be a successful naval blockade requires a 'two-ring blockade'.[121]

Let us start with the inner ring, which is the more dramatic of the two. In fact, the inner ring is a dead zone. In this region, which follows China's shorelines, the U.S. Navy would simply destroy, without warning, any ship that dares to sail through. It is a no-go zone, one in which U.S. submarines follow a sink-on-sight policy. In this scenario, Washington expects that U.S. submarines are its most powerful weapon. Surface ships are much more problematic so close to the Chinese mainland because the People's Liberation Army's has Anti-Access and Area Denial (A2/AD) systems that can target those with a barrage of missiles. Submarines, however, are much more difficult to hit. The U.S. Navy could also decide to use smart mines to mine major Chinese ports that are important to international shipping.[122]

Moving further away from Chinese territory, the inner ring is lined by an outer ring. The function of this outer ring is to act like a filter. Its job is to block ships involved in Chinese trade while letting all others sail through. To do so, this ring consists of a series of checkpoints that cover important shipping routes like the Malacca Strait and the other key passageways in East Asia.

The two rings are both important because there are many ways to deal with a blockade. Ships can always change their destination, and resources like oil can be bought and sold on international markets while the oil tanker is at sea. For example, a tanker carrying oil to South Korea will pass the outer ring because its destination is not China. But if the cargo — the oil — on that ship is then bought by a Chinese company, the ship, having passed the outer ring, can then change course and sail to a Chinese port. So, whereas the outer ring will already filter out most of the ships destined for China, the inner ring will prevent anyone from trying these kinds of tricks.

Although this sounds like an effective strategy on paper, it creates dangerous possibilities for escalation. Take the inner ring, for example. Washington expects that its submarines will give it a decisive advantage over the PLA Navy. The myth of Western military's technological supremacy, however, has been shattered in Ukraine in the war against Russia. A long list of Western weapons that were expected to dominate the battlefield have been successfully dealt with by the Russian army. Although U.S. officials

---

[121] For a good discussion on the complexities of a naval blockade, see *Collins, G. B. & Murray, W.S. (2008). No Oil for the Lamps of China, Naval War College Review, Vol. 61, No. 2*. See also *Fiona S. Cunningham (2020). The Maritime Rung on the Escalation Ladder: Naval Blockades in a U.S.-China Conflict, Security Studies, 29:4, 730-768*.

[122] Sean Mirski (2013). *Stranglehold: The Context, Conduct and Consequences of an American Naval Blockade of China, Journal of Strategic Studies, 36:3, 385-421*.

believed that the sight of a Bradley fighting vehicle or a Leopard tank would instill such fear in Russian soldiers that they would drop their weapons and run away in a panic, the only thing the world got to see is how well these vehicles burned after they had been destroyed by Russian drones, mines, missiles, and artillery. Faced with such humiliation, Washington did what it always does, namely to escalate by sending in more deadly and controversial weapons. This scenario can easily be repeated in the waters around China. When U.S. submarines do not prove to be as effective as Washington expects, for example because they are successfully countered by one of China's new weapon systems such as its secretive mini-submarines, U.S. leaders will simply escalate with more dangerous weapons and strategies. And make no mistake about it, they already have a list of targets they will go after.[123]

U.S. strategists have made other plans to weaken China's economy. These plans focus heavily on China's energy needs, especially its imports of oil. The idea here is that a country not only needs crude oil, but it also needs to refine the oil and then transport it to where it is needed. This requires all kinds of processing plants and infrastructure, all of which can be destroyed in targeted strikes. What these U.S. strategists imagine are missile strikes on Chinese oil refineries, pumping stations, storage facilities, and pipelines. With such key infrastructure destroyed and out of order for months, Beijing may ship in all the crude oil that it wants, it has lost the ability to use the oil for its civilian economy and its military. In this case, even without a naval blockade that chokes off China's oil imports, the Chinese energy sector will be severely hampered.[124]

Another strategy, which may be used together with a naval blockade, is to prevent Beijing from coping with a loss in overseas oil. Imagine that the U.S. Navy carries out a successful blockade and oil tankers no longer dock in Chinese ports. But if China can import its oil through overland pipelines, what is the point of the naval blockade? Luckily for Washington, they know where these pipelines are located. There are several major ones, including pipelines that come from Russia, Central Asia, and Southeast Asia. They all transport oil or gas into China to help satisfy the latter's energy needs. In fact, these pipelines would go some way in relieving the pressure on the Chinese economy and its military in case of a successful naval blockade, especially when these pipelines are upgraded and expanded in the future.

---

[123] Sutton, H. I. China's New Submarine Is Unlike Anything In Western Navies. Naval News, February 15, 2022.
[124] Collins, G. B. & Murray, W.S. (2008). No Oil for the Lamps of China, Naval War College Review, Vol. 61, No. 2

Washington, after having implemented their blockade, may be tempted to strike these targets as well. For example, the U.S. could use missiles to destroy the oil and gas pipeline that travels from Myanmar into Yunnan province, China. They may do the same to the oil pipelines that go from the Central Asian countries into Xinjiang. And if U.S. leaders behave particularly recklessly, they may even strike pipelines connecting Russia to China. With the destruction of Nord Stream being a U.S. secret operation, as investigative journalist Seymour Hersch has revealed, nothing seems too dangerous to U.S. fanatics in the White House.[125]

Beijing's response to all of this is anyone's guess. But many U.S. analysts believe that a naval blockade that is intended to strangle the Chinese economy will be regarded as an act of economic warfare, and even an act of war itself. Things can also escalate very quickly. Suppose a Chinese oil tanker decides to ignore the blockade. What will the U.S. do with a 300-meter-long oil tanker weighing several hundred thousand tons that refuses to stop? Having a U.S. attack submarine sink it with a torpedo is one option, but that most likely means war. Sending in the Navy Seals to take control of the ship using minimum violence may be less risky, but not by a lot. Just ask yourself, how would Washington react if Beijing started sending in military forces to board U.S. vessels, overpower their crews, and confiscate their cargo?

When it comes to economic warfare, a military blockade of important trade routes is just one of several methods that the U.S. can use. Washington has other options as well, all of them with the dangerous potential of turning into full-scale military conflict. Besides blockading trade, the U.S. seems especially keen to use two other types of economic warfare. These involve technology and finance.

In the next few sections, the way how the United States tries to cut off China from essential technology will be discussed in detail. The focus will be on advanced technology such as semiconductors — which according to technology experts form the backbone of any modern economy. Like a trade and oil embargo, this "chip war," as some call it, has the potential to spark Pearl Harbor-style moves by Beijing, which would ignite World War III. Yet despite these risks, Washington has already taken the first steps in waging a technological war against China. This makes it even more important to understand exactly what is happening and what the consequences may be.

Finally, the last sections of this chapter focus on a newly designed weapon to attack and bring down entire economies. It moves us deep into the realm

---

[125] Sean Mirski (2013). *Stranglehold: The Context, Conduct and Consequences of an American Naval Blockade of China,* Journal of Strategic Studies, 36:3, 385-421.

of economic and financial sanctions. Sanctions may sound neutral, but they are vicious, destructive, and deadly. Specialists in the U.S. Treasury who design and implement sanctions say plainly that they are intended to inflict pain and suffering. Consequently, sanctions have been devastating to entire societies. Interestingly, as the recent use of sanctions against Russia in 2022 has shown, the collateral damage may be enormous as well, and can harm Western populations too. Unfortunately, it is highly likely that Washington will use this weapon as well in their misguided attempt to bring down the Chinese economy and the Chinese Communist Party.

Not Oil but Chips

Did you know that during most years since the year 2000, China spent more money importing chips than oil? The reason is simple. Chips, also known as semiconductors or integrated circuits, can be found in all devices, from smartphones and computers to microwaves, machine tools, and cars. China is highly dependent on them, both for the goods its people consume at home and for the electronics the country exports abroad. Unfortunately for Beijing, China's dependency on foreign-made chips stems from two massive problems that are extremely hard to fix. These then create major vulnerabilities — ones that Washington is eager to exploit.

The first problem that China faces is that its own position in producing chips is not very strong, especially when it comes to the more advanced and cutting-edge chips. When you look at the chip supply chain — which refers to all the steps that are necessary to produce a chip — it becomes immediately clear that, overall, Chinese companies play a small role. And when it comes to choke points, which refer to specific points in the supply chain that are so difficult and specialized that only one or a few tech companies can do it, China is mostly or completely absent. Let us take a closer look at what this means in practice.

Producing a chip is a difficult and elaborate process. In fact, it takes so much knowledge and resources that there is no single company anywhere on Earth that can do it alone. Instead, for each of the required steps there are a few highly specialized businesses. The software used to design chips is mostly made by U.S. companies, while Chinese businesses own less than 1% of the global market. When it comes to producing chip-making materials, China has only 4%. For tools to fabricate chips this is 1%, and for chip design it is 5%. China only produces 7% of the global supply of chips, and none of them involve the most advanced ones. When taking everything together, China's share across the entire chip supply chain is only 6% of the global market, compared to 39% for the United States, South Korea's 16%, and Taiwan's 12%. Yet despite this glaring dependency on foreign chips due to China's limited role in the chip supply chain, this is not the worst part for Beijing.

Chinese leaders would sleep much better at night if the chip supply chain were dominated by their allies or countries that are politically neutral in the U.S.–China Cold War. Imagine if Russia were a major player in the global chip market. Sure, it would not solve China's dependency, but then at least Beijing could rest assured that their supply of chips is safe, because Russia is a close ally. But unfortunately for President Xi and his colleagues, this is not the world we live in. In fact, the overwhelming share of the global chip supply chain, including all the most advanced chips and related technology, is dominated by the United States and its allies.

The chip industry first took off in the United States in the 1960s, and to this day, the U.S. retains a leading role. Virtually every chip that is produced anywhere in the world has a connection to Silicon Valley, California. Besides the United States, the other major players are European countries, Japan, South Korea, Singapore, and Taiwan — all U.S. allies.

For example, chips are designed by American companies such as Intel or Nvidia, using computer software from other U.S.-based businesses like Cadence, Synopsys, and Mentor. This design is then sent to Taiwan Semiconductor Manufacturing Company (TSMC) — the leading fabricator of the most advanced chips. TSMC produces chips using sophisticated machine tools produced by a Dutch company ASML and by using other specialized materials from Japan or the United States. Many chips are then packaged and tested in Southeast Asia before being sent to China to be assembled in electric goods such as a phone or computer.

These supply chains differ a little bit for different chips. The production of memory chips, for example, which are used by devices to remember information, is dominated by South Korea and Japan. The biggest chip makers of analog chips, which perform a variety of functions such as processing visual and audio signals, are American, European, and Japanese. Logic chips, which run processes on computers and smartphones, are mostly designed by American firms and fabricated in places like Taiwan, especially by TSMC.

And when it comes to the most advanced high-technology chips, China is entirely reliant on American software and design; Dutch, Japanese, and American machinery; and South Korean and Taiwanese fabrication. No wonder Chinese leaders are stressed about a potential U.S.-led attempt to cut off China from vital technology. Given the composition of the global supply chain, Washington is in an immensely powerful position to pull this off. And this is exactly what U.S. leaders are signaling.

Before discussing the evolution of American technology policy vis-à-vis China and how it has taken on an increasingly aggressive form, it is important to answer the following crucial questions: Why are U.S. leaders concerned with China's technological rise? And why is Washington trying to prevent China from developing its own chip industry?

History gives us the answer. At least twice before has Washington blocked the economic and technological development of another country that it perceived as a serious competitor. The first case was the technological blockade that the United States imposed on the Soviet Union during the Cold War. The same playbook was then repeated in the 1980s and 1990s against none other than Japan — an official U.S. ally. Japanese industry, which had developed spectacularly under the guidance of the Ministry of International Trade and Industry (MITI), was becoming "too successful" in the eyes of U.S. officials. Japanese chip, automobile, and electronic firms were beginning to out-compete U.S. businesses. This had to stop. Nobody, not even official allies, are allowed to challenge American hegemony.

Consequently, in the mid 1980s, Washington began limiting Japanese exports to U.S. markets. They also forced Japan to overvalue its currency in order to make Japanese exports more expensive and thus less attractive. The United States could do these things because U.S. leverage over Japan was enormous. This included a vast U.S. military presence on Japanese soil, a U.S.-dominated Middle East from which Japan gets much of its energy supplies, and the importance of the U.S. market to the Japanese economy. Japan's government, as high-level Japanese officials remember, was put under so much pressure that they were forced to go along. And, as they feared, it did not take long before economic growth collapsed and crisis began. Japan's "Lost Decades" were thus engineered by Washington. The sole purpose was to crush any serious challenger to U.S. dominance, and it worked with great success. In fact, Japan has yet to recover.[126]

Going back to China, the U.S. goal is again to prevent another nation from catching up or overtaking the United States. U.S. officials, therefore, do not want China to succeed in building up its high tech industry. They want China to be subordinate and forever weak, vulnerable, and dependent on the United States. And to accomplish their goal, U.S. officials have taken an increasingly aggressive and dangerous approach, especially in recent years.

---

[126] Jeffrey D. Sachs. The US economic war on China. *The Jordan Times*, Aug 26, 2023

Strangling China's Tech Sector

Sitting behind a huge table, Foreign Minister Qin Gang (December 2022 to July 2023) presided over a room packed with journalists, both Chinese and foreign. It was March 7, 2023, and the newly appointed minister was about to talk about China's foreign policy, with a special focus on relations with the United States. Speaking calmly and softly, as Chinese leaders often do, he nonetheless sent a strong and powerful message.[127]

As can be expected, Qin Gang quickly began discussing the United States. He recognized that China and the U.S. are in a race for technological development and technological dominance. He then made an interesting comparison to sports to illustrate how the two sides are going about it. Imagine two athletes competing against each other in an Olympic race. One athlete, China, according to Qin, is giving its best by trying to run faster. The other athlete, the United States, tries to win by injuring the opponent instead. This is unfair and illegal, Qin continues.

Of course, what the Chinese Foreign Minister means is that the United States, to ensure its own technological dominance, always tries to undermine China's development through illegal means such as technological sanctions.

Interestingly, and perhaps not by coincidence, Qin Gang was not the first to use this sports metaphor. It goes back to the Obama administration. It was then that U.S. officials became more concerned about how to deal with the rise of the Chinese chip industry. The approach they decided to take to ensure American technological dominance was, in their own words, "win the race by running faster." Recognizing that the two superpowers were in competition with each other, the Obama administration planned to boost investment and innovation so that America could stay ahead.

There were some, however, who did not agree with this policy. Within the National Security bureaucracy, there were voices that spoke of a more aggressive and cynical approach. Then, when Trump took office, their view became the dominant one. "It would be great for us to run faster," one national security official stated, but it is not enough. In order to stay ahead in the race, the United States also has to try and injure its competitor. Consequently, Washington took a more aggressive, zero-sum path forward to technology development in general, and chips in particular.

What happened next is that during the Trump administration, several Chinese companies were targeted, including the most famous ones like Huawei, ZTE, and Fujian Jinhua Integrated Circuit Co. Over time, the

---

[127] Foreign Minister Qin Gang makes the following points during a press conference on March 7, 2023. See https://www.fmprc.gov.cn/mfa_eng/zxxx_662805/202303/t20230307_11037190.html

number of companies targeted by U.S. sanctions has grown, and U.S. actions also increased in intensity.

Take Jinhua, a producer of memory chips located in Fujian, a province on the southeastern coast of China. Because the company itself has been accused of stealing U.S. chip designs, an allegation that may very well be true, it was an easy case for Washington to justify testing out its technological sanctions.

In October 2018, Washington put the company on the so-called Entity List. This is a trade restriction list published by the United States Department of Commerce's Bureau of Industry and Security. U.S. businesses have to get approval (an export license) from the U.S. government if they want to sell goods to a company on the Entity list. It meant that Jinhua could no longer just buy goods with components, software, or technology originating from American firms. As a result, Jinhua was unable to buy from the United States highly specialized equipment and tools needed to produce advanced chips. The only alternative producer of these tools is Japan, but Washington coordinated with Tokyo so that they too stopped selling these items to China. Within months, Jinhua, China's most advanced memory chip firm, was in serious trouble, with production grinding to a halt.

Having succeeded in injuring an important Chinese chip maker, Washington set its sights on an even bigger target: Huawei. This company is one of the biggest success stories regarding China's technological development. Huawei produces all kinds of cutting-edge telecommunication equipment and technologies such as 5G. Interestingly, in order to justify U.S. attacks on the company, American officials have repeatedly referred to the possibility that Huawei's 5G networks are designed to allow the Chinese government to spy on its users. This is, however, mostly a distraction according to Chris Miller, author of the book the Chip War. The real reason why the United States acted to undermine Huawei is, first and foremost, all about the struggle for technological superiority and dominance. Huawei was positioning itself as a central player in sectors that used to be dominated by U.S. businesses, and Washington was not about to let that happen.

It is important to note that Washington's motivation is purely geopolitical and solely based on continued U.S. hegemony. Although U.S. politicians say that they are imposing sanctions because Huawei and the Chinese government are using "unfair" economic practices to develop advanced technology, this is a lie. In fact, Huawei's business model is very similar to that of Samsung, Sony, and other East Asian tech companies. The Chinese economic development model is also strongly based on that of Japan, and Japan got much of its inspiration from looking at how the United States developed its economy. No, the reason why U.S. officials want to destroy Huawei and other firms like it is because they simply cannot stomach the fact that a Chinese company has developed into a tech giant rivaling American tech companies. They also feel angry and frustrated that Huawei's success is stimulating China's technological capabilities in key areas.

For these reasons, on May 15, 2019, the Trump administration put Huawei on the Entity List, in effect banning the sales of U.S.-made chips to the Chinese company. This was a blow to Huawei, because it lost access to advanced U.S.-designed chips, for example from Intel and Nvidia. But there were still some openings left. Huawei could, for example, still buy chips from Taiwan's TSMC, if the design of those chips was not American. But this loophole did not last long.

The next year, in 2020, the Trump administration doubled down and extended the restrictions on chips manufactured by foreign firms that use U.S. software or equipment. This meant that TSMC, which uses U.S. software and equipment to produce chips, was no longer allowed to sell chips to Chinese companies — even if the chip designs themselves were not American.[128]

Then in 2022, the U.S. government, under the Biden administration, imposed new and more aggressive restrictions. They extended the 2020 ban on Huawei to the entire Chinese tech industry. Any firm anywhere in the world that produces chips with American technology now must ask the U.S. government for permission to sell to China.

Meanwhile, Biden set out to block China from buying machinery, materials, and software required to produce chips. For example, the U.S. pressured the Dutch government and ASML — a Dutch company that stands alone in producing complex machinery to make the most advanced chips — to stop their sales of machinery and equipment to Chinese firms. The Biden administration did the same to Japan — another important supplier of advanced equipment and materials to produce chips.[129]

In the same month, Biden also decided to stop approving export licenses to U.S. companies that sell to Huawei. Under Trump, only the sales of advanced chips and equipment to Huawei were refused, but under Biden,

[128] Dylan Martin, US sanctions drain Huawei of homegrown advanced chips, *The Register*, 21 December, 2022. See https://www.theregister.com/2022/12/21/us_sanctions_huawei_chips/

[129] Sevastopulo, D. & Fleming, S. Netherlands and Japan join US in restricting chip exports to China, *Financial Times*, January 28, 2023. https://www.ft.com/content/baa27f42-0557-4377-839b-a4f4524cfa20

all chips, including the lesser advanced ones, can no longer be sold to the Chinese tech giant.[130]

Moves like those listed above reveal that it is no longer a limited technology war targeting specific Chinese companies. Washington has declared war against the entire Chinese tech industry. According to the New York Times, the Biden administration aimed to "use U.S. influence over global technology and supply chains to choke off China's access to advanced chips and chip production tools." Washington's goal was to slow down Chinese economic and technological development and keep it "far behind" that of the United States.[131]

This is different from Trump's trade war with China. What Donald Trump did was at least partially motivated by nationalist sentiment about bringing back manufacturing jobs to the United States. Trump's restrictions on technology were also limited in scale and in scope. The Biden administration, however, has moved well beyond this. Their actions have nothing to do with stimulating the U.S. economy or creating jobs. Instead, it is all about undermining China's economic development and slowing its growth. The Financial Times refers to this as a move to "isolate China's entire high-tech sector," both military and civilian. The goal is to deny China the "basic building blocks for an advanced, globally competitive economy," according to Foreign Policy magazine, a move akin to "economic containment" or, as many analysts describe the effects of sanctions: economic and technological strangulation.[132]

The consequences of such actions can be severe, and the benefits are small. These technological sanctions certainly will delay China's development, but they cannot stop it. In fact, as many analysts conclude, they encourage and thereby stimulate Beijing's efforts in developing a strong and successful Chinese chip industry. Meanwhile, the U.S. is taking an enormous risk and creating dangerous conditions for escalation and conflict.[133]

---

[130] Freifeld, K., Alper, A. & Nellis, S. U.S. stops granting export licenses for China's Huawei - sources, Reuters, January 31, 2023. https://www.reuters.com/technology/us-stops-provision-licences-export-chinas-huawei-ft-2023-01-30/

[131] Swanson, A. & Wong, E. "With New Crackdown, Biden Wages Global Campaign on Chinese Technology," New York Times, October 13, 2022, https://www.nytimes.com/2022/10/13/us/politics/biden-china-technology-semiconductors.html

[132] Luce, E. "Containing China is Biden's explicit goal," Financial Times, October 19, 2022, https://www.ft.com/content/398f0d4e-906e-479b-a9a7-e4023c298f39; Bateman, J. "Biden Is Now All-In on Taking Out China." Foreign Policy, October 12, 2022, https://foreignpolicy.com/2022/10/12/biden-china-semiconductor-chips-exports-decouple/;

Cotton, T. (2021). Beat China: Targeted Decoupling and the Economic Long War. United States Senate.

[133] Miller, C. (2022). Chip War. Routledge. Simon & Schuster Ltd, see comment by Dan Wang

One thing that stands out when it comes to sanctions is that the trend is always towards more escalation. It starts with limited sanctions on one Chinese company, but then they expand to more businesses and become more restrictive. Soon, the U.S. is targeting the entire Chinese tech sector and is blocking access to all kinds of chips and technology.

It is important to note that these are harmful moves aimed against Chinese people. Advanced chips are not only important for technologies like artificial intelligence and robotics that can have military applications, which is what U.S. officials talk about in trying to justify the sanctions. These chips also play a vital role in medical imaging, pharmaceutical development, climate research, and many other civilian applications.[134]

In this sense, it is a quite remarkable feat of restraint that the Chinese government has shown during these years, although as of May 2023 that has changed. That month the Chinese government told Chinese companies to stop purchasing products from Micron Technology, a U.S.-based manufacturer of memory chips for mobile phones, computers, and other electronic devices. Given its very limited scope, these Chinese sanctions were a warning to Washington to stop escalating their economic war against China.[135]

U.S. officials, however, had no intention of backing down. In the next few weeks, they successfully pressured the Netherlands and Japan to stop selling specialized equipment and machinery to China for the production of advanced chips. Just days after the Dutch and Japanese governments announced these export restrictions, the Chinese government, having already warned the West that it would do so, ordered export restrictions on gallium and germanium metals and several of their compounds, which are key materials for manufacturing chips.[136]

The Chinese media reported again that this move serves as a warning that China is not simply going to let itself be cut off from the international chip supply chain, and that Western leaders should stop their economic war. Chinese officials are saying the same thing. Wei Jianguo, vice president of China Center for International Economic Exchanges, explained that "this is just the beginning of China's countermeasures, and there are many more

[134] Levits, E. Biden's New Cold War Against China Could Backfire The U.S. is now committed to thwarting China's development. At what cost? *New York Magazine*, November 14, 2022, https://nymag.com/intelligencer/2022/11/biden-economic-war-china-chips-semiconductors-export-controls.html

[135] Chang Che. *China Bans Some Sales of Chips From U.S. Company Micron*. New York Times, May 21, 2023.

[136] Liu Zhen. *China curbs critical metal exports in retaliation for Western restrictions on chip industry.* South China Morning Post, July 3, 2023; Shunsuke Tabeta. *China weighs export ban for rare-earth magnet tech.* Nikkei, April 6, 2023.

means and types of sanctions that China can use. If the high-tech restrictions on China continue to escalate, China's countermeasures will also escalate."[137]

While Western politicians like to believe that they can control where these things are going, the reality is that this sense of control was an illusion, and now China has started hitting back. It would be wise for us to realize that Beijing, contrary to most other targets of Western sanctions, is certainly not defenseless. They have already demonstrated that they can come up with their own sanctions, and they do not have to limit themselves to technology.

The United States, for example, gets much of its medical equipment and medicine from China. The same can be said for many rare earth minerals that are essential for modern technology, from smartphones to cars and airplanes. If this technology war escalates into something bigger, the effects on complex international systems are impossible to predict. There will be winners and losers, but, as always, the most vulnerable groups in society will be harmed the most when supply chains are disrupted, prices rise, and global technological and economic development slows down.[138]

But there is another danger lurking in the shadows. While the above economic picture may look bleak, economic wars can turn into military confrontations. In fact, the chip war the U.S. is waging may spark a Pearl Harbor style move by Beijing and a subsequent all-out war between the two superpowers.

The Next Pearl Harbor

On November 26, 1941, six aircraft carriers left Hitokappu Bay, a natural harbor on Iterup island located just northeast of Japan's main islands. Although negotiations between the United States and Imperial Japan were still ongoing, Japanese leaders did not expect diplomacy to solve the ongoing conflict between the two.

In the following days, the battle group sailed towards its destination and prepared for a surprise attack. Thanks to Takeo Yoshikawa, a spy who had infiltrated U.S. military installations on Hawaii, the Japanese commanders

---

[137] GT Voice: *US, its allies need to listen to China's warning on key materials exports.* Global Times, July 4, 2023; Junhua Zhang. *China's export controls are set to backfire.* GIS, July 31, 2023

[138] Inkster, N. (2020). *The Great Decoupling.* Hurst & Company; Cotton, T. (2021). *Beat China: Targeted Decoupling and the Economic Long War.* United States Senate; Feng, J. The Costs of U.S.-China Semiconductor Decoupling, Center for Strategic & International Studies, May 25, 2022, https://www.csis.org/blogs/new-perspectives-asia/costs-us-china-semiconductor-decoupling; Levits, E. Biden's New Cold War Against China Could Backfire The U.S. is now committed to thwarting China's development. At what cost? New York Magazine, November 14, 2022, https://nymag.com/intelligencer/2022/11/biden-economic-war-china-chips-semiconductors-export-controls.html

knew the composition of the U.S. fleet in Pearl Harbor. Then, on December 7, 1941, they launched their famous attack. The rest, as they say, is history.

The most important lesson we can learn from this event is that Japan did not attack Pearl Harbor out of the blue. In the years prior to the attack on Pearl Harbor, the United States and Japan had been waging an escalating economic war. Indeed, the attack on December 7, 1941, was a military escalation of an existing conflict between the two. Alarmingly, there are important similarities with the current competition between Beijing and Washington. It is not unthinkable that an economic war between China and the United States can lead to military conflict as well.[139]

The economic war between Japan and the United States escalated when President Roosevelt decided to cut off oil sales and froze Japanese assets and money that was held in the United States. This was a blow that, according to Japanese officials, threatened the continued existence of their country. Japan lacked oil resources of its own and thus was highly dependent on oil imports from the United States. With this supply now blocked, they intensified their search for other oil suppliers such as British Malaysia and the Dutch East Indies (Indonesia). But Washington was one step ahead of them and pressured Britain and the Netherlands to join the oil embargo and the assets freeze, which they did. Japan's oil and dollar supplies, both needed to fuel and buy resources for the army and economy, were now in serious trouble.[140]

In a desperate move, Japan tried to create other fuel sources, for instance by converting coal into oil. Unfortunately for Tokyo, they failed in setting up a synthetic fuel industry large enough to supply Japanese needs. Thus, being unable to buy the oil or produce it themselves, Japan's leadership decided that they simply would have to take it by force. Otherwise, their country's economy would go down the drain and, in the face of a severe economic crisis, their own position of power would come under severe strain. Feeling backed into a corner, Japanese leaders decided they had no choice but to lash out. And they did when they ordered a series of invasions and the attack on Pearl Harbor.[141]

Now let us shift attention to China. As described above, the Chinese economy has a great demand for (advanced) chips and chip-making technology, which Washington is actively trying to block. Not only has the United States itself prohibited sales of advanced chips, but they have also

---

[139] Calhoun, G. War With China? The Economic Factor That Could Trigger It. Bloomberg, https://www.forbes.com/sites/georgecalhoun/2021/09/12/war-with-china-the-economic-factor-that-could-trigger-it/?sh=6f9aee455d26
[140] Miller, E. S. (2007). *Bankrupting the Enemy*. Naval Institute Press.
[141] Stranges, A. N. Synthetic fuel production in prewar and World War II Japan: A case study in technological failure. *Annals of Science*, Vol 50, 1993, Issue 3, p. 229-265

pressured other suppliers such as Korea, the Netherlands, Taiwan, and Japan. The European Union may very well follow. Since 2019, they have designated China a "systemic rival." There are even people in the West calling for the creation of a "NATO for trade," an alliance of countries all determined to undermine China's economic and technological development. As we move closer and closer towards something like this, the question becomes: how will Beijing respond?[142]

As one might expect, just as Japan attempted to build up its own energy industry in the face of the oil embargo, China is trying to set up its own chip industry. Whether this will succeed, and will succeed fast enough, is anyone's guess. Suffice it to say, if China cannot buy enough of the chips that its economy and military need, and if they can't produce enough chips themselves, the Chinese leadership may conclude, like their Japanese counterparts so many decades ago, that they have no choice but to take them, by force.

In the case of Japan in the 1940s, the targets of their military campaigns were obvious. Both Malaysia and Indonesia were oil-producing regions. These countries were in the neighborhood, and Japan's military was strong enough to invade them. To Japanese leaders, it was the only way to break free of economic containment.

For China, there also is an obvious target. Taiwan is the world's leading producer of advanced chips. It is located next door, and Beijing has been upgrading and training its military to take the island by force. As discussed in the previous chapter, if such an attack were to be carried out, it is not inconceivable that the Chinese military will carry out surprise attacks on U.S. military bases in the region to prevent them from interfering in the invasion. In other words, another Pearl Harbor.[143]

This certainly is a worst-case scenario, but it falls within the realm of possibilities. What long-lasting economic wars and rising tensions do is to boost the power and influence of more aggressive groups within a political system. In every society, there are the so-called moderates, who prefer peaceful settlements, and militants, who feel that the time for talks and negotiations has passed, and the moment has come to use military force.

---

[142] Atkinson, R. D. & Prestowitz, C. China's Reaction to the Pandemic Shows Why the U.S. and Its Allies Need a NATO for Trade. Information Technology & Innovation Foundation, May 21, 2020; EEAS, EU-China Relations factsheet, April 1, 2022, https://www.eeas.europa.eu/eeas/eu-china-relations-factsheet_en

[143] Yen Nee Lee, 2 charts show how much the world depends on Taiwan for semiconductors, CNBC, March 15, 2021, https://www.cnbc.com/2021/03/16/2-charts-show-how-much-the-world-depends-on-taiwan-for-semiconductors.html

In the case of the Vietnam War, for example, the North Vietnamese government was dominated by moderates for many years. But as attacks by the U.S.-supported South Vietnamese regime increased in brutality, the moderates like Ho Chi Minh, in the end, had to make way for the more militant political forces within the Vietnamese political system. This is a completely natural dynamic, one that may very well play out similarly within the Chinese political system as it is facing escalating economic warfare coming from the United States.[144]

A U.S. economic war against China, such as trying to starve the Chinese economy of vital components, will give militants and hardliners within China's government, military, media, and society more influence, especially when attempts by Chinese moderates fail to resolve the conflict. If that happens, then escalation and military conflict become much more likely.

A military conflict over Taiwan motivated by chips and technology not only puts the world on the brink of World War III, but it would also have major global economic repercussions. Some U.S. strategists have put forward a very bold plan to thwart China from solving its chip problem by invading Taiwan. They call it a "targeted scorched-earth strategy." The primary goal would be to "destroy facilities belonging to the Taiwan Semiconductor Manufacturing Company." This would only take a few cruise or ballistic missiles; the U.S. military estimates. Destroying the world's leading chip-producing facilities would not only undermine Beijing's quest of solving their country's chip problem, but it would also collapse the global supply of chips at a moment in time when the Chinese army is at war and needs them the most.[145]

But what the destruction of TSMC, the leading fabricator of the most advanced chips, also does is to take away a third of the world's computing power. TSMC produces 37 percent of the logic chips, including the most advanced ones. Computers, phones, data centers, and most electronic devices simply do not work without them. If the company were destroyed in a Nord Stream-like attack, the impact on the world economy would be catastrophic. With digitized economies being the norm now, especially in the Western countries themselves, the damage would be enormous. This goes to show, once again, that a war between China and the United States will negatively affect people everywhere, including ordinary people and businesses in the West itself.

---

[144] Asselin, P. (2013). *Hanoi's Road to the Vietnam War.* University of California Press, see p. 3-47.

[145] McKinney, J. M. & Harris, P. *Broken Nest: Deterring China from Invading Taiwan.* The US Army War College Quarterly. Parameters 51, no. 4 (2021): 23-36.

Unfortunately, not only technological sanctions can evolve into military conflict. Financial and other economic sanctions can do the same, and these too are among the favorite tools that Washington uses against its rivals. In the remaining sections of this chapter, we dive into the realm of financial and economic warfare and explore yet another way how Washington can start its war against China.

The Art of Financial Warfare

"Sanctions are intended to create hardship — or to be blunt, 'pain'," describes Richard Nephew, a leading economic sanctions expert who wrote a book on the topic, *The Art of Sanctions*. He lists several kinds of sanctions that one country might impose on another. There are diplomatic sanctions, such as suspending a country from international organizations or imposing travel restrictions on politicians. With military sanctions, you can prevent a country from acquiring weapons and other military equipment. Then there are also technological sanctions, which deny a country access to specific technology. Finally, there are economic and financial sanctions, and they may be the most destructive of them all.[146]

Nephew goes on to describe, in a mechanical and emotionally detached manner, how to use economic sanctions to inflict the necessary amount of pain. The trick, he concludes, is to find the "Goldilocks" zone in which you apply enough pain to make the actor do what you want — a practice quite like torture. Nephew's account is remarkably honest for someone who used to be deeply embedded within the U.S. government. Economic sanctions, he says, are a form of siege warfare in which you try to isolate an economy, take away its ability to trade, do business, and buy and sell things that a country and its people need. Although economic sanctions may sound neutral and far more benign than military conflict, they can be just as deadly, Nephew states. Make no mistake about it, "sanctions are a form of violence."[147]

In an impressive show of self-reflection, Nephew, who has been a principal coordinator of economic sanctions policy for the U.S. State Department, goes on to say that he and his colleagues, while designing sanctions, often downplayed this idea of inflicting pain and suffering on an entire people. They did so to avoid feeling responsible for the humanitarian consequences. The U.S. government has always lied about this fact, Nephew writes. They always say that U.S. sanctions only target evil governments and other bad actors. But when you are intentionally harming an entire economy,

---

[146] Nephew, R. (2018). *The Art of Sanctions.* Columbia University Press, p. 9, 44-47.
[147] Nephew, R. (2018). *The Art of Sanctions.* Columbia University Press, p. 10-11, 124-125; Davis, S. & Ness, I. (2022). *Sanctions as War.* Brill.

the population will inevitably suffer too. In fact, very often, that is precisely the intention.[148]

One declassified internal policy document shows this more clearly than anything else. On April 6, 1960, after Fidel Castro had risen to power in Cuba, an internal memorandum of the State Department recommended a course for U.S. intervention. Because "The majority of Cubans support Castro," the memo reads, a U.S. military invasion is bound to fail. Therefore, the only way to get rid of Castro is to make life for ordinary Cubans so miserable that they will rise up and overthrow him: "every possible means should be undertaken promptly to weaken the economic life of Cuba", in order to "decrease monetary and real wages, to bring about hunger, desperation and overthrow of government." Hunger and desperation have indeed brought down governments, and by inflicting these conditions on the Cuban population, Washington was hoping for exactly that outcome. For more than six decades, starting in the 1960s, this has been the official U.S. policy of all U.S. presidents, both Democrat and Republican.[149]

It is not always easy to determine how many people have been harmed or killed by economic sanctions. In the case of Cuba, economic sanctions have held the country's economy back for over 60 years. This will have a negative impact on health, (child) mortality, disease, housing, education, and other social indicators. How many people died or were harmed unnecessarily because of this? That is much more difficult to determine than counting the dead and wounded on the battlefield. But in some cases, economists have indeed tried to answer such questions on exactly how deadly U.S. economic sanctions are.

One such study looks at Venezuela, a country located just south of Cuba. Since 2017, U.S. economic sanctions have, by design, taken away the country's ability to earn money from oil exports — Venezuela's main source of income. The resulting economic catastrophe, according to the authors, took the lives of tens of thousands of people and harmed hundreds of thousands more. The main reason is shortages of medicine and medical equipment. Venezuela used to buy these from abroad with its earnings from selling oil. But with oil sales plummeting, this became impossible. Consequently, people, especially young children and other vulnerable groups, were having a hard time getting the medication they needed, which then resulted in unnecessary and excess death.[150]

---

[148] Nephew, R. (2018). *The Art of Sanctions.* Columbia University Press, p. 11-12
[149] Davis, S. & Ness, I. (2022). *Sanctions as War.* Brill, see chapters on Cuba
[150] Weisbrot, M. & Sachs, J. (2019). *Punishing Civilians: U.S. Sanctions on Venezuela,* Challenge

In Iraq, another target of U.S. sanctions, economic sanctions in the 1990s led to a near collapse of all trade, resulting in the deaths of hundreds of thousands of people, many of them children — an act of genocide according to former United Nations officials. But although economic sanctions harm and kill — especially vulnerable groups like children, the sick, and the elderly — this does not hold Western countries back from using them.[151]

In fact, in the last few decades, economic sanctions have become a favorite tool of Washington. It is less costly than a military invasion, yet it can make foreign governments do what the U.S. wants. And as is important to realize, the United States and Europe are also in a unique position to use economic sanctions. A combination of factors gives the West a clear advantage over anyone else.

For one, the sheer size of the U.S. and European economies means that if they decide to deny a country trade and investment, it is a severe blow to that country. But the opposite is not true. Most U.S. businesses, for example, do not care much if they cannot do business with Cuba, because the island has such a small economy. But for Cuba to lose access to the huge U.S. market, that is a severe blow capable of grinding Cuba's economy to a halt.

Also, given Europe's and the United States' long history of dominating international trade, much of the economic and financial infrastructure is owned and controlled by them. SWIFT is a notable example. Located in Belgium, Brussels, SWIFT was created in 1973 to standardize the communication of international financial transactions, and as such it forms the "communication backbone" of the global financial system. If a transaction between two banks crosses a border, SWIFT makes sure the transaction is swift (hence the name) and safe, and that it has all the necessary information about where the transfer is coming from, how much money it is, and where it is supposed to go. Western banks manage this particularly important system, and there is no other system like it.[152]

Although SWIFT is supposed to be apolitical and neutral, it is sharing information with the U.S. Treasury. This allows Washington to track and trace money flows. And in the context of sanctions, on the orders of Washington and the European Union, a whole series of banks of Western enemies have been cut off from the system. This makes it exceedingly diffi-

---

[151] UNICEF—Results of the 1999 Iraq Child and Maternal Mortality Surveys. Federation of American Scientists, https://web.archive.org/web/20001025101709/https://fas.org/news/iraq/1999/08/990812-unicef.htm; von Sponeck, H. C. *A Different Kind of War: The UN Sanctions Regime in Iraq*; Siegal, Mark. *Former UN official says sanctions against Iraq amount to 'genocide'*, Cornell Chronicle, September 30, 1999.
[152] Zarate, J. C. (2013). *Treasury's War*. Public Affairs, p. 49-50.

cult for those banks to conduct normal business operations, which can have a huge impact on a country's economy, as we will see later.[153]

Other examples of how the West dominates the global infrastructure for financial services include maritime insurance. London and other Western maritime insurance companies insure much of the world's shipping. Without insurance, ships cannot sail or dock. Now, imagine what would happen to a country that depends on selling oil or other resources to the world market, and it suddenly finds itself being cut off from these Western insurance companies. Without insurance, they cannot ship their goods, they cannot make money, and the economy may collapse. And, of course, institutions like the World Bank and the IMF, which can provide countries with loans and investment, are controlled by Western countries as well.[154]

Washington and Brussels thus have a variety of economic and financial tools at their disposal which they use to inflict pain on others. In the next section, we will have a look at several examples to see exactly how sanctions are designed to cause pain, and how destructive the effects can be, not only to the targeted country but to the world in general, including people in the West themselves. And make no mistake about it, China, already under fire from the Western countries, is Washington's and Brussels' next big target for an all-out economic war.

The Financial Assault

In 2006, high up in the air on board the airplane of U.S. Secretary of State Condoleezza Rice, Stuart Levey was called to the front of the plane to give a briefing on a new weapon. In front of Rice and her advisors, Stuart laid out his views on how the United States could wage a new kind of economic warfare based on its dominant position in the international financial system. Instead of cutting a country off from trade with the rest of the world — the classic embargo — the U.S. could also cut off a country from the financial system through a targeted attack on its banks. Levey, in effect, had discovered a powerful weapon Washington could use to deal with rivals and disobedient governments. Now it was time to test this new weapon, and Levey already had a target in mind.

---

[153] Zarate, J. C. (2013). *Treasury's War.* Public Affairs, p. 53-54, 283-284
[154] Zarate, J. C. (2013). *Treasury's War.* Public Affairs, p. 304-306. The United States is the only country that has veto power over important decisions by the IMF and World Bank, see https://www.worldbank.org/en/country/unitedstates/overview and Congressional Research Service, The International Monetary Fund, March 7, 2022, https://sgp.fas.org/crs/misc/IF10676.pdf

Having laid out the basics of financial warfare, Levey then shifted attention to Iran, a country that the United States had wanted to subdue ever since the Shah, the pro-Western dictator, was overthrown over forty years earlier in 1979. Levey proposed a "financial insurgency" to "squeeze" Iran's economy. In carefully orchestrated steps, so Levey envisioned, Washington would use sanctions and threats to make it clear to the world that they had to stop doing business with Iran. It would be like "prey caught in a boa constrictor's lethal embrace."

Condoleezza Rice loved the plan and it went into effect almost immediately. In the following months and years, Levey did exactly what he had proposed. He traveled to over a hundred major banks and financial institutions all around the world. He sat down with the CEO and top-level management and told them in no uncertain terms that Washington did not want them to do business with Iran. They had better close the accounts and unplug all their Iranian customers and stop doing business with Iran altogether. If they refused, they would find themselves cut off from accessing the U.S. market.

Predictably, already in 2006 and 2007, major European banks fell in line and ended their transactions with Iran, its government, and its businesses. For all of them, access to the U.S. market was much more important than doing business with Iran. In this way, it was an easy choice, although many of them were unhappy about it. And while all of this was happening, the U.S. Treasury too began cutting off Iranian banks from the international financial system.

But this was not all. To prevent Iran from exporting its oil, Levey began visiting the major insurance companies that covered cargo ships in places like London and Germany. After Levey's presentation — characterized by intimidation and threats — the CEOs of the major insurance companies would terminate their dealings with any Iranian shipping company. As a result, it became exceedingly difficult for Iran to sell its oil and other goods.[155]

To complete what U.S. sanctions experts called a "financial assault," the Iranian central bank was targeted. Any foreign bank that made transactions with the Iranian central bank would be punished. It was the first central bank to be sanctioned, ever, and in the case of Iran, it was a very severe blow. Iran's central bank had become an unusually important institution because it had taken over much of the activity that other Iranian banks were no longer able to perform due to U.S. sanctions. Overall, it was a "full financial strangulation."[156]

---

[155] Zarate, J. C. (2013). *Treasury's War*. Public Affairs, p. 291-306
[156] Zarate, J. C. (2013). *Treasury's War*. Public Affairs, p. 296, 315, 333, 336

Then, several years later in 2012, Europe cut off Iranian banks from SWIFT, and the European Union decided that European countries were no longer allowed to buy Iranian oil. President Obama also threatened every country in the world from buying oil from Iran. If they bought too much, they would be cut off from the international financial system. And to prevent Iran from finding other ways to make money besides exporting oil, Washington cleverly designed sanctions that undermined Iran's automotive industry and the 500,000 jobs this sector provided to the Iranian people.[157]

The effects of the sanctions on the economy were dramatic, especially for ordinary people. In a short time, the prices of many products soared. Household items, food, and medicines doubled or tripled in price. Families struggled and many plunged into poverty. At the same time, the government was less able to provide them with food subsidies and other help. As Iran's economy was squeezed, bankruptcy tripled, and around 40 percent of men living in the cities were unemployed.[158]

Another effect of the soaring prices and unstable supply of goods was that it became almost impossible for people to plan for the future. The economy was simply too unpredictable to make any long-term plans. Buying a house or a car, planning to get married or have a baby, saving money for education, all these things became much more difficult. People were forced to view life day by day instead of making plans for themselves, their children, and their families.[159]

The health-care system was also severely impacted. The sanctions prevented Iran from importing medicine and medical equipment. Although these items themselves were not sanctioned, Iranian banks were cut off from the international payment system, and foreign banks were too scared of being punished by Washington that they refrained from doing business with Iran. Their fears are warranted. Indeed, the U.S. Treasury has a history of prosecuting pharmaceutical companies for selling medical supplies to Iran. The result was that, as of 2014, over 6 million people suffered due to medical shortages. Over 30 drugs that, according to the WHO, are "essential," were in short supply. Even during the Covid pandemic the sanctions were not eased. As the United Nations has pointed out many times, health crises always impact children, the elderly, and the poor and vulnerable the most, and this is indeed what happened in Iran.[160]

---

[157] Zarate, J. C. (2013). *Treasury's War.* Public Affairs, p. 338; Nephew, R. (2018). *The Art of Sanctions.* Columbia University Press, p. 108, 112-113

[158] Lam, K. (2020). *Collateral Damage.* New Degree Press, chapter 3 and 5

[159] Lam, K. (2020). *Collateral Damage.* New Degree Press, chapter 3

[160] Lam, K. (2020). *Collateral Damage.* New Degree Press, chapter 4

In another extremely cynical yet 'artful' sanctions move, the United States government deliberately did not use sanctions to undermine the ability of Iran to purchase mobile phones. Washington wanted Iranians to be miserable, desperate, out of work, *and* able to communicate with each other to spread the word on how dire the situation in their country had become. Communication also enables citizens to organize and revolt against their government — which was exactly what Washington wanted: to get regime change in Iran.[161]

President Obama understood the effects of the sanctions very well. In a speech on March 4, 2012, he boasted that despite the many people who had doubted him, the sanctions had accomplished "grinding the Iranian economy to a halt." [162]

The economic sanctions campaign spanned multiple U.S. administrations. It started under Bush, then continued under Obama, who kept the same sanctions team in place, and then Trump and Biden. It did not matter whether the White House was Democrat or Republican, everyone was on board to use this new and wonderful weapon. Feeling emboldened and invincible by their ability to take down an entire economy, it was unsurprising that Washington's and Brussel's next target was a much bigger and stronger country than Iran.[163]

From 2014, the West's economic cross hairs shifted towards Russia. Interestingly, the sanctions against Russia, which escalated in 2022, are causing not only hardship in Russia but they are also especially destructive to the West, most notably Europe. It is from this example of excessive collateral damage that we can start to appreciate even more how harmful a full-scale economic war with China is going to be.

Sacrifices

On August 24, 2022, the President of France Emmanuel Macron announced to his people that they should prepare for "the end of abundance." Macron delivered this sober speech after returning from his luxurious vacation residence Fort de Brégançon, where he enjoyed his free time hanging out on yachts and jet skis. But with soaring prices for food and energy plaguing Europe and his beloved France, the abundant lifestyles of Europeans are ending, so the French President explained, and will be replaced with growing poverty and economic insecurity. Interestingly,

---

[161] Nephew, R. (2018). *The Art of Sanctions.* Columbia University Press, p. 112-113
[162] Davis, S. & Ness, I. (2022). *Sanctions as War.* Brill, p. 181
[163] Zarate, J. C. (2013). *Treasury's War.* Public Affairs, p. 316

Macron did not say why this was happening, although he did hint at the fact that it had something to do with the war in Ukraine.[164]

Macron was not the only bringer of bad news. Josep Borrell, the High Representative of the Union for Foreign Affairs for the European Union, the EU foreign minister in other words, had also made it clear that things would be different in Europe from 2022 onwards. Europeans, Borrell stated, are going to "pay a steep price." Yet he also failed to say why people in the European Union should suffer economically from a conflict over Ukraine.[165]

The answer, a surprisingly revealing one, came from the German Foreign Minister Annalena Baerbock. Speaking at a conference in Prague on August 31, 2022, she explained that, as winter approaches and food and energy will be much more expensive, the German people, together with other Europeans, "will go on the street and say 'we cannot pay our energy prices', and I will say, 'yes, I know, so we help you with social measures'. But what I don't want to say is, ok, then we stop the sanctions against Russia... the sanctions will stay." [166]

What Baerbock and her fellow EU politicians are admitting here is that they know the economic sanctions against Russia are having a boomerang effect and are severely harming the European people and the European economies. They are also saying that they do not care, and the sanctions will stay, no matter what, for many more years to come. How did it come to this?

Following the February 24, 2022, Russian invasion of Ukraine, the Western countries decided to wage "an all-out economic and financial war on Russia." In sanctions package after sanctions package, until even journalists and commentators lost count, the aim was to "cause the collapse of the Russian economy," according to French Finance Minister Bruno Le Maire. But the ultimate goal was to accomplish regime change in Russia, something many Western leaders have dreamed of for a very long time. In their minds, the sanctions would collapse the Russian economy, and angry and desperate Russians would then revolt against their government. Putin

---

[164] France24, Macron warns France of 'the end of abundance' and tough times ahead, August 24, 2022, https://www.france24.com/en/france/20220824-macron-warns-french-of-tough-times-ahead-end-to-energy-price-cap; Manning, J. President of France sparks outrage after celebrating "end of abundance" on yacht. EuroWeekly, 26 August, 2022, https://euroweeklynews.com/2022/08/26/president-of-france-sparks-outrage-after-celebrating-end-of-abundance-on-yacht/

[165] Borell, J. Defending Ukraine in its hour of maximum need, March 1, 2022, blog post on EEAS, https://www.eeas.europa.eu/eeas/defending-ukraine-its-hour-maximum-need-0_en; Borell, J. The war in Ukraine and its implications for the EU, March 14, 2022, blog post on EEAS, https://www.eeas.europa.eu/eeas/war-ukraine-and-its-implications-eu_en

[166] Forum 2000, speech by Annalena Baerbock on August 31, 2022. See the video from 1:24 minutes until 1:27 minutes on https://www.forum2000.cz/en/forum-2000-conferences-2022-videos-democracys-clear-and-present-danger-how-do-we

would be overthrown and replaced by a new and pro-Western leader. If it reminds you of the 1960 memorandum about Cuba, it should. It is the same old game all over again.

But just like with Cuba, the West seriously underestimated the resilience of the Russian economy. European and American leaders believed that, as a German leader once famously told his generals in the early 1940s, "We have only to kick in the door and the whole rotten structure will come crashing down." They were wrong, but not for a lack of trying. Indeed, the economic assault on Russia by the West was among the fiercest in history.[167]

Russian banks, including its Central Bank, were cut off from the international financial system, lost access to SWIFT, and their money and assets were seized. Western businesses were forbidden to operate in Russia, and trade was severely restricted. Sales of technology, equipment, and spare parts for key Russian industries were prohibited, and so was buying key Russian commodities including coal, steel, and from December 2022, oil. Yet it did not work.[168]

To the astonishment of Western officials, Russia's economy withstood the attack. Russia is simply shifting its economic relations away from the West and towards the East, where they are welcomed with open arms. Russia is also upgrading its own technological and industrial base to be less dependent on Western technology. But as robust as Russia's economy has proven itself to be, the same can not be said of many Western countries. As predicted, the economic sanctions imposed by the EU and the U.S. wrecked havoc across the world, and ironically, especially in Europe itself. They did, in fact, cause a major food and energy crisis.[169]

Western leaders have, of course, denied that the sanctions are having anything to do with the soaring food and energy prices. But this is a lie. While it is true that the sanctions do not directly target Russia's food and fertilizer exports, which are important to the global food system and much bigger than Ukraine's, the sanctions are having a very strong indirect effect: they seriously limit normal trade in these commodities. As explained in the

---

[167] Lough, R. French minister declares economic 'war' on Russia, and then beats a retreat, Reuters, March 1, 2022, https://www.reuters.com/world/france-declares-economic-war-against-russia-2022-03-01/; Middleton, D. The New York Times. HITLER'S RUSSIAN BLUNDER, June 21, 1981

[168] European Council, EU sanctions against Russia explained, https://www.consilium. europa.eu/en/policies/sanctions/restrictive-measures-against-russia-over-ukraine/ sanctions-against-russia-explained/; Connolly, R. (2018). *Russia's Response to Sanctions*. Cambridge University Press

[169] European Council, EU sanctions against Russia explained, https://www.consilium. europa.eu/en/policies/sanctions/restrictive-measures-against-russia-over-ukraine/ sanctions-against-russia-explained/; Connolly, R. (2018). *Russia's Response to Sanctions*. Cambridge University Press

Iranian case, you do not directly have to sanction food and medicine to create a shortage in these goods. When you disrupt normal financial operations, everything gets affected.

Already in early March 2022, major international shipping companies like Maersk and others began avoiding Russia. They were afraid that if they participated in Russian trade, they risked punishment by Western sanctions. Holland & Knight, an American law firm specializing in advising the world's biggest corporations, informed their clients on March 7, 2022, that "Russian-related sanctions are already beginning to impact all shipping segments, including commodity traders, tankers, containers, dry bulk and gas." On financial transactions with Russia, their report states that "banks have reportedly paused their Russian activities and may refuse to issue, confirm or advise letters of credit directly or indirectly connected with Russian parties and Russia-related transactions." Even Reuters reported that "Sanctions have disrupted sales of fertilizer and crops from Russia. Many Western banks and traders are steering clear of Russian supplies for fear of running afoul of the rapidly changing rules." When trade with Russia, the leading exporter of wheat (twice that of Ukraine) and fertilizer, becomes severely disrupted, it is no wonder that prices soar, and shortages occur.[170]

And when it comes to energy, the situation is serious too, especially for Europe. What people like Ursula von der Leyen, who is the President of the European Commission, and other EU and Western leaders have done, is that they have destroyed any chance of having a working relationship with their main energy provider, namely Russia. And, in their short-sightedness, they did so without having an alternative energy source.

The German economic minister Robert Habeck, for example, traveled to Qatar to seek a major liquefied natural gas (LNG) deal to replace Russian pipeline gas. Following his visit, Habeck proudly claimed he had been victorious and had struck a deal. This turned out to be a lie, and Qatar has since stated that they cannot provide Europe with the energy it needs. And, even if

---

[170] Pribyl, S. T., Epstein, J. M., Nolan, C.R., Cavanaugh, J. M. U.S. Sanctions on Russia: Impact on Shipping Business and Contractual Considerations. Holland & Knight, March 7, 2022, https://www.hklaw.com/en/insights/publications/2022/03/us-sanctions-on-russia-impact-on-shipping-business; Reuters Staff, Reuters, UPDATE 1-Russian ministry recommends fertiliser producers halt exports, March 4, 2022, https://www.reuters.com/article/ukraine-crisis-russia-fertilizers-idINL2N2V7IJG; Polansek, T.& Mano, A. As sanctions bite Russia, fertilizer shortage imperils world food supply, Reuters, March 23, 2022, https://www.reuters.com/business/sanctions-bite-russia-fertilizer-shortage-imperils-world-food-supply-2022-03-23/; World Integrated Trade Solution. Fertilizers, mineral or chemical; nitrogenous, urea, whether or not in aqueous solution exports by country in 2021; FAOSTAT trade data for wheat for Russia and Ukraine in 2020.

it could, which it cannot, it would take many years for Europe to replace its natural gas infrastructure with a new energy infrastructure based on LNG.[171]

This charade continued for months. European leaders traveled to all kinds of places to seek energy, only to be turned down again and again. Yet they pretended they were making deals and there was nothing to worry about. Their obsession with weakening Russia and overthrowing Putin, combined with their overconfidence that economic sanctions would accomplish this, has made them unprepared for the energy crisis that they now find themselves in.

They did manage, in 2022, to buy enough Russian natural gas to fill up the European underground reserves, so Europe made it through the winter. They were also lucky that the winter was mild. But European leaders failed to find a suitable alternative supplier. And any new supplier, let us say the United States, cannot supply Europe with cheap Russian pipeline gas. Instead, Europe must buy more expensive LNG. This means that the EU has exchanged a cheap natural gas dependency on Russia for an expensive LNG dependency on the United States — a development solidified by the destruction of the Nord Stream pipelines.

With cheap energy gone, Europe's manufacturing sector will be less competitive, and as European industry starts to close or move to Asia and the United States, the de-industrialization of the European Union is a real possibility. German industry, the engine of EU economies, will be especially hard hit.[172]

All of this, of course, has not led European leaders to back down on the sanctions. The sanctions will stay, as the German Foreign Minister Annalena Baerbock made clear to the German people and her fellow Europeans. Instead, Western leaders will simply put the blame on Russia. For politicians, to blame others for their own failures is second nature, and that is exactly what they are doing. For example, British Prime Minister Rishi Sunak, in a speech at the G20 in November 2022, said that "the IMF predicts a third of the world's economy will be in recession this year or next." This "global economic asphyxiation," Sunak continued, "has been driven by the actions

[171] El Dahan, M., Mills, A., Rashad, M. Qatar says almost impossible to quickly replace Russian gas, Reuters, Feb 22, 2022, https://www.reuters.com/world/middle-east/qatar-can-divert-up-15-its-gas-exports-2022-02-22/; Qatar to help Germany cut Russian gas reliance, March 20, 2022, https://www.dw.com/en/qatar-to-help-germany-cut-reliance-on-russian-gas-says-minister/a-61191584; Miller, J., Kazmin, A., Borrelli, S. C. Germany clinches long-term gas supply deal with Qatar, Financial Times, March 20, 2022, https://www.ft.com/content/1192517b-e405-486f-a743-51b5be356024; Statement by Statement Qatar Energy does not mention anything about a deal, March 20, 2022, https://www.qatarenergy.qa/en/MediaCenter/Pages/newsdetails.aspx?ItemId=3704

[172] Energy crisis will erode Europe's competitiveness in 2023, Economist Intelligence, 13 October, 2022.

of the one man unwilling to be at this summit — Vladimir Putin." It is all because of "Putin's war." Sunak made no mention of economic sanctions.[173]

The failed and disastrous attempt by the West to collapse the Russian economy with economic sanctions has backfired spectacularly. It has created a food and energy crisis that is harming people in the Global South, in Europe, and in the United States. Yet Western leaders are unwilling to put an end to their obsession with Putin and Russia. They press on, harming and ruining the lives of their own citizens, economies, and countries in the process. We can expect no less when these same leaders, or like-minded successors, shift their aim towards China. And although Russia has not really retaliated with economic sanctions of its own, China, because it is a much bigger economy, has many more cards to play. If another disastrous miscalculation by Western leaders results in an all-out economic war between the West and China, Americans and Europeans may experience truly "the end of abundance."

---

[173] Speech by Rishi Sunak at the G20. PM statement at G20 press conference: 16 November 2022. https://www.gov.uk/government/speeches/pm-statement-at-g20-press-conference-16-november-2022

CHAPTER 4: COLD WAR IN HOT PLACES

John Stockwell carefully examined the walls of the small church school. The whole complex was marked by mortar rounds and bullet holes. As he stood up and walked outside, his eye caught the smoldering remains of a BDRM-2, a Soviet combat vehicle. Yes, a major firefight had taken place here. According to Colonel Roberto, the FNLA leader and Stockwell's assigned contact person on the ground, the capture of the town had been a major victory. Stockwell did not know what to make of that. The Colonel, who was always eager for more American weapons and military aid, took every opportunity to boast about his achievements. Take what happened earlier that day. The Colonel's men had captured several enemy soldiers who had clearly been lost and disoriented and had accidentally stumbled upon an FNLA position. The Colonel called that a major victory, too. Indeed, it was hard to get good intelligence on what was happening. But that was precisely why the CIA had sent Stockwell here, to Angola, an African country in the midst of civil war.[174]

Several weeks later, while on the plane back to the CIA's headquarters in Langley, Virginia, Stockwell drafted his report. There were three groups fighting for power in Angola. Washington, in all its wisdom, had decided to support the FNLA. Their main enemy, the Soviet-backed MPLA, were poorly armed and disorganized, Stockwell had realized. If the U.S. were to rush in weapons and supplies, the FNLA could take the capital and win the war.[175]

---

[174] Stockwell, J. (1978). *In Search of Enemies*. W. W. Norton & Company, p. 124-133. For a good description of the civil war, see Marcum, J. (1969). *The Angolan Revolution Volume 1: The Anatomy of an Explosion (1950-1962)*. The M.I.T. Press and Marcum, J. (1978). *The Angolan Revolution Volume 2: Exile Politics and Guerilla Warfare (1962-1976)*. The M.I.T. Press.
[175] Stockwell, J. (1978). *In Search of Enemies*. W. W. Norton & Company, p. 134-135.

Unfortunately for Stockwell, who headed the CIA's Angola Task Force, Secretary of State Henry Kissinger, or Dr. Kissinger as the man preferred to be called, was not intent on winning. Kissinger believed the war was already lost. The only reason he had ordered the CIA to secretly arm the FNLA was to make it more difficult for the Soviets to win. The whole point of supporting the FNLA, as CIA director William Colby later admitted to Congress, was that the Soviet Union was supporting the other side. Angola was not even strategically or economically important. But the United States had just lost the Vietnam War in 1975, and the White House wanted to show the world that America would continue to oppose Moscow anywhere and any time.[176]

Only a few people in Washington really understood the Angolan civil war. Kissinger was not one of them, yet he made the big decisions. In Kissinger's mind, if the Soviets wanted Angola, then he would oppose it. It was as simple as that. To these Cold War warriors who waged the war from behind their desks, Angola was simply a spot on the map that they wanted to color NATO blue, not Soviet red. In this pursuit, Kissinger blocked opportunities for peace, and the weapons the United States delivered only "added fuel to the bloody conflict," according to Stockwell.

Nonetheless, being a career-minded CIA agent at the time, Stockwell and his team of paramilitaries, intelligence officers, and propaganda experts worked overtime to carry out Kissinger's orders. They emptied CIA stockpiles of foreign weapons that could not be traced back to the United States — these always came in handy when Washington wanted to secretly support a (para)military group somewhere in the world. The CIA then had to come up with clever schemes to secretly transport them to Angola. The large C–141 transport planes from the U.S. Air Force would be most efficient, but they would also expose American involvement. Therefore, the CIA first sent the weapons to Mobutu, the U.S. supported dictator of the Congo and Angola's neighbor. Then, using borrowed and stolen small civilian aircraft, the CIA paid Angolan pilots to fly these weapons into Angola itself.[177]

To train the FNLA in how to use these weapons, the CIA placed its own military advisors among them. This was strictly forbidden. The CIA was not allowed to provide military training; they were only permitted to collect information. But it was simple to circumvent this restriction. By calling these military advisors "intelligence gatherers," the CIA fooled the U.S. Congress

[176] Moreira de Sa, T. (2019). "The World Was Not Turning in Their Direction. The United States and the Decolonization of Angola. *Journal of Cold War Studies*, Vol. 21, No. 1, pp 52-65; Marcum, J. (1978). *The Angolan Revolution Volume 2: Exile Politics and Guerilla Warfare (1962-1976)*. The M.I.T. Press, p. 257, 260; Stockwell, J. (1978). *In Search of Enemies*. W. W. Norton & Company p. 43-46; Blum, W. (2004). *Killing Hope*. Zed Books, p. 251.
[177] Stockwell, J. (1978). *In Search of Enemies*. W. W. Norton & Company, p. 58-59, 208-209.

and others who wanted to limit U.S. involvement in the Angolan civil war. And when a European journalist in the Congo was close to finding out that Washington was bringing in weapons, the CIA quickly devised a plan that got the journalist kicked out of the country.[178]

In the meantime, Moscow responded by sending in weapons and supplies of its own to the MPLA. What started out with modest aid quickly turned into an arms race. As a result, the internal conflict of Angola turned into a hot war between the two superpowers with America supporting one side and the Soviets the other. It was one of the many hot wars that were fought over the course of the U.S.–Soviet Cold War.

With weapons and foreign troops pouring into Angola, chances for a negotiated peace were ignored or blocked. After intense fighting and with an FNLA defeat imminent, the CIA and other Cold War warriors wanted to escalate things by sending in sophisticated weapons, tanks, artillery, C-47 gunships, foreign mercenaries, U.S. advisors, and even U.S. combat forces. If that were to happen, the world would witness another Vietnam. But contrary to that hot war, this time U.S. Congress would not permit it. Nonetheless, Angola, just like Vietnam, had felt its internal conflict inflamed by super-power competition. And all that it did was to turn an internal conflict into something far more destructive, bloody, and deadly.[179]

Angola's case illustrates an important and often forgotten side to super-power competition. Although most people in the West think the U.S.–Soviet Cold War was a stand-off in Europe, where both sides had amassed enormous armies, the two superpowers were actively fighting each other all around the world. That is why the people who suffered the most during this period were the people of the Third World. From the Vietnamese jungle to the arid steppes of Africa, Washington and Moscow competed over resources and strategic locations. Sometimes, they simply got involved to undermine the other. In the process, they brought pain, misery, and death to the people of the Global South. With a new U.S.–China Cold War in the making, this region may again be turned into a Cold War battlefield.

Two Railways

Two railway tracks cut through the beautiful landscape of Kenya, all the way from Mombasa at the coast to the inland capital Nairobi over 300 miles away. One of these tracks was built by Britain during the time when

---

[178] Stockwell, J. (1978). *In Search of Enemies.* W. W. Norton & Company, p. 176-177, 200-201.
[179] Marcum, J. (1978). *The Angolan Revolution Volume 2: Exile Politics and Guerilla Warfare (1962-1976).* The M.I.T. Press; Stockwell, J. (1978). *In Search of Enemies.* W. W. Norton & Company, p. 216-217.

Kenya was one of many colonies making up the British Empire. Nicknamed the "Lunatic Express," the railway served important functions to the British colonial government.

Right next to this remnant of colonial rule lies a brand-new railway track. Constructed by the China Road & Bridge Corporation and finished in 2017, it has taken over the task of transporting people and cargo. This railway is one of several Belt and Road Initiative (BRI) projects in Kenya. The BRI is a centerpiece of Chinese foreign policy, and includes many more projects in Africa, the Middle East, Asia, and beyond. Interestingly, in the West, it has sparked the question of whether Africa is again facing colonialism, this time not by the European powers who divided the continent between them during the famous 1884–85 Berlin conference, but by the Chinese Communist Party who devised the Belt and Road Initiative from their headquarters in Beijing.

U.S. government officials view the BRI as China's way of expanding its power and influence in the world, thereby undermining the dominant position of the West in places like Africa. To prevent the Chinese from eroding U.S. power, Washington may again decide to wage hot wars, only this time against China. And to get the people in the West to go along with this, they present Beijing's BRI activities in Africa and other places as a modern attempt at colonization. Without shame or a sense of irony, American and European politicians say it is now up to the West to protect the Third World against occupation and exploitation.

But is China colonizing Africa? And if colonization is not a good description, what then is China doing there? And how and where in the Global South can Beijing and Washington come to blows?

Before discussing future hot wars in more detail, we should unpack what China is doing in places like Africa, and to what extent these BRI activities resemble colonization. We have all heard of the term 'colonialism', and we understand it is part of Western history. But to grasp the true meaning of the word, we must listen to its victims, whose voices often have been ignored or suppressed in the Western version of history. Only then will we be able to judge whether Africa really needs our protection, or whether Western leaders are trying to coax us into supporting a series of hot wars to protect their own power and dominance against a rising China.

The Faces of Colonialism

Panic overwhelmed Nderi Kagombe the moment the guards dragged him and the others out of the truck. In normal circumstances, Nderi and his fellow prisoners would have been happy to finally breathe some fresh air. But what they had seen, looking outside from the truck, had shocked them to their bones.

While standing under the blistering afternoon sun, the white British officers ordered them to take off their clothes. Afraid of suffering yet another anal cavity search, Nderi and the others refused. Their brave little stance did not last long. Rifle butts began hammering down upon them. Screams turned into desperate murmurs as the guards shoveled sand into their mouths. Nderi remembers how they ripped off his clothes and shaved off all his hair. Next, he was stuffed into a uniform and then pushed into one of the cages. This was the welcoming ceremony of Mwea, a heavily guarded prison camp on Mageta Island. It was just one camp of many, and part of a much bigger system that the British colonial office in Kenya called the "Pipeline." [180]

Nderi used to live a quiet life in the capital city of Nairobi, where he owned two small shops selling restaurant supplies. Business was good. It allowed him to support his wife and children, and even save some money on the side. But life in an Apartheid-like state in which Africans were treated as second-ranked citizens did not feel right with Nderi. He developed sympathy for those who resisted the British occupation. One day, he made the decision to secretly help the resistance by giving them some supplies. But unfortunately for him, his secret got out. When the British security forces came for him, Nderi was arrested and moved to Manyani, one of the more notorious camps in the Pipeline.

In total, Nderi was sent to seven different camps. Shackled in chains and with little or no food, the Lunatic Express transported him from one camp to the next. Everywhere the routine was the same. Forced to sleep in filthy barracks, a piercing siren and the shouts of guards would wake the prisoners up suddenly. On a lucky day, Nderi and the others got some watery porridge before the guards started marching them out to the worksite for yet another day of forced labor in the boiling sun. After the sun had set and exhaustion was near, they were marched back to the camp, driven forth by clubs and rifle butts. After a restless night, the whole sequence would repeat itself. These, of course, were the good days.

On a bad day, Nderi witnessed or was subjected to all kinds of torture. The British settler who ran Nderi's compound in Manyani regarded all Africans as animals, and he treated them as such, and worse. Together with his right-hand man Wagithundia, a guard whose skin disease made him look like Satan, they devised creative ways of torture. They preferred to do this

---

[180] Elkins, C. (2005). *Imperial Reckoning.* Henry Holt and Company. See p. 154-155, 157-158, 161, 170-171, 175, 177, 179, 185, 191, 311-316

in public. Seeing the fear and shock in the eyes of the onlooking prisoners amused them greatly.

But as Nderi recalled, Manyani was not the worst. One of his most terrifying memories came from Mwea, a special camp on Mageta Island, which was surrounded by a vast swamp. There the British guards would chain a prisoner to a post, take the sap from a special leaf, and rub it all over him. Next, the mosquitos that filled the swamp and the camp would completely cover the victim and devour him slowly. Although Nderi showed exceptional mental strength and determination during his imprisonment, the Pipeline ultimately broke him, just as the British conquest and occupation had crushed so many before him.

The conquest of Kenya was the work of force and violence the inhabitants had never seen before. The conquering forces consisted of a core of British officers and soldiers, reinforced by African mercenaries (often referred to as 'nigger soldiers') and colonial armies from British India. The conquest lasted for over a decade, and it took dozens of military operations to crush all resistance.[181]

Many of these operations were punitive expeditions, which the British considered as a necessary part of 'educating' Africans. Burning entire villages and their food stores, accompanied sometimes by the killing of every inhabitant, was standard practice. Theatrical shows of violence were considered an effective way to intimidate people into submission.[182]

But there were those who did not give up easily. One of the groups who fiercely resisted the British conquest were the Giriama. They had taken up working the fertile lands near the coast and did not want to abandon their existence as independent farmers. When the British came and tried to force them into subordinate wage labor, they resisted bravely. To the British it was clear what needed to be done. The Giriama needed to be 'educated' in the ways of the white man and the superiority of British force.

What followed was a public display. A dynamite team from the British Public Works Department walked into the Gaya, an important cultural site of the Giriama. Under the silent gaze of the tribal elders, they planted charges all around the main trees and gates. Then they were blown to bits. The remaining trees and dwellings were burned, and the entrance, or what

---

[181] Berman, B. & Lonsdale, J. (1992). Unhappy Valley. James Currey Ltd, Heinemann Kenya, Ohio University Press. See Book 1, chapter 2; Walter, D. (2017). *Colonial Violence*. Hurst & Company, p. 63, 77

[182] Lonsdale, J. M. (1977). The Politics of Conquest: The British in Western Kenya, 1894-1908. *The Historical Journal*, 20(4), 841–870. http://www.jstor.org/stable/2638411 See p. 852; Walter, D. (2017). *Colonial Violence*. Hurst & Company, p. 123, 151

was left of it, barricaded. Unknown to the Giriama, this was only the opening salvo.[183]

Having destroyed sacred ground, British patrols began sweeping through the countryside, burning villages in their path. They fired upon anyone in sight, whether they were hostile or not. In systematic sweeps, thousands of homes were burned and all cattle confiscated. The bows and arrows of the Giriama were no match for British guns. This once determined and united tribe was reduced to a divided and helpless lot, many of whom were forced to flee.[184]

Now that all resistance had been stamped out, the British wanted to turn their brand-new colony into a profitable enterprise. But this proved to be difficult. Most British settlers, who of course took possession of the most fertile lands, had not come to Kenya to work. Physical labor was below these lords and ladies. What they required were servants and laborers. In "White Man's Country," blacks were supposed to work the fields and clean the house while the whites entertained themselves at the bar, the racetrack, and on the polo fields. Indeed, the settlers were hoping to recreate in Kenya the slave-plantation model of the American South. But having killed and displaced so many Kenyans, the British had a tough time finding enough of them. And those they did capture often did not want to work for them.[185]

The natives had proudly owned and worked their lands for generations. Possession of land had enormous importance to them. It was a big part of their culture and customs. In many ways, owning land and being independent farmers defined them as human beings. Only with coercion and violence were the British able to break these ancient traditions. They implemented laws designed to bankrupt Africans, to drive them off their lands, and into the arms of the British settlers.[186]

Surprisingly, at least to the settlers, many Africans began to resist these "civilizing" methods. A vicious circle of assaults and murders quickly took hold. White Man's Country, instead of being a paradise for the British, got tainted by a climate of paranoia and fear.

The lords and ladies, dressed in expensive suits and silk dresses, now carried around with them loaded rifles and shotguns and only dared to go to sleep at night with a gun at arms' reach. Children were kept at home

---

[183] Brantley, C. (1981). *The Giriama and Colonial Resistance in Kenya, 1800-1920.* University of California Press, p. 110-111

[184] Brantley, C. (1981). *The Giriama and Colonial Resistance in Kenya, 1800-1920.* University of California Press

[185] Elkins, C. (2005). *Imperial Reckoning.* Henry Holt and Company, p. 3-4 and 10-12.

[186] Elkins, C. (2005). *Imperial Reckoning.* Henry Holt and Company p. 15-16; Njoh, A. J. (2007). *Planning Power.* UCL Press. p. 175

and indoors. Nobody felt safe. But revenge came swiftly. For every settler murdered by an African, the British murdered three or four times as many. Large scale massacres started to be a common occurrence.[187]

Fortunately for the British, they had vast experience in controlling resentful peoples. Their empire was not built on cooperation and trust with the locals. They were also in luck because at that time, which was the 1950s, Britain was also very busy trying to eliminate a resistance movement in Malaya, another British colony. Governor Baring, British highest official in Kenya, decided to use similar tactics that were working out great in Malaya. The key was to move all those who resisted, or who were suspected of having sympathy for the resistance, into heavily guarded concentration camps. In Kenya, this quickly developed into a vast network of prisons and forced labor camps. There, surrounded by barbed wire, watch towers, and armed guards, the Africans could not further spoil the fun for the British in White Man's Country. In total, there were more than a hundred camps, some of them gigantic in scale. Britain created its own gulag, not in the icy cold of Stalin's Siberia, but in the sweltering heat of British Kenya.[188]

The camps were strategically placed along the Lunatic Express, so prisoners could easily be moved from one camp to the next. British security forces raided villages and even entire cities, battered down doors, and dragged the inhabitants outside. Men, women and children were separated and their were possessions taken away. The men were then put on a truck or a train and moved to the euphemistically named transit camps, or "cruelty camps" in the words of Christian missionaries.[189]

Inside these transit camps people were "screened," which meant tortured, until they 'confessed'. Until this day, screening remains a dirty word in the Kenyan language. Those who refused to confess, people such as Nderi, were send to more notorious camps where the British were more creative in their methods of torture. The entire system was referred to as the "Pipeline" — a system to process and root out all resistance to British rule.[190]

Although the horror finally ended in the late 1950s, for many men, women and children, the physical and mental scars remained. Of course, they were the lucky ones. The death toll in the camps had been high. For those families who never got to see their loved ones again it was difficult to find closure because the British had buried most in anonymous mass graves. For far too

---

[187] Elkins, C. (2005). *Imperial Reckoning.* Henry Holt and Company p. 42-45.
[188] Elkins, C. (2005). *Imperial Reckoning.* Henry Holt and Company p. 101-103, 150-151
[189] Elkins, C. (2005). *Imperial Reckoning.* Henry Holt and Company p. 63.
[190] Elkins, C. (2005). *Imperial Reckoning.* Henry Holt and Company p. 151-152 and chapter 5

many this burden was too great to bear, and suicide proved to be the only way out.[191]

Kenya's experience with colonialism was typical in most ways. Some countries and peoples fared a little bit better, others experienced a worse fate. This brings us to what colonialism is. Colonialism, at its very core, is a system of conquest and domination, fear and humiliation, and ruthless exploitation. The numbers of deaths and destroyed families in Kenya tell one such tale, the ten million who perished in the Belgian Congo another. So do the twelve million Africans who were chained and shipped to the America's by British, French, Spanish, Portuguese, and Dutch slave traders to replace the tens of millions of people who did not survive the colonial conquest of Latin America. Historians estimate that the African slave trade, which included countless raids and wars to capture slaves, killed another thirty or forty million more, cutting population growth of the entire African continent in half. These numbers, of course, are only the beginning of an awfully long list.[192]

But these statistics are just that: numbers. They do not convey the tragic stories of the victims, who, like Nderi, had encountered Western colonialism. It makes you wonder what kind of human beings could design such a system of cruelty and death. Their names, however, are familiar to all of us.

One such name is Christopher Columbus. His lust for gold inspired him to invent a system of slave labor that punished children by cutting off their limbs if they failed to mine the desired amount. Another champion of colonialism was Winston Churchill, who ordered the use of chemical weapons "against recalcitrant Arabs as an experiment." Churchill, while dutifully carrying the White Man's burden, proudly stated he was "strongly in favor of using poisoned gas against uncivilized tribes." John Quincy Adams, the sixth President of the United States, ruthlessly exterminated the native Indians. In his personal diary he wrote about "that hapless race of native Americans, which we are exterminating with such merciless and perfidious cruelty." That admittance did not stop him though. In fact, it is

---

[191] Elkins, C. (2005). *Imperial Reckoning.* Henry Holt and Company p. 269-271

[192] Hochschild, A. (2006). *King Leopold's Ghost: A Story of Greed, Terror and Heroism in Colonial Africa.* Pan Books; Mannix, P. D., Cowley. M. (2002). *Black Cargoes: A History of the Atlantic Slave Trade 1518-1865.* Penguin Books; Maddison, A. (2001). *The World Economy: A millennial perspective.* Development Centre of the Organisation for Economic Co-Operation and Development, 2001. See p. 243; Sanabria, H. (2007). *The Anthropology of Latin America and the Caribbean.* Pearson Education, Inc., p. 82-83.

extremely hard to find Western leaders who resisted the attempt by Europe and the United States to colonize the world.[193]

But besides such famous individuals, to most of the victims, colonization simply meant a white face beating them down with a rifle butt, a curly red-haired sailor waiting for them on the beach with a chain in his hand, or a tanned face on the other end of a whip in one of the Caribbean 'plantation machines'.

Never has the world seen such systematic injustice on a global scale. This then brings us to what China is doing in Africa. To make the comparison with colonialism, something that ironically many Westerners are doing, means losing sight of what colonialism was. This does not mean, however, that Beijing's actions are therefore innocent. On the contrary, they may have numerous harmful effects.

Belt and Road: Business Imperialism?

If you want to understand who benefits from an economic or political system, a good place to start is to identify who designed it. The Belt and Road Initiative (BRI), being a Chinese Communist Party (CCP) creation, is there to benefit the CCP. Although the BRI does so in many different ways, they can all be traced back to the core issue of the communist party — making sure the CCP continues to rule and dominate China. Everything the CCP does ultimately comes down to this simple fact. So how does the BRI help the party? It does this by stimulating China's economy. As long as the Chinese economy grows and people's standards of living rise, the Chinese population will accept CCP rule. The BRI is supposed to ensure continued Chinese economic success, and in doing so, continued CCP dominance. This then brings us to the next question: what is the BRI?

The BRI is a system in which China loans money to other governments who then make use of Chinese construction companies to build roads, railways, bridges, ports, industrial parks, hydroelectric dams, electric grids, and other infrastructure. This then serves a range of different Chinese goals.[194]

For one, it provides work for Chinese construction, engineering, and high-tech businesses, both private and state-owned, who have outgrown

---

[193] McConnell, M. and Mueller, P. (1991). *Dangerous Memories: Invasion and Resistance Since 1492*. Chicago Religious Task Force on Central America, p. 51; Thomas, A. (1985). Effects of Chemical Warfare. SIPRI. See p. 33-35; Weeks, W. E. (1992). *John Quincy Adams & American Global Empire*. The University Press of Kentucky, p. 193;

[194] For books on the BRI, see Miller, T. (2019). *China's Asian Dream*. ZED Books; Blanchard, J-M. F. (2021). *China's Maritime Silk Road Initiative, Africa and the Middle East*. Palgrave Macmillan

the Chinese market and now must look abroad to make money and provide employment to the Chinese people.

The infrastructure that they built also helps to connect China with other countries. Creating connections is key to the BRI. While it is true that sometimes the BRI connects other countries with each other, for example land-locked Ethiopia with the port of Djibouti, the most important thing is to connect China with the rest of the world so that Chinese businesses can continue to sell their manufactured goods and buy much-needed resources.[195]

On a grander geopolitical level, the goal of the BRI is to integrate countries into a China-centered system. As the Chinese presence grows in a country, their dependence on China also increases. Over time, countries and governments may find themselves 'locked-in' an economic system that revolves around China. For Beijing, this is also an attempt to move countries away from the Western-dominated world order and closer to a new global order centered around China.

But does this mean that, for example, African countries have no choice in the matter and are merely being exploited by China? A quick answer is it depends. African countries can use the BRI to boost their own economic development, but they will have to negotiate with China, make demands, and insist on the right kind of policies. Without that, the BRI may bring them more harm than good.

This is what countries should not do. Suppose a government joins the BRI to simply loan money from a Chinese bank to have a Chinese construction company come in and build a railway. Will that guarantee the country's economic development? Here the answer is at best a maybe, and in many cases, the answer will be no. Just like in colonial times, the construction of infrastructure in a Third World country without a solid development plan can accelerate its de-industrialization and increase its focus on exporting raw materials. A railway can make it easier for advanced industrial countries to sell their manufactured goods all over the region and to transport raw materials to the coast for export. This may be bad for a country's overall economic development. But interestingly, it may still be very tempting for politicians to agree to something like this. They can present a modern railway to their people, claim they are modernizing the nation, and, if the people fall for it, receive praise, and extend their time in office.[196]

Real development, however, will only take place when the host government makes sure that technology and skills are transferred from the Chinese

[195] Blanchard, J-M. F. (2021). *China's Maritime Silk Road Initiative, Africa and the Middle East.* Palgrave Macmillan, p. 53-80.
[196] Batou, J. (1991). Between Development and Underdevelopment. Geneve, Librairie Droz 11, pp. 15-16

to their own country. For example, governments that join the BRI should insist that the Chinese engineering firm partners with a local one, and that technical training and technology is shared. An industrial park constructed by Chinese firms that allows Chinese companies to produce for local African markets will only boost development if these companies must share their expertise and technology with African businesses. This strategy, in fact, was used by none other than China to further its economic and technological development, and they did so with immense success. African countries should insist, though, on a meaningful transfer because Beijing will be perfectly happy to not share its technology. And although China is an economic whale and the individual African countries are much smaller minnows, the BRI is very important to the CCP, and that gives leverage to Africa and other countries in the Global South to make their own demands. The Chinese like to talk about win-win cooperation, and the BRI can bring that about, if governments do the right thing.[197]

How does the BRI compare to other grand international schemes? It lacks the kind of coercion and violence that comes with colonialism. But there is one historical example involving the British Empire that the BRI has much in common with. In important ways, China's BRI in Africa and elsewhere is like Britain's activities in Latin America in the 1800s. And there are important lessons to learn from that.

When the nations of Latin America became independent from their colonial masters Spain and Portugal around the 1820s, the newly formed governments decided to partner with Britain. They struck a whole series of economic deals that included the construction of infrastructure and increased trade, in a way not too different from the BRI. To illustrate, compare these two statements, the first from the U.S. ambassador to Brazil in the 1830s: "Great Britain supplies Brazil with its steam and sailing ships, and paves and repairs its streets, lights its cities with gas, builds its railways, exploits its mines, is its banker, puts up its telegraph wires, carries its mail, builds its furniture, motors, wagons..."[198] And the second from A 2018 CNN report describing China's influence in Ethiopia: "Cars chug through the city on smooth Chinese roads, Chinese cranes lift the skyline, sewing machines hum in Chinese factories in Chinese-owned industrial parks, tourists arrive

---

[197] Blanchard, J-M. F. (2021). *China's Maritime Silk Road Initiative, Africa and the Middle East*. Palgrave Macmillan, p. 81-110; Brautigam, D. (2009). *The Dragon's Gift*. Oxford University Press, p. 145

[198] Galeano, E. (2009). Open Veins of Latin America: Five Centuries of the Pillage of a Continent. Serpent's Tail, p. 178.

at the Chinese-upgraded airport and commuters ride modern Chinese trains to work."[199]

As it turned out, in the 19th century, Latin America boosted British industry, finance and trade. British manufacturers happily produced railway materials, which were then shipped to America by British shipping companies and insured by British financial institutions. And with the railways in place, it became easier to transport raw materials and agricultural crops to the coast and move British manufactured goods in. British merchant houses arranged their transport, which again was carried out by British ships and insured by British insurance companies. Most of the profits left Latin America and moved to banks in London, where they were invested in the British economy, not in the economies of Latin America. The Latin American governments pretended that they were modernizing the continent, but in fact, it only delayed and harmed economic development. These politicians chose to go down this path without the British forcing them, at least for the most part, and happily partnered with Britain to further their own — not their country's — interests.[200]

If a comparison with colonialism must be made, then the BRI best resembles this type of "business imperialism." And as this proved to be greatly beneficial for 19th-century Britain, so the BRI is designed to benefit China. Other countries, including those in Africa, can use it for their own purposes, but they should not expect Beijing to lend them a helping hand.

In terms of a U.S.–China Cold War, the BRI raises another particularly important issue. Now that Chinese businesses and investments have gone overseas, Beijing feels a growing need to safeguard them. Chinese security forces and the military are now starting to follow wherever the BRI leads them. The first experiments of Chinese military forces operating on the global scene have been in Africa, and nothing suggests that they will stop there.

The Flag, the Merchant, and the People's Liberation Army

Under a clear blue sky in the desert heat, three hundred Chinese soldiers and sailors stand at attention. In the middle of the square, two poles rise. One flies the Chinese Five-star red flag, the other the light blue and light

---

[199] Quoted from Blanchard, J-M. F. (2021). *China's Maritime Silk Road Initiative, Africa and the Middle East.* Palgrave Macmillan, p. 85

[200] Platt, D. C. M. (1977). *Business Imperialism 1840-1930: An inquiry based on British experience in Latin America.* Oxford at the Clarendon Press. For Argentina, see Rock, D. (1985). *Argentina 1516-1987: From Spanish Colonization to Alfonsín.* University of California Press, pp. 119, 149-150, 168, 177, 181-183. See also Frank, A. G. (1967). Capitalism and Underdevelopment in Latin America. Monthly Review Press.

green flag of Djibouti. Indeed, this small African nation is home to China's first official foreign military base.

Opened in August 2017, the base can host several hundred soldiers, together with armored vehicles and armed helicopters. Its location near the Chinese constructed Doraleh port gives it a naval capability too, that includes the docking of frigates, destroyers, and amphibious assault ships.[201]

The choice for Djibouti as the first site of a Chinese military base abroad comes in part because of its strategic location at the Gulf of Aden — a vital waterway for shipments of oil. The Gulf of Aden also connects the Suez Canal and Europe in the West with the Indian Ocean and China in the East. Yes, for China's BRI, Djibouti's location is very important.

Interestingly, China's base is located only 12 miles away from Camp Lemonnier, a United States military base that is home to the Combined Joint Task Force Horn of Africa of the U.S. Africa Command. Camp Lemonnier is much larger than China's military base and can host up to 4,000 U.S. troops. The fact that China located its base nearby is no coincidence, though.

As in everything that Chinese leaders do, the choice for Djibouti was made very carefully. Because this small African country already hosts several military bases from the United States, Britain, France and Japan, China's military presence does not stand out. Deng Xiaoping famously said that China's foreign strategy should follow the maxim of "*taoguang yanghui,*" which means "keep a low profile and bide your time." To some extent Beijing still likes to keep a low profile, but there are important signs that this is changing. With more investments and businesses operating overseas, Beijing wants to guard those interests. As a result, China's military and security presence overseas is growing, and its actions have become more assertive.[202]

Protection of China's overseas interests by Chinese security and military forces really took off in the wake of the 2013 crisis in Libya, when Beijing was caught mostly unprepared and acted indecisively. Following the outbreak of civil war and NATO's military attack against the country, 36,000 Chinese had to be evacuated suddenly. The Chinese government realized that a failure to protect Chinese citizens anywhere in the world could threaten its legitimacy to rule in the eyes of its population. Therefore, they decided to turn the PLA into a more global force and included in its mandate the protection of China's overseas citizens, investments, and property.[203]

---

[201] Ghiselli, A. (2021). Protecting *China's Interests Overseas.* Oxford University Press, p. 1, 229
[202] Ghiselli, A. (2021). Protecting *China's Interests Overseas.* Oxford University Press, p. 71-75
[203] Hodzi, O. (2019). *The End of China's Non-Intervention Policy in Africa.* Palgrave Macmillan, chapter 4; Ghiselli, A. (2021). Protecting *China's Interests Overseas.* Oxford University Press, p. 59-60

In the years following 2013, China acted more decisively in two other conflicts in Africa, namely in Mali and Sudan. The conflict in Sudan was especially concerning to Beijing because Chinese oil corporations have major investments there. The Chinese government got so worried that they even abandoned their non-interference policy. Beijing likes to brand itself as a government that does not interfere in the internal affairs of other countries. But with important interests at stake, this principle, just as keeping a low profile, was conveniently put aside for a while.

The situation in Sudan has been dynamic, to say the least. Beijing started out supporting the central government in the north. Already in the early 1990s, China became a major weapons supplier, providing missiles, tanks, helicopters, and fighter aircraft. With these weapons, the Sudanese government tried to keep its southern province under control. The south of Sudan, where most of the oil is, wanted independence, but the central government in the North did not want to let that happen.[204]

But Beijing's position changed after 2005, when it became clear that South Sudan had a real chance of gaining independence. Instead of keeping to their non-interference policy, Chinese officials began meeting politicians from the South. Beijing wanted to make sure that, if South Sudan would win against the north, relations with the South would be friendly, to ensure the safety and operations of Chinese oil companies. But in doing so, China was actively interfering in the internal affairs of Sudan.

Things really got out of control in 2013, two years after South Sudan had gained its official independence. As is often the case in newly formed countries, there are rival groups competing for power. In the case of South Sudan, a civil war broke out that threatened to bring destruction to China's oil, construction, and telecommunication companies. Beijing decided to help negotiate between the warring parties but was mainly motivated to protect its own economic interests. When a United Nations operation in South Sudan was launched, China took the opportunity to send in its own military forces under the UN banner. Beijing also made sure that the UN mandate included the protection of Chinese oil installations. By cleverly making this intervention part of a larger United Nations operation, the Chinese government can claim legitimacy and, to some extent, disguise its true motivations and intentions behind talk about bringing peace and assisting the United Nations.[205]

---

[204] Hodzi, O. (2019). *The End of China's Non-Intervention Policy in Africa*. Palgrave Macmillan, chapter 5 and 6

[205] Hodzi, O. (2019). *The End of China's Non-Intervention Policy in Africa*. Palgrave Macmillan, chapter 6

Besides protecting its BRI interests, another reason China has been eager to participate in UN operations is to gain combat experience in military operations in far away places. Beijing knows its military has fought only a few wars in the past decades. Consequently, they are now looking for opportunities to gain experience in real military operations. Therefore, both UN missions in Mali and Sudan involved Chinese combat troops. In Sudan this was a considerable force (battalion size), and they were equipped with modern weapons including drones, armored infantry carriers, and antitank missiles.[206]

Compared to the 2003 war in Iraq, when 130,000 U.S. troops simply invaded and occupied the country, these actions by China may seem rather dull. But that would be missing the point. China's foreign policy is very carefully planned, and the direction in which it is moving is clear. Gradually, step by step, Beijing is increasing its military presence around the world. Until now, Chinese leaders used United Nations operations to let their military gain experience and, at times, protect its BRI interests. But that may very well be about to change.

Looking at the future, as China's overseas investments and trade continue to grow, so does the need to have foreign governments in place that are loyal to Beijing and eager to do business with China. If you combine this with China's growing military power, the next logical step for Beijing would be to completely drop its non-interference policy and, just like the West, actively start maneuvering pro-Chinese governments into power. For the continued success of the BRI, this may become important, because as recent events have already shown, a change in government can have big implications.

One very good example is Tanzania, where China was planning to construct the largest deep seaport in East Africa. But when Tanzania got a new President in 2015, this new government showed far less enthusiasm to continue such projects. Plans for billion-dollar Chinese loans for the construction of railways were canceled. Instead, Tanzania contracted firms from Turkey and Portugal. The Beijing of 2015 accepted its losses, but would a future and far more powerful Beijing do so as well? As China's power grows, the Chinese government will be increasingly tempted to use its military power to prevent such things from happening. And to make matters worse, examples like Tanzania will inspire and tempt the United States to try to overthrow pro-Chinese governments and replace them with more anti-Chinese and pro-American ones. Naturally, this then can lead to a

---

[206] Hodzi, O. (2019). *The End of China's Non-Intervention Policy in Africa.* Palgrave Macmillan, p. 205, 245 ebook; Ghiselli, A. (2021). Protecting *China's Interests Overseas.* Oxford University Press, p. 210-218

whole series of hot wars between the two superpowers, just as it did in the first Cold War between the United States and the Soviet Union. And as the next two sections show, nobody wants to repeat those, especially not the people who live in those unfortunate countries that may be targeted.[207]

Falling Dominos

On August 9, 1965, a Chinese air defense unit shot down an American F-4 fighter near the Yen Bai area in North Vietnam. It was the first U.S. plane downed by a Chinese anti-aircraft (AAA) unit. It would not be the last. Soon after this first kill, a second Chinese AAA division crossed the border from Guangxi province into Vietnam. Together, the two divisions totaled 21,000 AAA troops. Over the course of the war, these and other Chinese units shot down 1,707 American planes. The Cold War had turned hot as the superpowers fought each other for control over Indochina and many other places in the Third World.[208]

The Vietnam or Indochina War is the most dramatic and destructive example of superpowers competing against each other over a region in the Third World. Historians refer to this era this as the 'Global Cold War'. The Cold War was far more than a standoff between Soviet and Western forces in Europe, which tends to be the focus of Cold War history. Most of the fighting occurred in the Third Word. From Asia to Africa and Latin America, no region escaped. But nowhere was it as bad as in Indochina.[209]

In Vietnam, the United States, China, and the Soviet Union were trying to get a loyal and obedient government in power. Simply put, Washington wanted a pro-U.S. and anti-Soviet/anti-China government in Vietnam, and Moscow and Beijing wanted the opposite. They showed little to no concern for what the Vietnamese people wanted. Vietnam had become a pawn in a geopolitical game and, in the process, was virtually destroyed.

The story starts all the way back in 1858, when France had begun colonizing Indochina. Following military conquest, the French turned Vietnam into a police state that suppressed basic freedoms; exploited workers to exhaustion; locked up anyone who resisted in a brutal prison system; and taxed the Vietnamese heavily so they paid for their own occupation and exploitation. In other words: colonial business as usual. Between

---

[207] Blanchard, J-M. F. (2021). *China's Maritime Silk Road Initiative, Africa and the Middle East.* Palgrave Macmillan, p. 138-164

[208] Xiaobing Li (2019). *Building Ho's Armies.* University Press of Kentucky, p. 168 and 235, note 9

[209] Westad, O. A. (2007). *The Global Cold War.* Cambridge University Press. For earlier books see Kolko, G. (1988). *Confronting the Third World.* Pantheon Books and works by Noam Chomsky such as Deterring Democracy and Manufacturing Consent.

1940 and 1945, however, France briefly lost control over Indochina to Japan. But after the Japanese were defeated, the French quickly set out to reconquer their profitable colony. It is here that the superpowers became involved.[210]

Beijing preferred that the French would not reconquer their former colony, that instead Vietnam would be independent, and that the country get a communist government under the leadership of Ho Chi Minh. To prevent France from reconquering Vietnam and imposing its own pro-Western colonial regime on the country, China began helping the Vietnamese. The goal was to transform Vietnam's peasant militia into a modern regular army capable of defeating the French. Beijing provided heavy weapons together with training in strategy, logistics, communication, and all other things that a modern army requires. Meanwhile, Chinese military advisors actively assisted the Vietnamese military in planning and conducting operations against the French army. With China's help, Vietnam defeated France at Dien Bien Phu in 1954. It looked like Beijing was about to get its way, but then the United States joined the fight.[211]

Actually, Washington had already been involved for quite some time. Although in public American politicians claimed they were not helping Paris, they were in fact providing the French army with massive amounts of military equipment. Overall, the U.S. funded up to 78% of all the costs. Both China and the U.S. were thus pouring in weapons and money, which made the conflict all the deadlier and more destructive.[212]

After France left the scene in 1954, Washington continued to support the regime of Bao Dai which ruled over South Vietnam. Bao Dai had been a loyal French puppet and had also assisted the Japanese. He had no difficulties in shifting his allegiance yet again to another master, this time the United States. Bao Dai was not the last widely unpopular leader that Washington supported in the South. His successor, Ngo Dinh Diem, America's 'miracle man' in Vietnam, was despised by most South Vietnamese too. As such, it took effort to keep these men in power. But with the help of the notorious CIA chief Colonel Edward Lansdale, who became Diem's trusted advisor, and together with increased military support from the United States, Diem's rule was secured at least for a while. Meanwhile, China aided the North

---

[210] Brocheux, P. & Hemery, D. (2009). *IndoChina an Ambiguous Colonization, 1858-1954.* University of California Press; Zinoman, P. (2020). *The Colonial Bastille.* University of California Press.

[211] Xiaobing Li (2019). *Building Ho's Armies.* University Press of Kentucky.

[212] Kahin, G, McT. (1986). *Intervention: How America Became Involved in Vietnam.* Alfred A. Knopf. Inc.

Vietnamese in their attempt to rid themselves of this pro-American regime in the South.[213]

What followed was a brutal war that lasted until 1975. China and the United States poured in massive amounts of weapons and ammunition. At its peak, there were around 500,000 U.S. troops in Vietnam and over 100,000 Chinese. None cared much for the Vietnamese, although they certainly did pretend. Beijing, for example, began blocking negotiations after Washington sent in ground forces in 1965. They were hoping that the war would be a drain on American resources and weaken it in the process. For its part, Washington had prevented a peaceful end to the conflict by violating the 1954 Geneva Agreement and by blocking democratic elections in 1956.[214]

As the war raged on, the moderates within the Vietnamese Communist Party who had been in charge for years were overtaken by the more militant factions. The militants viewed the moderates as naive for hoping negotiations could bring peace, and they wanted to use more aggressive action. Meanwhile in the South, a series of military dictators took over after Diem showed some signs that he was considering negotiating. Washington continued to make sure to replace anyone who was edging towards diplomacy until there was no government left to speak of, except for a group of hard-line military generals.[215]

While Vietnam was sliding into oblivion, the superpower competition spread to the rest of Southeast Asia. To Washington, this was not only a fight over Vietnam. Interestingly, Vietnam was not even vital to American interests. Yes, the country had some resources and markets, but nothing out of the ordinary. This begs the question, why did consecutive U.S. presidents continue to invest so much in this war? The answer to this question is crucial, because it illustrates how easily these hot wars can develop into something much bigger and much more destructive.

When President Lyndon Johnson asked his advisors whether all the efforts in Vietnam were worth it, he was confronted with the view of the Joint Chiefs. They answered that if the U.S. lost in Vietnam, they would lose Southeast Asia. Like falling dominoes, so they reasoned, "country after country on the periphery would give way and look toward Communist China as the rising power of the area."[216]

---

[213] Kahin, G, McT. (1986). *Intervention: How America Became Involved in Vietnam.* Alfred A. Knopf. Inc; Logevall, F. (2012). Embers of War. Random House.

[214] Qiang Zhai (2000). *China and the Vietnam Wars.* University of North Carolina Press, p. 165-166

[215] Asselin, P. (2013). Hanoi's Road to the Vietnam War. University of California Press; Kahin, G, McT. (1986). *Intervention: How America Became Involved in Vietnam.* Alfred A. Knopf. Inc.

[216] Kahin, G, McT. (1986). *Intervention: How America Became Involved in Vietnam.* Alfred A. Knopf. Inc., p. 239

That would mean similar developments in neighboring Laos and Cambodia, and then perhaps Indonesia, with its rich resources and sizable markets, would follow. Finally, a communist Southeast Asia could pull Japan, the "Super-domino," towards a pro-China and pro-Soviet Asian bloc outside of U.S. control. Like a virus, in the words of Henry Kissinger, Washington must stop the spread. And so they did, in a ruthless manner.[217]

In Thailand and Myanmar, the United States supported military dictators like Ne Win (Myanmar) and Phibun and Sarit (both Thailand). They returned the favor by aligning their governments with the United States and against China. In Thailand, the U.S. was allowed to establish military bases to fight the Vietnam War. Both Phibun and Sarit cracked down on newspapers, journalists, and anyone else who criticized the United States. In return, Washington provided them with economic aid through the World Bank and loads of military equipment. The CIA also ran a secret program to transform the Thai police into another army to make sure the dictators remained firmly in power.[218]

In Malaysia, Washington was fortunate that the British had already made sure their former colony got a pro-Western government. In fact, the U.S. copied some of the tactics Britain had used and applied them in Vietnam. For example, the U.S. military used chemical weapons to destroy foliage that served as cover to Vietnamese guerilla fighters and destroyed food crops to starve out the enemy — techniques pioneered by the British in Malaysia.[219]

Laos and Cambodia also did not escape. Both had governments that tried to keep their countries out of the war, but their efforts were ruined by Washington. Next, the U.S. supported several military dictators, and bombed the countries back to the stone age — actions that fueled brutal civil wars. For good measure, the CIA built up a large paramilitary force in Laos to fight against anyone who resisted pro-U.S. rule. Starting in 1961 and under the code name Operation Momentum, the CIA ended up running a 30,000-man fighting force at a cost of $3.1 billion (in 2016 U.S. dollars).[220]

The CIA was also busy propping up a pro-U.S. president in the Philippines. The famous (or notorious) Colonel Edward Lansdale, who later would lend his services to Vietnam, "invented" President Ramon Magsaysay, who ruled the Philippines from 1953 until 1957. The CIA ran his election

[217] Dower, J. W. Pentagon Papers, 1972. vol. 5. 08. The Super Domino in Postwar Asia
[218] Foley, M. (2010). *The Cold War and National Assertion in Southeast Asia*. Routledge; Fineman, D. (1997). *A Special Relationship: The United States and the Military Government in Thailand, 1947-1958*. University of Hawai'i Press; Zawacki, B. (2017). *Thailand: Shifting Ground between the US and a Rising China*. Zed Books
[219] Grob-Fitzgibbon, B. (2011). *Imperial Endgame*. Palgrave Macmillan.
[220] Kurlantzick, J. (2017). *A Great Place to Have a War*. Simon & Schuster; Clymer, K. (2004). *The United States and Cambodia, 1969-2000*. Routledge.

campaign, drugged his political opponent, and wrote his speeches. One time, when Magsaysay deviated from the CIA script, a frustrated Lansdale knocked out the incumbent president. Once in power, the CIA made sure he passed a law (written in Washington) that banned the Communist Party in order to, ironically, prevent the country from falling "under the control and domination of an alien power." Later, Washington threw its weight behind Ferdinand Marcos, who ruled the Philippines as a pro-U.S. dictator until the 1980s.[221]

Finally, in Indonesia, the most important domino (except perhaps for Japan), Washington first tried to strip off the outer islands where most of the resources are by supporting several renegade anti-communist military leaders. When that failed, the U.S. supported General Suharto, who went on a killing spree to annihilate anyone suspected of having Soviet or Chinese sympathies. Suharto would rule as a military dictator for 31 years until 1998. With people such as him firmly in place, the entire region of Southeast Asia was made immune to pro-Soviet and pro-China governments. And in the meantime, Vietnam itself, the source of the virus, was being destroyed.[222]

Constructive Bloodbaths

Seminyak Beach in Southwest Bali looks and feels like paradise. But hidden underneath the soft white sand and gentle blue ocean lie the remains of a dark and deadly secret. The wellness and mindfulness centers where tourists come to meditate and relax hide a bloody and violent past. Only on rare occasions, when a tourist strolling along the beach seeking shells stumbles upon a human skull buried in the sand, can you get a glimpse of what happened here in the winter of 1965–66.

General Suharto's rise to power was a murderous event of epic proportions. In a frenzy, whipped up by relentless fake news and propaganda, Suharto's supporters and his military went after anyone suspected of having Soviet, Chinese, or other communist sympathies. "Operation Annihilation," as the Indonesian army called it, was supported enthusiastically by Washington. The CIA describes it as "one of the worst mass murders of the 20th century," yet the agency provided detailed "kill" lists with the names of thousands of people that Suharto and his men should murder. Already a few months into the killings, the State Department estimated that several hundred thousands of people had been killed. But U.S. support never wavered. As machetes were

---

[221] Brands, H. W. (1992). Bound To Empire. Oxford University Press; Blum, W. (2004). *Killing Hope*. Zed Books, chapter 4.

[222] Kahin, A. R. & George McT. Kahin. (1995). Subversion As Foreign Policy. The New Press; Bevins, V. (2020). The Jakarta Method. PublicAffairs.

brought into Bali, Suharto's military began dragging people to Seminyak Beach. There they were hacked to death or simply shot, and their bodies piled up and left to rot. As white sand turned red and paradise became hell, Indonesia moved away from Moscow and Beijing and closer to Washington — an event much celebrated in the Western media.[223]

What happened in Indonesia in 1965–66 was a "constructive bloodbath," according to Edward Herman and Noam Chomsky. They identify two other types, namely benign bloodbaths, which are mass killings that have no impact on Western power and so Western leaders do not care about them, and nefarious bloodbaths, which are conducted by official enemies of the West and are therefore strongly condemned and typically much exaggerated. The constructive type, however, are killings that benefit Western power and are the ones that we like and support. Indonesia was simply one such case of many.[224]

Historian Vincent Bevins has found such constructive slaughters in at least twenty-two countries between 1945 and 1990. When superpowers compete over Third World territories, mass murder is often the outcome.

Cambodia, for instance, was carpet bombed by the United States with 2.7 million tons of bombs. From the 500,000 dead bodies and out of the ashes of a destroyed society rose the Khmer Rouge of Pol Pot (similar to how ISIS arose from a destroyed Iraq), and they killed over two million more. Meanwhile, in Laos, on average the U.S. carried out a bombing run every 8 minutes, every day, for almost a decade. With much of the population hiding in caves desperately trying to survive, chances for a pro-U.S. government increased. Ten percent of the population did not survive this constructive bloodbath.[225]

But it was Vietnam that suffered most, and it is worth studying in detail because this is what the Third World may face again when the United States and China really go at it.

The butchery in Vietnam did not limit itself to people. It included nature and the land itself. "The Vietnam War differed from previous wars," geographer Joseph Hupy writes, "because now the destruction of key components of the country's physical environment became a deliberate military strategy." Sarah DeWeerdt, writing for World Watch, agrees and writes that "US

[223] The New Press; Bevins, V. (2020). The Jakarta Method. PublicAffairs. See also Kahin, A. R. & George McT. Kahin. (1995). Subversion As Foreign Policy and
[224] Chomsky, N. & Herman, E. S. (1979). The Washington Connection and Third World Fascism. Spokesman.
[225] Kiernan, Ben (2008). The Pol Pot Regime: Race, Power, and Genocide in Cambodia Under the Khmer Rouge, 1975–79. Yale University Press p. 16-19; Clymer, K. (2004). The United States and Cambodia, 1969-2000. Routledge

actions in Vietnam gave rise to the concept of 'ecocide' — the deliberate destruction of the environment as a military strategy." The U.S. carried out bombing on a scale never seen before, dropping 14,000,000 tons of bombs on the country between 1965 and 1971. "Carpet bombing" and "saturation bombing" left behind more than 26 million craters, transforming Vietnam's tropical landscape into something resembling "a moonscape of craters and scorched earth," environmental experts observed. A U.S. soldier who witnessed such destruction described it as "bombers and artillery pound the [land] into the gray porridge that the green delta land becomes, when pulverized by high explosives."[226]

Meanwhile, the U.S. sprayed 79 million liters of poisonous chemicals over one-seventh of the land in South Vietnam, destroying trees and food crops, killing animals, and contaminating the ground, food, and water. Between 1961 and 1968, around 1,293,000 people were contaminated. In the years after, medical specialists observed an increased number of birth defects in babies born from contaminated parents. Some newborn babies missed a nose or eyes, lacked forearms or parts of their brain, and were born without an anus or without belly skin so that their organs were visibly exposed. Some mothers gave birth to formless bloody lumps.[227]

Vietnamese officials estimate that around three million people, including 500,000 babies, continued to suffer from these toxic chemicals after the war ended. Scientists discovered that the contamination effects are passed onto future generations, destroying the lives of people and families even thirty years after the war officially ended.

Although nobody knows exactly how many people were killed during the war, when you look at the range of studies, the most likely estimate is around 2 million dead Vietnamese civilians. Around 5.3 million people were wounded, a third of them women and one-quarter children under the age of thirteen.

Of course, the number of dead and wounded tells just one story in a much larger tragedy. As is always the case, the horrors of war forced people to leave their homes behind and flee into the cities. The South Vietnamese capital Saigon grew from 1.4 million people to 4 million, making it the most densely populated city on earth (twice that of Tokyo, which came in second place). This extreme case of overcrowding created enormous slums, gigantic

---

[226] Hupy, J. P. (2008). *The Environmental Footprint of War*. Environment and History 14 (2008): 405–21; DeWeerdt, S. (2015). *War and the Environment*. World Watch Magazine, Volume 21, No. 1.

[227] Wilcox, F. A. (2011). *Scorched Earth: Legacies of Chemical Warfare in Vietnam*. Seven Stories Press

garbage dumps, and vast waste fields in which infant mortality rate skyrocketed to 36% and diseases such as cholera, typhoid, and even the bubonic plague (nicknamed the black death) were rampant. In the chaos of war around 100,000 children got separated from their parents and were roaming and scavenging the streets. Meanwhile, 500,000 women found themselves forced into prostitution to survive.[228]

Back in the United States, young men were prepared to fight and kill the Vietnamese. The U.S. boot camp experience that trains recruits was carefully designed to achieve that effect. The goal was to make these new soldiers capable of killing without hesitation and regret. While they were marching, they chanted the song "kill, kill, kill." Drill sergeants exposed them to racist beliefs and dehumanizing nicknames for their enemy. A Vietnamese person became a dink, a gook, or a rice-eater. U.S. soldiers were taught that the enemy were not humans but more like animals. Turning the Vietnamese into something less than human made them easier to kill, even morally right to kill. "That's what they engraved into you. That killer instinct," one Vietnam veteran remembers. In the North Vietnamese Army, which was trained by China, things were no different. "They always promote hatred, because without hatred, nobody would fight," a former NRF guerilla recalls.[229]

Body count became "*the* measure of success," according to U.S. Assistant Secretary of Defense Alain Enthoven. The more kills the better, and the more rewards your unit and your officer would get. Body counts were openly displayed in army camps to encourage competitions. Killing anything that moved, whether it was a squad of Vietnamese guerillas or a family of farmers, was all part of the game. And when it turned out that U.S. soldiers had killed civilians, they simply put some Soviet or Chinese weapons near the dead bodies so they could falsely be listed as Viet Cong soldiers.[230]

In light of a potential new Cold War between the United States and China, the Vietnam War should serve as a dire warning to everyone. What took place there, and in the surrounding region, may happen again somewhere else in the world. And when it does, the long list of tragedies outlined above will repeat itself. It is to these future bloodbaths that we will turn now in the last remaining sections of this chapter.

---

[228] Turse, N. (2013). *Kill Anything That Moves*. Metropolitan Books, p. 112-113.
[229] Turse, N. (2013). *Kill Anything That Moves*. Metropolitan Books. See also Horton, B. L. *A Content Analysis of Viet Cong Leaflets as Propaganda, 1963-68.* Master Thesis, Texas University.
[230] Turse, N. (2013). *Kill Anything That Moves*. Metropolitan Books.

Xi Jinping's Warning

On the evening of September 14, 2022, the international airport of Samarkand, Uzbekistan, was a buzz of activity and anticipation. It was a special moment. Not every day does one of the most powerful people on the planet pay a visit to one of Central Asia's oldest cities.

Uzbek President Shavkat Mirziyoyev had ordered an exceptionally grand welcoming ceremony. Dozens of Chinese and Uzbek flags were waving in the evening breeze. An intricately dressed honor guard flanked a gigantic red carpet. The fanfare was standing ready to play traditional Uzbek instruments. The dancers, dressed up in their festive national costumes, were nervously awaiting the signal to begin their performance. President Mirziyoyev had left nothing to chance. He wanted his guests to feel welcome, honored, and respected. It was indeed a special day.

Once the foreign airplane had slowly come to a stop in front of the welcoming ceremony, the doors opened, and the Chinese President Xi Jinping stepped outside. Accompanied by some of China's most powerful men, including foreign policy giants Yang Jiechi and Wang Yi, Xi calmly took in the overwhelming festivities, shook hands with numerous Uzbek officials, and gave a speech on deepening China–Uzbekistan friendship. Then he left the airport to await a series of important meetings the next day. Xi was not the only high profile visitor to arrive at the airport. Presidents from fourteen countries, including India, Russia, and Turkey, arrived as well. Uzbekistan was about to stage one of the world's most important meetings: The SCO Samarkand Summit.[231]

The Shanghai Cooperation Organization (SCO) is the world's largest regional political, economic, and security organization. Its members cover 60% of Eurasia and 40% of the world's population. The SCO, with its headquarters in Beijing, marks China's growing international influence and leadership. But Xi did not come to the SCO summit in Uzbekistan just to talk about trade, investment, and the Belt and Road Initiative. Yes, these were important topics. But something else occupied his mind. China's supreme leader had come to Samarkand with a dire warning to his fellow Presidents. The West had developed, even perfected, a new kind of weapon.

The next day, on September 16, 2022, Xi Jinping sat down with the other presidents and delivered his speech. Xi talked about the glory of the ancient

---

[231] Ministry of Foreign Affairs of the People's Republic of China. President Xi Jinping Arrives in Samarkand to Begin State Visit to Uzbekistan and Attend the 22nd Meeting of the Council of Heads of State of the Shanghai Cooperation Organization. 2022-09-15. See https://www.fmprc.gov.cn/eng/gjhdq_665435/2675_665437/3255_664392/3257_664 396/202209/t20220915_10766231.html

---

silk road, and how it inspires the SCO and its member states to deepen collaboration in pursuit of economic development and political security. But there are threats on the horizon. "Cold War mentality and group politics are resurfacing," Xi concludes. Although he does not say where this mentality is taking hold, everyone present knows exactly about whom the Chinese President is talking about. "We should guard against attempts by external forces," Xi continues before delivering his warning message, "to instigate 'color revolution'." The Color Revolution, as Xi Jinping understands very well, is a relatively new Western weapon that has already set numerous countries ablaze with social unrest, violence, and the overthrow of entire governments. The next most likely target? Central Asia and other Chinese allies all around the world. And this worries China's supreme leader, perhaps the single most powerful man alive. And it should. Color Revolutions have the capability to destroy the SCO, paralyze the Belt and Road Initiative, and reduce China's power and influence everywhere.[232]

Color Revolutions and Hybrid Wars

A Color Revolution is an attempt by the Western powers to overthrow a foreign government and to replace it with a pro-Western one. Although the United States has been in the business of overthrowing foreign governments since 1898, the year it overthrew the government of Hawaii, a Color Revolution is new in the way this result is achieved.

A typical Color Revolution goes as follows: It starts with a small group of disorganized people without the means and popular support to bring down their government. These people may be motivated by real grievances, for example resentment towards authoritarianism and corruption. But the key thing to understand is that they are a minority and, as such, are not able to carry out a successful coup. A powerful external force, however, can tilt the balance in their favor. Western support, especially from the United States and Europe, can turn a protest movement into a successful Color Revolution. This then brings up two questions: why is the West doing this, and what kind of support can they give that turns the tide?[233]

To start with the first question, Color Revolutions can be traced back to the end of the U.S.–Soviet Cold War. Although countries in East and Central Europe had broken away from the Soviet Union, that did not automatically

---

[232] The State Council Information Office of the People's Republic of China. Full text of Xi's speech at SCO Samarkand summit. September 17, 2022. See http://english.scio.gov.cn/topnews/2022-09/17/content_78424890.htm

[233] Korybko, A. (2015). *Hybrid Wars: The Indirect Adaptive Approach to Regime Change.* Institute for Strategic Studies and Predictions.

mean their governments were eager to ally themselves with the West, join NATO, adopt Western-style economic policies, and copy Western political institutions. Yet this is exactly what Western leaders in Washington and Brussels wanted. Their hope was to get pro-Western leaders in power who would abandon socialist state-led economic policies, embrace neoliberal economic reforms a.k.a. "shock therapy," and move their countries into Western organizations like the European Union and NATO. Why? To isolate and weaken Russia — the eternal enemy in the eyes of Western Cold War warriors — and to open an area formerly closed to Western capitalism.[234]

This is not how Color Revolutions are presented in the West. Politicians and media organizations alike portray Color Revolutions as spontaneous and legitimate struggles by a population against an authoritarian government. As such, the West presents their support to such events as "democracy promotion." But, as we will see shortly, this is not backed up by the evidence.

This then brings us to the question of how. How does the West help a local movement in overthrowing their government, and how does the Color Revolution differ from other coup attempts that the United States has carried out since 1898 and all throughout the Cold War? The best way to answer these two questions is by discussing the first Color Revolutions carried out by the West. Not only do they show the techniques and methods used, but they also reveal which U.S. and European institutions and organizations are involved.

Although scholars agree that the first Color Revolutions took place in the early 2000s, the United States already had gained valuable experience in Eastern Europe in the decade prior.

Hoping to get pro-Western governments in power in the former Soviet countries, the U.S. government, supported by a range of non-governmental organizations (NGOs), interfered in foreign elections in Bulgaria (1996), Romania (1997), Slovakia (1998), and Croatia (1999). One technique favored by Washington was to mobilize the political opposition around one pro-Western political candidate and to support that candidate's bid for power using sophisticated propaganda techniques and close opinion polling. For example, in Bulgaria in 1996, one U.S. NGO — the International Republican Institute (IRI) — convinced the Bulgarian opposition parties to rally around the pro-Western politician Petar Stoyanov. This strategy proved to be successful, and Stoyanov won and served as the Bulgarian president from 1997 to 2002. These and other successes paved the way for further experi-

---

[234] Sussman, G. & Krader, S. (2008). *Template Revolutions: Marketing U.S. Regime Change in Eastern Europe.* Westminster Papers in Communication and Culture, Vol. 5(3): 91-112.

mentation in "democracy promotion." These early attempts culminated in Serbia, the site of the first real Color Revolution.[235]

The plan to depose the Serbian President Slobodan Milosevic in the 2000 elections already started the year before, in 1999. A Western-funded international congress was held to plan Serbia's future and to bring together pro-Western Serbian entities with Western NGOs and the European Union. Milosevic, they concluded, looked vulnerable. Perhaps he could be overthrown. What followed was a U.S.-and-European-sponsored-and-led campaign that combined politics, non-violent resistance techniques, and modern propaganda. The usage of these techniques to overthrow a foreign leader and replace him with a pro-Western government is the hallmark of a Color Revolution.

First, the U.S. polling firm of Penn, Schoen and Berland conducted a study and concluded that the anti-communist and pro-Western lawyer Vojislav Kostunica was the most likely candidate to beat Milosevic. Consequently, the U.S. State Department brought the two other major opposition candidates to Budapest, where they were pressured to drop out of the race. Washington wanted the Serbian opposition to unite behind its candidate.

Next, the National Democratic Institute (NDI) (another U.S. NGO) flew the Serbian opposition — the Otpor movement — to Poland where they met and learned important lessons in campaigning and activism from more experienced Polish political activists. Also, throughout the year 2000, another U.S. NGO, the International Republican Institute (IRI), funded and organized seminars in Budapest to train Otpor activists in the teachings of Gene Sharp's work on non-violent regime change. Gene Sharp wrote a book that describes 198 methods of non-violent resistance to bring down governments. After this training, these Otpor members returned to Serbia to implement what they had learned.

Then, a very sophisticated media campaign was launched that drew upon modern Western propaganda techniques. For example, media training received a lot of attention. According to a Serbian marketing professional "every word of the opposition's one-minute and five-minute core political messages used by opposition spokesmen across the country was discussed with U.S. consultants and tested by opinion poll." The opposition, from local youth group activists to the actual political candidates, got intense training on how to answer questions from journalists and how to counter arguments by Milosevic supporters.

---

[235] Sussman, G. & Krader, S. (2008). *Template Revolutions: Marketing U.S. Regime Change in Eastern Europe.* Westminster Papers in Communication and Culture, Vol. 5(3): 91-112.

Also, U.S. public relations (PR) experts assisted and trained Otpor activists in the clever use of slogans and logos. These were first tested by opinion polling and after being approved by U.S. PR experts, they were recited by opposition spokesmen, graffitied on walls, printed on stickers, put on T-shirts, and spread in other ways. "The foreign support was critical," remembers an opposition marketing expert, "this was the first campaign where our strategy was based on real scientific research." After Milosevic's overthrow, Otpor's slogan and logo campaign received much international praise.

Overall, the U.S. government, through a variety of NGOs, spent $10 million on the Serbian opposition in 1999, and $31 million in 2000, the year of the election. This money funded media activities, protests, and polling, and managed the opposition election campaign. The U.S. also funded the opposition radio, the music campaign "Rock for Change, Rock the Vote," and a Serbian NGO that encouraged academics, journalists, and others to support the opposition. And the money was well spent. Milosevic was ousted, and the pro-Western candidate Petar Stoyanov won the election. The Color Revolution had worked. This success, of course, emboldened Washington and Brussels, and they quickly turned their eyes to their next targets: Georgia and Ukraine.

"I did not think I should have paid serious attention to these young people running around with flags and making graffiti on the streets. I was wrong," said Eduard Shevardnadze, the former President of Georgia after he was overthrown in a Color Revolution in 2003. Only three years after Milosevic was removed from office, the Georgian President suffered the same fate. He, like Milosevic and others, was unprepared for this new type of regime change.

The same techniques were used. Propaganda, non-violent resistance, and effective political organizing — all the ingredients of a successful Color Revolution. The United States and Europe arranged for members of the Serbian Otpor opposition movement to travel to places like Georgia and Ukraine to teach those opposition movements how to overthrow their government. "We trained them in how to set up an organization, how to open local chapters, how to create a 'brand', how to create a logo, symbols, key messages," one Otpor activist proudly explained.

Meanwhile, U.S. NGOs like the National Endowment for Democracy (NED) and others funded the Georgian opposition. They received a "start-up" cash payment of $350,000. Additional money was provided to fund a series of media campaigns, which included advertisements on TV, flyers, and other materials.

Following the successful overthrow of Georgia's president Shevardnadze, the NDI director in Kyiv, David Dettman, met with the NDI director
of Georgia to talk about whether a similar Color Revolution could be instigated in Ukraine. From these talks Dettman concluded that it could, and he
arranged training centers for the Ukrainian youth movement run by experienced Otpor activists. Georgian experts also arrived to assist the Ukrainian
opposition.

The same sequence of events took place in Ukraine as in Serbia and
Georgia. First, the NDI, to unify the political opposition in Ukraine, pushed
Yulia Tymoshenko to ally herself with Viktor Yushchenko instead of
running against him. Then, U.S. NGOs like Freedom House gave hundreds of
thousands of dollars to start up advertising campaigns throughout Ukraine.
In 2004 alone, the U.S. spent $34 million on the Color Revolution. These
funds were used for get-out-the-vote programs, including leaflet campaigns,
street theater, rock concerts, karaoke shows, and door-to-door campaigns.
The U.S. also brought the opposition to Washington for three weeks of
political training. To train the opposition in the 198 methods of non-violent
regime change, 12,000 copies of Gene Sharp's book were distributed among
the opposition in 2004. The result? Viktor Yanukovych was out, and the
pro-Western candidate Viktor Yushchenko, who aimed to get Ukraine into
the European Union and NATO, got in. Washington and Brussels could add
Ukraine to their list of successes.[236]

The examples above already give a taste of what Color Revolutions are all
about. But there is more to them than meets the eye. Overthrowing a government is not an easy task. Therefore, Color Revolutions are based on sophisticated principles, and they are quite different from the old-school CIA coup.
They also rely on a network of specialized organizations whose intentions
are anything but benign. Finally, the Color Revolution has a violent twin
brother or sister, and together they are part of the so-called Hybrid War. In
the remainder of this section, all these things will be explained.

One thing that makes Color Revolutions unique is their reliance on information and the ability to spread a message among the population. This can
make or break a successful revolution. Naturally, the main goal is to spread
a message that encourages people to help overthrow the government, or, if
that is not possible, to stop people from supporting the government. But
as anyone who spends time on social media knows, making a message turn

---

[236] See also Mitchell, L. A. (2012). *The Color Revolutions.* University of Pennsylvania Press
p. 49-91, and McFaul, M. (2007). *Ukraine Imports Democracy.* International Security, Fall,
2007, Vol. 32, No. 2, pp 45-83.

viral is easier said than done. Therefore, and very interestingly, the Color Revolution draws heavily on concepts first developed by Western experts on propaganda

One example is Edward Bernays, known as the founding father of public relations. In 1928, he wrote a book entitled *Propaganda*, in which he discusses in detail how a small group of individuals can shape people's beliefs and attitudes in order to make them behave in a certain way, even if they initially would be opposed to it. Bernays called this the "engineering of consent." On this he writes, "When the public is convinced of the soundness of an idea, it will proceed to action... but such results do not just happen... they can be accomplished by the engineering of consent." In other words, Color Revolutions can be created, or 'engineered,' by an external power through the use of clever propaganda.[237]

Bernays also recognized that with the use of technology that enables instant communication, persons can be "regimented" for common action even if they live many miles apart. This is highly relevant to Color Revolutions. Consequently, they rely heavily on modern developments in navigation and social media.[238]

For example, Facebook enables people to create closed groups in which they can discuss and prepare anti-government strategies and operations. Once people move into the streets to protest, they can use Google Maps to plan locations to assemble and routes to march. Twitter enables protesters to share information on how to avoid police forces, and videos of the protest or violent police responses can be recorded on people's phones and spread on YouTube. Social media is also key to getting the Western powers involved.

One of the main goals of such operations is to use social media to make the Color Revolution go viral so that it will be picked up by the Western media. Once the Western media throws its support behind the protesters, this provides an opening for the external power — e.g., Washington or Brussels — to get more heavily involved. It makes it easier for Western politicians and others to advocate for U.S. or EU action, for example by imposing economic sanctions on the targeted government, ramping up diplomatic pressure, and providing more direct support to the Color Revolution.

Already in the Serbian Color Revolution of 2000, before social media took off, information, instant communication, and the use of international media were already highly effective. U.S. agents on the ground directed the Serbian opposition movement during protests and helped them elude the

---

[237] Korybko, A. (2015). *Hybrid Wars: The Indirect Adaptive Approach to Regime Change.* Institute for Strategic Studies and Predictions.

[238] Korybko, A. (2015). *Hybrid Wars: The Indirect Adaptive Approach to Regime Change.* Institute for Strategic Studies and Predictions.

police using GPS information. They also trained the opposition leaders on how to use the internet and SMS messaging to exchange information and coordinate their efforts during marches to maximize their effect. Meanwhile, CNN journalists were informed in advance where to go so they would be in a good position to make favorable pictures and videos of the protesters.[239]

Color Revolutions are thus characterized by hidden Western involvement, non-violent resistance, and the use of modern information technology such as mobile phones, instant messaging, the internet, and social media. It is quite a different approach to overthrowing a government than what the United States used to do.

During the U.S.–Soviet Cold War, if Washington wanted to get rid of a government, they typically did something like the following: The CIA was instructed to identify pro-U.S. groups, which were typically right-wing in their political orientation, often with links to the military and/or police forces. Next, Washington offered them a deal: We support you in seizing power, and in return you will implement economic and geopolitical policies that are beneficial to us. Once an agreement was made, the CIA would take things to the next level.[240]

Typically, if an election was about to happen in the targeted country, Washington and the CIA would try to bribe people, stuff ballot boxes, infiltrate and undermine rival political parties, kidnap or kill political opponents, undermine or destroy their news organizations, and use economic sanctions to weaken the current government. Sometimes this would be enough to get the pro-U.S. regime in power.[241]

If an election or an election victory proved impossible, the CIA would start sending in money and weapons to the opposition movement. After having received training in combat operations, the violence began and would continue until a military coup succeeded in overthrowing the government. The new pro-American leader, often a military dictator, could then count on the CIA to continue training his security apparatus and the secret police to crack down on the population and solidify his grip on the country.

Naturally, all the victims of the violence, the coup, and its aftermath could easily be labeled and dismissed as communists, although they were often simply peasants, labor union leaders, students, and nationalists. And as long as the new regime obeyed Washington and followed pro-U.S. policies, the U.S. would continue to provide economic, diplomatic, and military support.

---

[239] Engdahl, F. W. (2009). *Full Spectrum Dominance*. Edition.Engdahl
[240] Engdahl, F. W. (2009). *Full Spectrum Dominance*. Edition.Engdahl
[241] See Blum, W. (2004). Killing Hope. Zed Books for many examples

Compared to a Color Revolution, the CIA method is much more crude, violent, and more humiliating for Washington when information leaks out. As such, the CIA does not play a leading role in instigating Color Revolutions. In the examples discussed above, we have already encountered some of the organizations that are. Many of them are in fact U.S. NGOs. The National Endowment of Democracy (NED), is the central player in this network. The NED also funds the NDI and IRI, and together they form a Color Revolutionary triad. Interestingly, when you analyze their involvement in Color Revolutions, it becomes clear that the real goal is not democracy promotion — as Western governments and their NGOs like to pretend — but instead is about furthering Western economic and geopolitical interests. The NED is a perfect example, and it is worthwhile to explore this in a little bit more detail.

The National Endowment for Democracy (NED) came into being in 1984. Its official mission is to help countries develop democratic institutions. It does so through grants. This means that the NED gives money to groups that are involved in political movements, election monitoring, media, and others. The expressed goal of promoting democracy in the targeted country, however, is a disguise. The NED's real agenda is quite different.

Although technically not an arm of the U.S. government, the NED is considered as such by many because it gets most of its funds from Washington and is staffed by many former U.S. government officials. But the connection runs much deeper. In fact, the NED is related to the CIA. After the CIA's reputation was severely damaged in the 1970s by a series of negative revelations, some of its secret activities were handed over to the NED. According to the former NED president Allen Weinstein: "A lot of what we do today was done covertly 25 years ago by the CIA." As such, for an organization that claims to be about promoting open and democratic systems, the NED prefers to operate in secret. Even the U.S. Congress has difficulties in keeping track of what the organization is up to.[242]

Interestingly, an analysis of the NED confirms the suspicion that the organization is not as benevolent as it makes itself out to be. By looking at hundreds of NED grants throughout the 1990s, a study on the NED concludes that there is no evidence that the NED was successful in promoting democracy, despite numerous grants and many millions of dollars. One consistent finding, however, was that the NED likes to operate in countries that are not open to U.S. business interests. The NED also tends to be present in countries that are designated by Washington as rivals or enemies. Either

---

[242] David Ignatius, "Innocence Abroad: The New World of Spyless Coups," Washington Post, September 22, 1991

these two findings are a giant coincidence, or the mission of the NED, like that of the CIA, is to influence political systems, interfere in elections, and help overthrow governments to further U.S. business and geopolitical interests.[243]

Patterns of funding by Western governments and their NGOs also reveal the true intent behind Color Revolutions. Another study shows that before and during the Color Revolution, Western money flowed to pro-Western opposition groups that tried to seize power from the current ruling government. These actions are labeled by the West as "democracy promotion." But once successful, and with the opposition in charge of the country, Western funds shifted away from civil society and "democracy promotion" and instead flowed towards this new government. While the West did not support the previous government, they do assist the new pro-Western one, after having supported them in seizing power. Apparently the West is more interested in promoting a particular outcome — the overthrow of a certain leader or government and replacing them with a pro-Western group — than in promoting democracy in general. Taken together, the NED and the CIA have something in common. They may use different methods but as organizations that carry out U.S. foreign policy, their goals are identical.[244]

To end the discussion on Color Revolutions, it is important to talk about its more violent twin. Color Revolutions are part of a bigger phenomenon known as Hybrid War. The Color Revolution, also known as a soft coup, may fail; if so, it can shift to Unconventional Warfare to bring about the overthrow of the government in a so-called hard coup. In this sense, Unconventional War is the Color Revolution's violent twin brother or sister.[245]

The U.S. Army handbook defines Unconventional War as "activities conducted to enable a resistance movement or insurgency to coerce, disrupt, or overthrow a government." It builds on the preceding Color Revolution and uses its established network and the social, financial, informational, and other infrastructure to support a violent campaign to topple a government. Propaganda is key to this transition from Color Revolution to Unconventional War.[246]

According to the U.S. Army manual, in the first phase of Unconventional War, the resistance and its external sponsor — e.g., the United States — use

---

[243] Hale, Eric, T. "A quantitative and qualitative evaluation of the National Endowment for Democracy. 2003, *LSU Doctoral Dissertations*. 2774.

[244] Stewart, S. (2012). *Democracy Promotion and the 'Colour Revolutions'*. Routledge. See chapter 8

[245] Korybko, A. (2015). *Hybrid Wars: The Indirect Adaptive Approach to Regime Change*. Institute for Strategic Studies and Predictions.

[246] *Special Forces Unconventional War*. Headquarters, Department of the Army, Training Circular No. 18-01. November 2010.

propaganda to psychologically prepare the population to move against their government, to support the resistance, accept their violent methods, and to permit the United States to become involved. Note that this propaganda campaign never stops. It continues even as the other phases of Unconventional War are initiated. Also, in phase one, U.S. special forces help train the resistance to use radio broadcasts, pamphlets, newspapers, and other mediums and techniques to shape popular beliefs and attitudes to support their effort of overthrowing the government.

Then, in phase two and three, the United States coordinates its efforts with the resistance, which are facilitated by U.S. special forces and CIA operators that have infiltrated the country and establish contacts on the ground.

Next, in phase four and five, these U.S. agents begin training and arming the resistance. Combat operations are planned until, in phase six, these are carried out. They may include sabotage, assassinations, and strategic attacks against government forces and buildings. Note that Unconventional War is not about armies of tanks and infantry moving in to seize cities and other strategic locations. It is more like urban guerilla warfare waged by small groups of lightly armed fighters. The aim is to degrade the government's ability to defend itself so that an urban uprising against the palace or presidential office is enough to topple the government.

Then, once the government is overthrown, phase seven starts, which is the final phase. The resistance forces are either disbanded or become part of the new government's formal military apparatus. Thus, Hybrid War can sometimes turn a failed Color Revolution into a successful Unconventional War.

To conclude this section, we return to Xi Jinping's warning. As you can see, the United States and Europe have a diverse toolbox at their disposal to interfere in other countries, influence elections, shape local and international opinion, and wage non-violent and violent campaigns to overthrow governments and replace them with pro-Wester ones. The list of targeted countries keeps on growing, and includes Kyrgyzstan (2005, 2010), Belarus (2006, 2020–2021), Moldova (2009), Russia (2011), Ukraine (2014), Kazakhstan (2022), and Georgia (2023). Not all of them were successful. Also, some were pure Color Revolutions while others, such as the Western sponsored overthrow of the Ukrainian government in 2014, displayed violent elements that point to Unconventional and Hybrid War. Indeed, it is one of the West's favorite weapons to target their rivals.

With this list in mind, we can understand why Chinese officials are worried. Although the West tended to wage Hybrid War in former Soviet

States to weaken and undermine Russia, Xi Jinping has come to understand that this weapon is now being targeted at him, China, the Belt and Road partners, and other countries that are strategically or economically important to Beijing. In fact, the West has already been waging Hybrid War against China, as we will see in the final section of this chapter.

Future Bloodbaths

Based on lessons learned from the first Cold War, you can make some educated guesses about where the United States and China will end up fighting each other and what these conflicts will look like. In fact, the battle has already started, mostly in non-violent Color Revolutionary ways. But if the competition between the two superpowers intensifies, it is likely they will become far more deadly and destructive. Let us look at a few examples.

In 2018, the president of the International Republican Institute (IRI), a U.S. think tank that receives its funding from the State Department and the National Endowment for Democracy, proudly told his audience how they had successfully influenced the Malaysian general election that was held several months earlier. It had resulted in a more pro-U.S. and anti-China government. In fact, one of the first moves of the new government was to freeze Chinese BRI infrastructure investments.[247]

Similarly, in Myanmar, the National Endowment for Democracy (NED) has dozens of programs that focus on media, education, and political campaigning. Some of their goals are to train journalists and fund news organizations that produce pro-U.S. and anti-Chinese news, and to train and fund anti-BRI protests. One major success was to support protests against the construction of a very large hydroelectric dam across the Irawaddy River (the Myitsone Dam), one of China's most important BRI projects in Myanmar. It led to the government feeling forced to cancel the dam's construction in 2011.[248]

But while these are nice little victories that undermine China's BRI, China continues to move ahead and, if past is prologue, the United States will escalate to increasingly violent Unconventional War strategies to undermine and weaken their rival. One standard technique is to exploit internal divisions within a country. Myanmar, for example, has ethnic minorities

---

[247] Republican-linked US think tank tells of long ties with opposition to bring down BN. FMT Reporters, August 6, 2018. See also this video for the statement by IRI's President Daniel Twining: https://www.youtube.com/watch?v=L4ilMqtkJJo

[248] Peng, N. (2021). *International Pressures, Strategic Preference, and Myanmar's China Policy since 1988.* Springer, p. 78; Strangio, S. (2020). *In the Dragon's Shadow.* Yale University Press, p. 188 and 205 ebook.

in the border regions who, for historical reasons, do not get along with the central government. Myanmar's military is worried that if the United States were to provide these groups with weapons, these ethnic groups could be transformed into a force capable of challenging military rule. In such a scenario, it is highly likely that China would start backing the military government, and with two superpowers flooding the country with weapons, a deadly civil war will be in the making.[249]

In such cases a clear U.S. victory may not even be necessary for Washington to achieve its goal. If Myanmar descends into a destructive civil war that reduces the country to a failed state like Libya, it can no longer function as China's strategic ally and important BRI partner. Myanmar's oil and gas pipelines that connect the Indian Ocean with China and bypass the vulnerable Malacca Strait — an important BRI project for China's energy security — may well be jeopardized or even destroyed in the process. These are all wins for the United States. Such tactics can also be used to destabilize central Asian countries that Beijing is in the process of trying to integrate into a China-centered bloc.

Another example to make a country turn its back on China would be to support a coup d'état that replaces a pro-Chinese government with a pro-Western strongman. In fact, perhaps such an event already took place in Guinea, a resource-rich country in West Africa that has vast bauxite and iron deposits that China is very interested in.

On September 5, 2021, an elite unit of Guinean Special Forces stormed the presidential palace. They deposed the president, Alpha Condé, and Colonel Mamady Doumbouya announced himself to be the new leader. Interestingly, at that time, U.S. Special Forces were training this elite unit. It is not difficult to imagine how such an event can turn into a hot war.[250]

Suppose U.S. forces were indeed instructed to train Guinean special forces to carry out a coup. This means they got rid of President Condé who had struck many infrastructure and resource deals with Beijing. His successor, if he is more pro-Western, may change this. For example, China has 14 state-owned and private companies operating in Guinea's aluminum business. Guinea also has the world's largest undeveloped iron deposit, and Chinese firms have invested heavily in a project to mine it. If the new presi-

[249] Peng, N. (2021). *International Pressures, Strategic Preference, and Myanmar's China Policy since 1988.* Springer, p. 42
[250] Walsh, D. & Schmitt, E. U.S. Forces Were Training the Guinean Soldiers Who Took Off to Stage a Coup. The New York Times, September 10, 2021

dent is beholden to Washington, what does that mean for these investments and China's resource dependency?[251]

Given the damaging implications to China, it is perhaps unsurprising that Beijing abandoned again its noninterference policy. Chinese politicians denounced the coup in Guinea and called for Condé to be released. But what would have happened if China had some of its own military forces in the region, as may be the case in the near future? In that case, they could have supported Condé or a strongman of their own. With two sides fighting for power, a civil war is in the making, one in which the United States supports one side and China the other — laying the groundwork in Guinea for a future bloodbath.[252]

The above examples illustrate the kind of conflicts that can unfold. It is impossible to predict where and when they will occur. Resource-rich countries in Africa and the Middle East that are important to China are also tempting targets for Washington. The Pacific Island nations may also be destined for Color Revolutions if they allow Chinese military bases on their soil. There is in fact a competition going on between Washington and Beijing to increase their military presence in the region.

Successful destabilization of countries in the vicinity of China is also be beneficial to U.S. goals. The Color Revolutions in Kazakhstan in 2022 and in Georgia in 2023, for example, were intended to create second fronts to Russia. In addition to ramping up Ukrainian aggression against ethnic Russians, especially since 2014, the U.S. and NATO turned to destabilizing countries that neighbor Russia in order to force Moscow to shift attention and resources to these events. Similarly, if the United States and China come to blows over Taiwan, expect equivalent attempts by the West to destabilize Central and East Asian countries around China. The goal would be to force Beijing to take action in response, in the hopes it weakens Chinese efforts to conquer Taiwan. These may even include stirring up further turmoil in Tibet and Xinjiang, thereby threatening a breakup of China. The deaths of tens of thousands of innocent civilians will not bother U.S. leaders one bit if it furthers their policy of weakening China.

To conclude, in a new Cold War, the Third World will again suffer much. When entire nations are reduced to pawns in a global geopolitical chess game, the wellbeing of the people who live there are of no concern to the competing superpowers. Western leaders will no doubt pretend their goal

---

[251] Global Times Staff Reporters. Risks of Guinea coup to Chinese projects manageable. Global Times. September 6, 2021. https://www.globaltimes.cn/page/202109/1233515.shtml

[252] Dunst, C. China Is OK With Interfering in Guinea's Internal Affairs. Foreign Affairs, September 8, 2021.

is to protect people, democracy, and freedom. But these are just ways to sell their aggressive interventions and wars to us, by making it seem they serve some noble purpose. As will be explained in the next chapter, we should not fall for such propaganda, lies, and deceit. The fate of people around the world depends on it.

Chapter 5: Information Warfare

Late in December 1979, the Soviet army attacked Afghanistan. It was a brilliantly executed operation. Spetsgruppa "A', also known as Alfa Group," together with other special forces that had been airlifted into the capital Kabul, carried out coordinated attacks against key government installations. The Tajbeg palace, once home to the Afghan royal family, was stormed and captured. Inside, Soviet troops shot and killed the Afghan leader Hafizullah Amin. His replacement, Babrak Karmal, was considered by the Kremlin to be a more obedient and pro-Soviet figure.

In the evening twilight, while Soviet special forces were preparing themselves to take Kabul, several Soviet motorized rifle divisions entered Afghanistan from the north. Moving along two axes, they quickly took control over major cities and other strategic locations. Within weeks, over 100,000 Soviet military personnel, supported by thousands of tanks and armored fighting vehicles, moved in. The occupation of Afghanistan had officially begun.

For nine years, the Soviet military waged a bloody and brutal war in Afghanistan. Soviet military forces carried out search and destroy missions against villages that were suspected of assisting the Afghan resistance. Following an artillery barrage, Soviet forces would move in and systematically destroy the remaining buildings, the food supply, agricultural lands, livestock, irrigation systems, and water wells. Sometimes all male inhabitants were executed.[253]

---

[253] For books on the Soviet-Afghan War see Arnold, A. *Afghanistan: The Soviet Invasion in Perspective*; Amstutz, J. B. *Afghanistan: The First Five Years Of Soviet Occupation*; The Russian General Staff. *The Soviet-Afghan War: How a Superpower Fought and Lossed*

The result of this campaign of violence and terror against the Afghan population was horrifying. By the time the Soviet military withdrew in 1989, about 1.3 million Afghans had died. Another 5.5 million had been forced to flee the country while another 2 million had been internally displaced. The land itself was devastated as well. The entire agricultural infrastructure was either damaged or destroyed, and wildfires caused by aerial bombardments had laid waste to almost a quarter of Afghanistan's forests. Today, the country faces almost total deforestation — one of several legacies of the Soviet-Afghan war.

In the Soviet media, however, a quite different tale was told. In their news report, there was no "invasion of Afghanistan." Instead, Soviet media organizations reported that their military had been invited in by the Afghan government "to help the hapless Afghan people to defend their freedom." While the Soviet military conducted its search and destroy missions to eliminate any and all resistance, the military campaign was described as a "noble cause of helping a friendly nation." All Moscow wanted to do was "protect the friendly Afghan people" from Western "aggression." [254]

This shocking display of propaganda certainly is not unique. In fact, the world had witnessed a similar façade fourteen years earlier. In 1965, when President Lyndon Johnson sent American ground forces into South Vietnam to keep the pro-U.S. military dictatorship in power, Johnson did so because the regime was on the verge of collapse following years of popular resistance from much of the Vietnamese people. Yet the Western media did not speak of an U.S. invasion or an U.S. attack against South Vietnam. Instead, they reported that the United States military had been invited in by the democratic government of South Vietnam. In the following years, the U.S. military carpet bombed the countryside, used chemical weapons against villages and peasants, and systematically destroyed the environment — actions described in the Western media as "an excess of righteousness and disinterested benevolence." All Washington wanted to do was to lead "the free world's fight to contain aggressive Communism." [255]

In the Soviet media, the attack on Afghanistan never happened. Similarly, in the Western media, the United States never attacked Vietnam. It was the defense of Afghanistan, and the defense of Vietnam. And when Soviet and American forces were finally forced to retreat, the wars were described as mistakes motivated by noble intentions — certainly not a war crime. Of

---

[254] Lanine, N. and Media Lens. *Invasion - A Comparison of Soviet and Western Media Performance.*
[255] Herman, E. S., Chomsky, N. *Manufacturing Consent: The Political Economy of the Mass Media.* See p. 173-175, 187, 191, 199-200, 205 and 241 for some of the quotations used.

course, the American attack on Vietnam was widely condemned in the Soviet media, and so did the West condemn the Soviet invasion of Afghanistan.

It is astonishing that two media systems that are so different in numerous ways — one state-owned and the other privately managed — produce identical news. And it was not just the Afghan and Vietnam wars. In fact, this kind of news reporting characterized the entire Cold War. Both media systems parroted the Cold War narrative set out by their respective governments. And they did so enthusiastically, passionately, and consistently, until the story became so entrenched in the minds of everyone, that it turned into official history and fact. How is this possible?

Propaganda Systems

People in the West tend to quickly dismiss State-owned media like those that exist in China or the former Soviet Union. The thinking is that when the media is owned and controlled by those in power, the news cannot be trusted. Instead of presenting an objective and neutral view of events, the news will be carefully selected and manipulated to serve the interests of the government.

This line of reasoning is, of course, valid. But it would be a mistake to conclude that because Western media organizations are not owned by the State, their news can be trusted. This is what most Westerners like to believe. But one of the most fascinating aspects of news is that different media systems can in fact produce the same kind of news.

Let us begin by looking at the Chinese media system, and then compare that to the media in the West to see why the output they produce is so similar.

The Chinese propaganda system is like a pyramid. It is highly hierarchical and extends from a senior leader at the Politburo at the top all the way down to the provincial, city, and district level at the bottom. Within this system, the most powerful organization is the Chinese government's Central Propaganda Department (CPD). It is a secretive group — its address and phone number are both classified. Everyone who works for the CPD must be a Communist Party member. The main function of this organization is to ensure that the information systems in China, from television and print to art and scientific publishing, are all promoting the CCP party line. And it does so in several ways.[256]

First, the CPD appoints senior leaders within all major news and publishing organizations. This means that only people who obey (and, to

---

[256] Brady, A-M. (2008). *Marketing Dictatorship.* Rowman & Littlefield Publishers Inc, chapter 2

a large extent, agree with) the party line and follow CPD instructions are given such important positions. In this way, the CPD can rest assured that all the major news organizations in China are led by people on whom they can count on to produce the kind of news that the Communist Party wants. But this is not all the CPD does.[257]

The CPD also organizes "update meetings" in which they tell editors and journalists what they should report, how they should tell these stories, and, of course, what they are not allowed to publish. The CPD also publishes a classified journal in which all these things are thoroughly explained. This internal report is then circulated among the different news organizations.[258]

Interestingly, with these different mechanisms of control and guidance in place, the need for censorship in the Chinese propaganda system is much smaller than you may think. While the CPD does have major censorship powers, it is more of a tool of last resort. Most senior leaders, journalists, and editors simply know what they can and cannot say.[259]

Now compare this to the Western media system. The theory that is best supported by the evidence is the so-called "Propaganda Model" proposed by Edward Herman and Noam Chomsky. It starts off with the simple fact that almost all major Western media organizations are big corporations and they earn most of their money through advertising from other major corporations. They also rely on the government and the business world for most of their information and news. What this tells you is that Western news organizations are not fully independent entities, but that they are part of a network that includes the most powerful and wealthy groups in Western society. And this is just the beginning.[260]

It is well-known that this corporate and political "power elite," which is most accurately described by sociologist Charles Wright Mills, are closely interconnected. Business leaders and politicians tend to move from government to high positions in corporations and vice-versa. Most come from wealthy families and study at the same elite universities. They know each other well, go to the same parties, intermarry, and work together. Consequently, they tend to share the same world view and, most importantly, hold similar interests. These members of the power elite also own the Western media.[261]

---

[257] Brady, A-M. (2008). *Marketing Dictatorship.* Rowman & Littlefield Publishers Inc, p. 16

[258] Brady, A-M. (2008). *Marketing Dictatorship.* Rowman & Littlefield Publishers Inc, p. 19

[259] Brady, A-M. (2008). *Marketing Dictatorship.* Rowman & Littlefield Publishers Inc, p. 94-95

[260] Herman, E. S. & Chomsky, N. (2006). *Manufacturing Consent.* Ballantine Books.

[261] Mills, C. W. (1956). *The Power Elite.* Oxford University Press.

So the Western media consist of corporations that depend on other corporations and they also depend on the government. They are owned and controlled by a small group of wealthy and powerful people, and those people are, together with other business and political leaders, part of the power elite. Now, suppose a major Western media organization like the *New York Times* (NYT) publishes news that undermines vital interests of this so-called power elite. What will happen?

The short answer is that several mechanisms will force the NYT back into line. Major corporations, whose interests are now being harmed by the NYT, will withdraw their advertising money. Politicians and business leaders will no longer provide the newspaper with information. Starved from resources, the NYT, if it wants to continue to make profit and survive, must shift its reporting to news that is acceptable to the power elite.

What you are going to end up with is a media system in which only media organizations can thrive that remain on good terms with the power elite. Consequently, they must employ journalists and editors who they know will follow the 'party line'. In a famous interview with BBC journalist Andrew Marr, Noam Chomsky made exactly this point. Marr came out saying that propaganda in the Western world is impossible, because nobody tells him what to report. Chomsky then explained that only those journalists that already believe the party line are allowed to stay, and that if you believe something different, you would eventually be cast out and replaced by a journalist who does. Generally they, too, simply know what they can and cannot say. Now compare this to the Chinese media system. Different mechanisms, but similar results.[262]

Yet the similarities do not end here. The institutional analysis above only scratches the surface. In fact, and perhaps much to your surprise, as we will see in the next section, much of China's propaganda system is actually based on its Western counterpart. Indeed, Chinese Communist propaganda is inspired and based on techniques first developed and applied in the West.

Thought Control with Western Roots

Although we like to believe that propaganda is something that only happens in dictatorships, modern day propaganda techniques were developed in the United States of America. Only later did the Soviet Union and China learn about and copy these methods.

---

[262] Noam Chomsky on Propaganda - The Big Idea - Interview with Andrew Marr, February 1996. See https://www.youtube.com/watch?v=GjENnyQupow

The roots of modern-day propaganda go back to 1917, the U.S. President Woodrow Wilson, and the Committee of Public Information — a fitting Orwellian name. At that time, World War I was raging throughout Europe and America had just declared war against Germany. The U.S. population, however, was not interested. They did not want to become entangled in a European war. As such, the American people were not eager to fight. This presented Woodrow Wilson, who wanted the United States to join the war, with a major challenge. To solve this problem, the White House set up the Committee on Public Information (CPI) — its brand-new propaganda agency.

Staffed by experts in public relations (PR) and journalism, the CPI directed the Western media into publishing highly emotional anti-German news. Much of it was fake and made up, as they later admitted, but many of these exaggerated stories about monstrous German war crimes proved to be highly effective. In only six months, the attitude and beliefs of the American people changed completely. Americans began hating Germans. They stopped teaching the German language in school and stopped listening to music from famous and formerly well-respected German composers like Wagner and Bach. Anyone who dared to suggest otherwise was accused of being anti-American and a potential German spy. Infected with anti-German hysteria, the U.S. population was ready, even eager, for war. To Wilson and the members of the CPI, it was a staggering success. One that opened the door to many more possibilities. From that moment onwards, propaganda techniques have only become more sophisticated, and have been used in every conflict since, often with similarly stunning results.[263]

To those who believe in democracy, manipulation of people's attitudes to make them accept government policy that they otherwise would reject sounds wrong. In this sense, propaganda undermines democracy. But from a power elite point of view, this was precisely why propaganda is so important in a democratic society. All the Western propaganda experts, starting from the Committee on Public Information, shared this belief.

According to Walter Lippmann, a member of the Committee on Public Information and known as the 'father of modern journalism', those in power should shape public opinion to get the population to support policies they otherwise might not. Propaganda was the perfect tool — a "revolution in the art of democracy." Edward Bernays, the father of public relations and propaganda, called this the "engineering of consent," which he believed was crucial

---

[263] Chomsky, N. Media Control: The Spectacular Achievements of Propaganda; Jowett, G. S. & O'Donnell, V. (1999). *Propaganda and Persuasion.* Sage Publications, Inc., p. 162-163; Snow, N. (2010). *Propaganda Inc.* Seven Stories Press, p. 79-84.

for "regimenting the public mind every bit as much as an army regiments the bodies of its soldiers." The ultimate goal was to use propaganda "to control and regiment the masses according to our will without their knowing it."[264]

Another pioneer was Harold Lasswell, the director of the American Political Science Association. He realized that there is a need for more propaganda in modern democratic Western societies, not less. When the power elite no longer can use violence to control people, thought control and propaganda become essential control mechanisms. Unsurprisingly, the works of Lippmann, Bernays, Lasswell, and others have been carefully studied by the Chinese Communist Party. It inspired them to transform Chinese propaganda.[265]

China experienced its revolution in the use of propaganda much later than the United States. Early Chinese and Soviet Communist propaganda were very crude and ineffective. It was too obvious, too theoretical, and persuaded few people. Propaganda that explained party ideology in an abstract and complicated manner did not appeal to the average person. An attempt to create heroes of communism — people who worked incredibly hard, possessed no flaws, and blindly obeyed the Party — came across as unreal and fake, and did not inspire people to copy that behavior. But luckily for the Chinese, they could draw inspiration from the West to uplift their propaganda game to new levels.[266]

The realization among the Chinese government of the need for more effective propaganda fully crystallized in 1989. It was the Tiananmen Square incident that set everything in motion. During this crisis, Chinese leaders relied on the military to deal with a large protest movement. Although effective, Beijing realized that their position of power was not as secure as they previously thought. What they should do, the Chinese government concluded, is put in more effort to prevent such crises from developing in the first place. And what better method to control any population in a non-violent manner than effective PR, that is, propaganda? It had worked wonders in the West. Consequently, the CCP turned to Lippmann, Bernays, Lasswell, and other early pioneers of Western propaganda to learn exactly how to manipulate thoughts, beliefs, and attitudes.[267]

---

[264] Bernays, E. L. (1928). Propaganda; Chomsky, N. Media Control: The Spectacular Achievements of Propaganda.

[265] Carey, A. (1997). *Taking the Risk out of Democracy.* University of Illinois Press, p. 81; Brady, A-M. (2008). *Marketing Dictatorship.* Rowman & Littlefield Publishers Inc., p. 65, 68, 71.

[266] Brandenberger, D. *Propaganda State in Crisis: Soviet Ideology, Indoctrination, and Terror under Stalin, 1927-1941.* Yale University Press.

[267] Brady, A-M. (2008). *Marketing Dictatorship.* Rowman & Littlefield Publishers Inc., p. 65, 68, 71

Nowadays Chinese propaganda, like that of the West, uses reason, appeals to emotions, conveys positive and negative messages, and allows discussion within strict limits. Certain ideas can be expressed freely, others cannot. Scripted debates may seem real and meaningful, yet they are carefully designed to lure people's thoughts in a particular direction. Public image has become everything to Chinese politicians, perhaps as important as the kind of policies they implement. Chinese PR departments, like Western PR firms, teach politicians what to say, how to say it, what to wear, where to look, and what gestures to make. Public appearances are all carefully scripted so as to achieve the greatest effect. Chinese propaganda draws upon psychology, marketing, PR, communication theory, and advertising. And as Western governments and business have learned to do, the Chinese government monitors people's beliefs and attitudes through regular polling studies that tell them what the population is thinking and whether the propaganda is working.[268]

As a result, the Chinese propaganda system is formidable, perhaps close to being as sophisticated as that of the West. Modeled on the United States, Beijing has also expanded its "messaging" internationally. It has English-speaking news agencies broadcasting in foreign countries, and through the BRI, Chinese radio and television are introduced to millions of people around the world.

What this means is that in a New Cold War, both sides are in excellent positions to wage an intense information campaign using similar propaganda techniques. Much of it will be aimed at their own populations, but some of it is meant to shape global opinion. And although most people like to believe propaganda is something that happens only in dictatorships and not in modern Western societies, it is likely that the West will be waging the information war the hardest. This then brings up the question: what can we expect?

To get an idea in what ways the Western media system is already spitting out pro-Western anti-China propaganda, the best way to start is to examine its behavior during the previous U.S.–Soviet Cold War. The next sections will illustrate to what extent the media in the West willingly and enthusiastically serves Western governments, and how in the modern day and age the internet too has fallen under its control. Also, several case studies will show exactly what this propaganda looks like, in what ways it serves the

---

[268] Brady, A-M. (2008). *Marketing Dictatorship.* Rowman & Littlefield Publishers Inc., p. 78-79, 83. For a good read on how politicians are trained and events scripted, see McGinniss, J. (1988). *The Selling of the President.* Penguin Books.

power elite, and how it enables Western governments to demonize enemies, overthrow democratic governments, and wage a Cold War against China.

A Herd of Independent Minds

One fascinating example of the Western media following their government's lead took place at the very beginning of the Cold War, even before the U.S.–Soviet conflict had officially started. During World War II, Western intellectuals, writers, and opinion makers had built up and spread the belief that the Soviet Union was a force for good in the world. The reason was simple. The Soviets were allied with the West against Nazi Germany. But when the Cold War began to take shape following Germany's defeat in 1945, these same intellectuals were now asked by their governments to transform "Good Old Uncle Joe" — Joseph Stalin — from partner and valued ally into a villain ruling the Evil Empire — the Soviet Union.[269]

Although history shows that governments can usually count on the media and public intellectuals, writers, and even artists to lend their services willingly to whatever direction the government wants, in the early Cold War, political leaders in the United States and Britain decided to leave nothing to chance and constructed their own propaganda systems to guide these 'independent thinkers' in the right direction. They created their own version of state-controlled media, in many ways not unlike that which exists in Communist China.[270]

The CIA took the lead in the United States and created the Congress of Cultural Freedom, which it ran from 1950 until 1967. From the outside, the Congress looked like an innocent cultural foundation that promoted research, published magazines, and organized conferences and art exhibitions. At its peak, the Congress had collected an impressive membership consisting of a full range of famous Western intellectuals, writers, journalists, and artists. It also had offices in thirty-five countries, published dozens of political and other high-profile magazines and up to a thousand books. The Congress even owned its own news service.[271]

But behind the façade of cultural freedom lay the CIA and its geopolitical agenda of promoting U.S. interests. The goal was, as one of the CIA agents described it, to "produce people who, of *their own reasoning and conviction*, were persuaded that everything the United States government did was right." Not

---

[269] Saunders, F. S. (2013). *The Cultural Cold War.* The New Press, p. 49; Jenks, J. (2006). *British Propaganda and News Media in the Cold War.* Edinburgh University Press, p. 39-44.

[270] Jenks, J. (2006). *British Propaganda and News Media in the Cold War.* Edinburgh University Press

[271] Saunders, F. S. (2013). *The Cultural Cold War.* The New Press

unlike the Chinese Propaganda Department, the Congress achieved this by bringing together intellectuals, writers, and artists, and showed them that money, fame, and access to other rewards were available to them if they took a strong pro-American and anti-Communist line in their work.[272]

Meanwhile, the U.S. government ran other programs to inform these intellectuals and the news media that they would be serving their country and the greater good if they adopted a pro-U.S. and pro-Western way of thinking about the world. The goal, which they achieved with considerable success, was the creation of an intellectual class of people that *believed* the United States was a force for good. They reflexively and instinctively supported anything the U.S. government did in their writings, speeches, books, movies, and art. With such people running the major news media and other publications, censorship was no longer necessary.

Besides, at the same time, these intellectuals, writers, and journalists would also stamp out anyone who did not agree. Dissenters would be verbally attacked, smeared, and fired from their jobs until they either submitted or disappeared from the mainstream.[273]

Britain, which in the beginning of the Cold War was the major source of international news for most of the world, also followed this example. Organizations like the BBC and Reuters not only took an anti-Soviet and pro-Western line in their reporting, but they also policed themselves to make sure that journalists and editors who displayed communist sympathies were removed from the organization.[274]

Meanwhile, the British government circulated reports 'advising' the news organizations on what to report and what not to report. These Chinese Propaganda Department style "update meetings" were a valuable tool to keep the British media in line.[275]

And then there was the benevolent-sounding Information Research Department (IRD). This was the arm of the government that, like the Congress, played a key role in shaping the way news agencies and intellectuals reported on events. The IRD would conduct 'scientific research' in a way so that the outcome was always fixed: the Soviet Union is aggressive, evil, and expansionist, and the United States and the West are defensive and good in every sense of the word. Reports from the IRD, often deliberately

---

[272] Saunders, F. S. (2013). *The Cultural Cold War.* The New Press, p. 125, 290.

[273] Jenks, J. (2006). *British Propaganda and News Media in the Cold War.* Edinburgh University Press

[274] Jenks, J. (2006). *British Propaganda and News Media in the Cold War.* Edinburgh University Press, chapter 3

[275] Jenks, J. (2006). *British Propaganda and News Media in the Cold War.* Edinburgh University Press, p. 53 and see the D-Notice system.

written in a dry tone to make them seem more scientific and objective, were then distributed among journalists and news organizations so they would report on them. The BBC especially, given its link to the government, obediently went along with anything the IRD wished. Given the BBC's international reputation for independence and objectivity, it was the perfect vehicle for the IRD.[276]

Shorter and fresher-sounding news bites were also put together to reach a wider audience. The IRD would approach journalists or writers, give them a topic, provide them with anti-Soviet and pro-Western information, make it clear in what way the author was supposed to report that information, and then buy and publish their work.[277]

On the other side of the Atlantic, the CIA worked in a similar fashion. Former CIA officer John Stockwell, who served as the Chief of the Angola Task Force in the 1970s, describes that during the Cold War, the CIA had a station in many of the world's capitals, very often inside the U.S. embassy. From there, CIA operatives were in contact with that capital's major newspaper. Stories written by the CIA were passed along to a local journalist who then published it in the newspaper. The CIA would then inform CIA stations in other capitals to have their local media republish this story. With the story gaining more traction, the chances increased that it would be picked up by one of the major Western media organizations, and when that happened, a story written by the CIA became mainstream news all over the world.[278]

Although technically most Western media organizations were not under government control, you can see that there are many ways that governments and their intelligence agencies shape the news. Unfortunately, these acts to control information have not lessened in the modern day and age. If anything, in a globalized and digitalized world, information has become even more important, and so has the need by those in power to control it.

The Modern-Day Struggle for the Minds of Men

"Can we trust what we read in Wikipedia, the website you co-founded?," asked Freddie Sayers, the interviewer on Lockdown TV. Larry Sanger, of the famous website Wikipedia, answered: "Well, you can trust it to give a reliably establishment point of view on pretty much everything." What the

---

[276] Jenks, J. (2006). *British Propaganda and News Media in the Cold War*. Edinburgh University Press, chapter 4 and 5. For the BBC see p. 90-91.

[277] Jenks, J. (2006). *British Propaganda and News Media in the Cold War*. Edinburgh University Press, p. 69.

[278] Stockwell, J. (1978). *In Search of Enemies*. W. W. Norton & Company, p. 194.

media and Wikipedia do, Sanger explained, is to give you one version, one viewpoint, on what the truth may be — and that is more often than not the mainstream established government point of view. "Of course, that is not how Wikipedia used to be."[279]

In 2004–2005, Wikipedia's co-founder remembers fondly, when Wikipedia was just becoming a household name, you could find different points of view laid out on Wikipedia on every topic. It was a place of learning and exploration — as it should be, as Wikipedia was meant to be. But, the interviewer challenges Larry, is there not a sense that "when you look something up in an encyclopedia, that you want the establishment view?" It is certainly much quicker and easier, right? If the website gives you one truth instead of several different versions of it?

"Boy... I don't really think that is what you want," Sanger explains. "We, being free individuals, want to make up our own minds. And if we don't, then there is something wrong with us... Basically, if you are the sort of person who just wants to be told what... your party thinks, what the dictator thinks, then you're kind of in a bad situation. You're not fully human in that case. In fact, in situations when that happens, the word for it is propaganda when it is systematic. And that is really what we are dealing with on Wikipedia." And the danger and unfortunate reality, Wikipedia's co-founder states, is that "If only one version of the facts is allowed, then it gives a huge incentive to wealthy and powerful people to seize control of things like Wikipedia in order to shore up their power. And they do."

These comments by Larry Sangers expose that even in free and democratic societies, information systems can become hijacked by those in power. And when that happens, we end up in an Orwellian situation. George Orwell, in his book *1984*, referred to this as the government's Ministry of Truth that simply tells people what to believe. When information systems are organized in a way so they only present one truth, then people are no longer encouraged or challenged to think for themselves. Instead, people simply need to memorize and internalize whatever information their leaders present them with. And Wikipedia, and other information systems like it, are not immune to such pressures, as Sangers explained.

Social media systems are no different. Facebook, YouTube, Twitter, and others are, like the mainstream media, owned by powerful corporations with obvious ties and collaborations with the government, as the Twitter files reaffirmed once again. These social media giants may have started out as places intended for people to share information and learn about different

---

[279] See the interview with Larry Sanger on LockdownTV, July 14, 2021. https://www. youtube.com/watch?v=l0P4Cf0UCwU&t=887s

points of view, but it did not take long for them to go through the same process as Wikipedia.

Nowadays, a YouTube or Google search will give you the mainstream establishment point of view — the result of how the search algorithm is designed. Alternative ideas, forums, and channels no longer come up on the first few pages. In fact, people who present an alternative viewpoint that challenges the establishment government line are increasingly difficult to find. Often, you can only find them when you already know their names and the names of their channels. And when you do not, it is almost impossible to be exposed to their work.

Dissenting investigative journalists, commentators, and other non-mainstream intellectuals and artists also face other obstacles. Their videos are increasingly demonetized on YouTube, and their tweets removed. They may find themselves blocked from PayPal to take away sources of income. Their Wikipedia articles are removed to hide their existence from the public or are edited to make them seem unreliable. Some of them are de-platformed, which means that when you get banned from one social media site, you get blocked from all the major social media. Meanwhile, if you do toe the establishment line, your videos and articles are boosted by the algorithms, and you easily find a large audience. This creates enormous temptations and incentives to put your dissenting views and opinions aside, and simply go along with the mainstream.[280]

One example of how Facebook, Twitter, and Instagram are policing the internet to censor dissenting voices is the documented removal of posts and the suspension of accounts of people who opposed and protested U.S. government's actions against their countries. For example, after the White House implemented economic sanctions on Venezuela and Iran, these social media giants removed posts and accounts of those who spoke out against this. And following the illegal assassination by the Trump administration of Iran's top general — an act of war in itself — posts that signaled support for one of Iran's most popular figures were removed and an Iranian news organization had its account suspended. Like Wikipedia, these platforms that present themselves as neutral and independent, increasingly present one single pro-Western version of events to their publics.[281]

Meanwhile, the Western news media is continuing to cooperate with their governments, extending their longtime partnership that can be traced back to the early Cold War and beyond. Although typically done in secret,

---

[280] For a detailed account with examples see Norton, B. *Wikipedia formally censors The Grayzone as regime-change advocates monopolize editing.* The Grayzone, June 10, 2020.

[281] Norton, B. *Under US pressure, social media companies censor critical content and suspend Venezuelan, Iranian, and Syrian accounts.* The Grayzone, January 12, 2020.

information sometimes leaks out that reveals the extent of media-government collusion. One such example concerns the BBC and Reuters. Starting in 2017, these two news giants worked together with Britain's Foreign Office, specifically the secretive department of Counter Disinformation & Media Development. Together, they spread pro-Western news in and around Russia. In another secret government program, the BBC and Reuters signed up to spread pro-NATO and pro-Western 'news' in Ukraine. The goal of these two operations was to destabilize the Russian government, promote pro-Western opposition groups to rise up, and to encourage Ukrainians to join NATO. All of this is official Western government policy, and the media was recruited to help, which they did. If it weren't for the leaked documents, this operation would have remained unknown, which of course begs the question how many more of these programs exist.[282]

Of course, the fact that this information came out did not change anything. You might have expected that social media giants, having witnessed Reuters doing the government's bidding, would not cooperate with such news agencies. But this would be a mistake. Twitter, for example, announced in 2021 that it is now collaborating with Reuters to "elevate credible information" and to suppress information that tells a different story. In other words, Reuters will help run Twitter's censorship department. It does not take a genius to figure out the kind of information about which they were talking. Unfortunately, events like the Ukraine war in 2022, have accelerated all these trends.[283]

Journalists, intellectuals, and commentators who tried to discuss the Russian point of view on the war in Ukraine have been suppressed or removed from social media, their contents are increasingly difficult to find, and many have been verbally attacked and smeared as being Russian spies, working for Putin, or being "Putin understanders." Apparently, trying to understand the other side — the basis in any negotiation — has become borderline criminal in the free and democratic West. Russian media organizations like RT were also banned in Europe and the United States, and even the search engine DuckDuckGo, which brands itself as a censorship-free alternative to Google, has tweaked its algorithm to downrank sites that present the Russian point of view. Whatever you may think of content coming from Russian sources, the fact that Westerners no longer can access them brings us one step closer to an Orwellian society that only knows one single 'truth'. If a well-functioning free and democratic society depends on a

[282] Blumenthal, M. *Reuters, BBC, and Bellingcat participated in covert UK Foreign Office-funded programs to "weaken Russia," leaked docs reveal.* The Grayzone, February 20, 2021

[283] Norton, B. *Twitter partners with UK govt-backed, CIA-linked Reuters to censor alternative views.* The Grayzone, August 4, 2021

climate in which people are free to exchange information and discuss events, then the current trend is very worrisome. A second Cold War with China will surely boost censorship and propaganda to new levels in the West.[284]

This then brings us to actual cases of Western Cold War propaganda. How does this propaganda work? Can you recognize it? And, in the case of the Cold War with China, are we already being subjected to this kind of propaganda? The remainder of this chapter will answer these questions, and it may come as no surprise that indeed an anti-China propaganda campaign has already taken root in the West. But before we dive into that, let us first have a look at several classical examples that demonstrate the workings and effectiveness of Western propaganda during the U.S.–Soviet Cold War.

Cold War Cases of Western Propaganda

On May 30, 1954, the New York Times reported that an unidentified airplane had flown over the capital of Guatemala, a country in Central America. The plane appeared to have dropped paper leaflets over the city, messaging people to stand up and fight against their communist government. In the following weeks, the NYT mentioned several times that mysterious airplanes were flying over Guatemala. And each time they dropped leaflets telling people to revolt against their government. Three weeks later, on June 19, the leaflets went as far as to demand the surrender and resignation of Jacobo Arbenz — Guatemala's president. In one news report, the NYT identified the airplane as a C-47, a United States military transport plane.[285]

From June 1 until June 30, 1954, the NYT laid out a whole series of reports documenting the dramatic events that were unfolding in Guatemala. The United States government had blocked all weapon shipments going into the country. Meanwhile, the White House was flying military equipment into Honduras and Nicaragua — Guatemala's neighbors. From these countries, the NYT reported, an anti-communist movement launched an invasion to overthrow Arbenz and his communist-infiltrated government.

America's most respected newspaper also reported in detail a conflict between Arbenz and a giant U.S. corporation named United Fruit. United Fruit owned large swaths of the most fertile land in Guatemala, and Arbenz wanted to get this land back and distribute it amongst his people. In a

---

[284] Oremus, W. *In Ukraine, tech platforms abandon the illusion of neutrality.* Washington Post, March 12, 2022.

[285] Sydney Gruson, GUATEMALA GRIM AS TENSION RISES. New York Times, May 30, 1954; special to the New York Times, Blackout is Described. New York Times, June 19, 1954; Schlesinger, S. & Kinzer, S. Bitter Fruit: The Untold Story of the American Coup in Guatemala, p. 7.

country plagued by tremendous poverty and inequality, to many ordinary Guatemalans this was a most welcome development. To United Fruit's board of directors, however, it was a nightmare scenario.

Most interestingly, the NYT never did put the pieces of the puzzle together. Although events in Guatemala and the fall of the Arbenz government in a military coup dominated the news in the spring of 1954, the NYT, in the hundreds of articles it published, at no point reported or analyzed U.S. government involvement in the overthrow of a democratic government for geopolitical and economic reasons. To the contrary, the newspaper had been presenting Washington's side of the story most obediently.[286]

For years before the military coup took place, the NYT had painted the Arbenz government as communist, even though no communists held a high position. On June 8, 1951, the editorial board of the newspaper published an article titled "The Guatemalan Cancer." The news report, if you want to call it that, parroted Washington's line that Guatemala was in bed with the Soviet Union, and that Moscow wanted to use this small country as a springboard for an all-out invasion of Latin America. No evidence was presented of course; the fact that U.S. officials were saying it was evidence enough for the NYT. This story would be repeated endlessly until Arbenz was finally overthrown and replaced by a pro-U.S. military leader.[287]

Only decades later did the true story come out. The CIA had overthrown Arbenz in a military coup because the Guatemalan president had dared to challenge U.S. economic dominance over his country. A follow-up investigation by the CIA also concluded that there was no Soviet connection. The communist movement in Guatemala had been small, and it did not control the Arbenz government. Arbenz himself had no link to Moscow. There was no Soviet threat in Guatemala or anywhere else in the region during those years.[288]

---

[286] The New York Times archive has 259 articles on Guatemala from June 1 to June 30, 1954, the month of the coup. Except for a few statements published in the Times coming from the Guatemalan government itself, in which U.S. hostility towards Arbenz and its attempt to portray Arbenz as communist is mentioned, no other article goes into this fact. Typically such statements are published in very small articles deep into the newspaper, which makes them very hard to find. And given the non-stop portrayal of Arbenz's government as communist, readers would most likely not take statements from that government seriously anyway.

[287] Editorial Board, *The Guatemalan Cancer.* New York Times, June 8, 1951. See also Fisher, Z. C. (2007). American Propaganda, Popular Media, and the Fall of Jacobo Arbenz. University of Tampa. Master of Arts thesis for a great discussion on Western media reporting on Guatemala

[288] Schlesinger, S. & Kinzer, S. Bitter Fruit: The Untold Story of the American Coup in Guatemala; Blum, W. (2004). Killing Hope. Zed Books, see chapter on Guatemala; Rabe, S. G. *The Killing Zone: The United States Wages Cold War in Latin America.* See p. 32 and 45

The coup itself was a bloody affair. Thousands of people died. The CIA assisted in the killings by providing a "disposal list" with the names of people the military should go after. Arbenz's government would also be the country's last democratic government for decades. Over the period from 1954 until 1996, while resistance to a series of military dictatorships steadily grew, around 200,000 people were killed by government death squads. Overall, it was a very constructive bloodbath, made possible by the 1954 military coup, which the *New York Times* and other Western media outlets enabled by obediently reporting exactly what Washington wanted Americans to know.[289]

This case reveals that when the U.S. government wants to get rid of a foreign leader and his or her administration, one essential step that is always taken is to discredit and demonize them. Arbenz was painted as a communist and a dictator, someone who was in bed with or controlled by the evil Soviet Empire. Arbenz's communist government posed a threat to his country, the region, and, despite the country being dirt poor and having almost no military to speak of, it was even a threat to the United States. The endless repetition of this story and the complete absence of any counter argument ever being presented shaped American beliefs and developed into common knowledge. Even though no evidence was ever presented, the Guatemalan threat, or 'cancer,' became fact. As a result, a bloody military coup that overthrew a popular people-oriented government and replaced it with a pro-U.S. military dictator was turned into a welcome and positive change in the eyes of many Americans. All thanks to effective propaganda.

The Western media's performance regarding Guatemala's 1954 coup was not the first, nor would it be the last. In fact, in 1953, one year earlier, the CIA and the British MI6 had overthrown the democratically elected leader of Iran, Premier Mossadegh, and the media had played an important part.[290]

In the years leading up to the 1953 Iranian coup, the media neatly followed the line that Washington set out. Mossadegh was portrayed in the Western media as a crazy and discredited leader, someone who was about to hand Iran to the Soviets. The media ignored the fact that Mossadegh was a nationalist first, and that his main goal was to keep his country out of the hands of any foreign power, be it London, Washington, or Moscow. Mossadegh was no communist, nor was he sympathetic to Moscow, but the Western media painted him as such, nonetheless.

---

[289] Rabe, S. G. *The Killing Zone: The United States Wages Cold War in Latin America.* See p. 53
[290] Dorman, W. A. & Farhang, M. (1987). *The U.S. Press and Iran.* University of California Press. For a good book about the coup itself, see Abrahamian, E. (2013). *The Coup.* The New Press.

The media did not mention that the rise of Mossadegh and his popularity in Iran came from his opposition to British control over Iranian oil. Iranians were frustrated and angry that most of the profits from Iranian oil ended up in London banks. Mossadegh's attempt to gain back control over his country's own resources, a move widely supported by the Iranian people, frightened and angered London and Washington. Before ordering the coup, they used economic sanctions to try to collapse the Iranian economy. The hope was that it would lead to Mossadegh's downfall. The media, of course, ignored this part of the story and did not mention the sanctions. Instead, they put the blame for the collapsing economy solely on Mossadegh himself. In the meantime, Mossadegh's rival, the pro-Western Shah of Iran, was presented as a rational reformer who could bring back stability and economic growth.

In the six months leading up to the coup, the Western media were especially harsh on Mossadegh. More lies on his supposedly communist connections appeared, and they labeled him a dictator as well.

When the coup finally happened, the Western public had been well prepared to welcome the event. The Shah was celebrated as the new leader of Iran, and the fact that he allowed Britain and the United States to take control of Iranian oil did not lead the media to investigate and report on possible Western involvement. In fact, the opposite was the case, and the New York Times reported that "There is even a measure of gratitude [in Iran] toward the United States and British governments."

In the next 25 years until 1979, the Shah ruled Iran as a pro-Western dictator. The SAVAK, the Shah's notorious secret police, which was trained by the CIA, crushed all opposition. Its well-earned reputation for torture and executions kept people quiet and afraid. Naturally, no trace of this could be found in the Western media, which portrayed the Shah as a wise and concerned reformer. Although the democratically elected Mossadegh was routinely dubbed a dictator by the NYT in the months leading up to his overthrow, the Shah, during his 25-year rule, was only referred to as a dictator three times.

The coups in Iran and Guatemala in 1953 and 1954 are the most famous Cold War cases of the United States overthrowing a democratic government and replacing it with a pro-Western military dictatorship. In both cases, the Western media reported exactly what Washington wanted. The governments of Iran and Guatemala were demonized, and their leaders discredited. It did not matter whether the accusations were true or false. The statements were not even presented as accusations, but as mere fact. With endless repetition and without counter-arguments, these stories quickly morphed into popular beliefs and common knowledge. And once that happens, there is no longer any need to present evidence. Indeed, when anyone tries to present a counter argument, they can be easily labeled and dismissed as communists or Soviet spies.

By leaving parts of the story out, misrepresenting others, and by simply making up things and presenting them as fact, the media prepared the Western populations to accept or even welcome the downfall of popular governments and their replacement by military dictatorships. This kind of media support for Cold War policy was routine. In fact, if you study the dozens of interventions, coups, and wars that the United States carried out during the Cold War, you will find not one case of media opposition.

Media support for war has continued after the collapse of the Soviet Union. The Iraq war of 2003 is a case in point. Within two weeks after 9/11, the White House and the Pentagon were already making plans to invade Iraq, according to former Supreme Allied Commander Europe of NATO General Wesley Clark. At the time, there was no evidence for a connection between the terrorist attacks and Iraq, and there never was. Yet the media obediently followed Washington's line and reported on Iraq's possession of weapons of mass destruction (WMD) and Saddam's connections to Al Qaeda. News reporters who challenged these claims, such as Phil Donahue who ran a show on MSNBC, were fired.[291]

The reality is simple. When Washington or other Western governments decide to go to war, the media considers it as their duty to support it, and that it is what they do, every single time. All mainstream newspapers, TV news channels, and other outlets will speak with one voice. They present the same picture, repeat the same arguments, and counter or suppress any opposing views. The 2022 war in Ukraine is another such example of the entire Western media parroting the exact same government sponsored line — a feat that rivals the media performances in totalitarian countries.

Of course, one other conclusion you can draw from these examples is that the Western media outlets like the *New York Times* are simply incompetent and got the stories wrong. But there is one flaw in this argument. If the western media tends to be incompetent in its foreign policy reporting, you expect that mistakes are made randomly. Sometimes the NYT says something that benefits U.S. government goals, and sometimes it reports a story that contradicts or undermines them. This is, however, not what you find.

---

[291] For General Wesley Clark, see the Democracy Now interview on 2007: https://www.youtube.com/watch?v=z8ityb0Ips4; For see Phil Donahue see the Democracy Now interview on March 21, 2003: https://www.youtube.com/watch?v=ozxzNjRqCiE

In the case of Guatemala, Iran, and all other conflicts since, the reporting of the *Times* and other Western media outlets tends to be over 95% in favor of the U.S. government's goals. This then suggests strongly that these are not mistakes at all. It may not be the 99% that you can get in China or in other countries with tightly controlled State-owned media, but it does come remarkably close. And it is with this in mind that we now turn to Western media reporting on China.

In the next section, the most sensitive and explosive "China story" since 2018 will be discussed — the Uyghur genocide. Then, in the last section, the Western media campaign to turn the Cold War against China into a good vs evil story — one about democracy vs dictatorship — will be studied as well. In both cases, the goal is not so much to prove or disprove whether these stories are correct. Instead, the focus will be on how they serve as great examples of modern Western anti-China propaganda. It is up to you to make up your own mind on what you choose to believe and what not.

Genocide in Xinjiang: anti-China propaganda?

One story on China that has captured an enormous amount of attention and outrage in the West is the allegation that the Chinese government has imprisoned a million Uyghurs — a Muslim minority group in Xinjiang Province — and is subjecting them to indoctrination, brain washing, forced labor, and even mass sterilization in a genocidal attempt to wipe out the Uyghur culture or perhaps even the Uyghur people entirely.

At first glance, this type of news should ring a few alarm bells. This story demonizes a foreign government, one that has been designated as a rival or enemy of the West. The fact that all Western media outlets speak with one voice, present the same arguments, and repeat them endlessly also should not surprise you. But that does not mean this is merely propaganda. Maybe there is a genocide going on in Xinjiang. So how should we process such a story?

A good starting point would be the following. First, we know from history that governments are capable of carrying out such hideous crimes. We also know, however, that governments can lie, and that the Western media has a tendency to obediently parrot these lies. As already discussed, there are many examples of stories put out by Western governments and the Western media that falsely demonized countries and governments that are rivals or enemies of the West.

The false and made-up horror stories about German war crimes in WWI that dominated the Western media is one such example. The WMD lie about Iraq, and the lies about Mossadegh and Arbenz are others. A more cynical case, one that shares important similarities with the alleged Uyghur genocide, is that of the 1991 allegation that Iraqi soldiers, after their conquest of Kuwait, had killed hundreds of babies by throwing them out of their incubators and leaving them on the floor to die. A brutal crime, perhaps as monstrous as genocide. The most convincing evidence for this story came from a girl simply identified as Nayirah. In a very emotional testimony in front of the U.S. Congress, she informed the Western world about having been a witness to these horrible crimes. This story, like other propaganda stories, played a key role in getting people in the West to approve, even welcome, a war against a rival or enemy nation. Only later, after the story had served its purpose, did the truth come out. The girl Nayirah was the daughter of the Kuwaiti ambassador to the United States. She was coached and trained by the U.S. PR firm Hill and Knowlton to tell a lie. She did not witness these alleged crimes. In fact, the crimes never happened. It was all made up. Even the *New York Times*, which ran enthusiastically with the story before the war, was forced to admit this after the U.S. had launched its military attack against Iraq.[292]

Going back to the Uyghur story, it is important to keep these two things in mind: governments are capable of extreme crimes, and governments and media organizations also run fake stories to demonize their rivals in order to get their populations to support war. What this means is that you should approach the Uyghur story by carefully examining the evidence and having a close look at the people and organizations who are putting forward this evidence.

Related to this last part, it is helpful to adopt the approach taken by the Western mainstream media. They never accept stories from organizations that are linked to the Chinese or Russian government. Usually these are dismissed out of hand as Russian or Chinese propaganda that serves some ulterior motive. So, let us apply this and other healthy critical thinking to the analysis of the Uyghur story.

What follows below is a lengthy analysis of all the major reports and research on which the alleged Uyghur genocide is based. The Western media ran with these stories continuously. In fact, they have dominated their headlines for years. Indeed, these were the driving force behind the Uyghur genocide story. Note that these reports are on the internet and are free and accessible to everyone. If you want to judge what to believe and what not, you can read and analyze them yourself, and study how they influenced

---

[292] John, R. MacArthur. Remember Nayirah, Witness for Kuwait? The New York Times, January 6, 1992

Western media reporting. It makes an extremely interesting case study of propaganda, as you will see shortly. Lastly, before we begin, the point of the analysis below is not to prove or disprove what is happening in Xinjiang. It merely serves as an illustration of how the Western propaganda system works.

The first news reports in the Western media about a million Uyghurs being detained in secret detention or re-education camps appeared in 2018. These early claims, presented as fact and repeatedly endlessly, were based on two reports.[293]

The first report comes from the Network of Chinese Human Rights Defenders (CHRD), which is a Washington-based organization that receives most of its money from the U.S. government through the National Endowment for Democracy (NED), which itself is an organization deeply involved in destabilizing rival foreign governments. According to the former NED president Allen Weinstein: "A lot of what we do today was done covertly 25 years ago by the CIA."[294]

The CHRD report claimed that a million Uyghurs are detained in camps. It was based on interviewing eight ethnic Uyghurs living in Xinjiang. They guessed how many people they believed were detained in their village. The authors of the report then generalized these findings to the 11 million Uyghurs living in the Chinese province, and so the figure of million was born.

To take this as credible and convincing evidence, you have to assume that those eight villagers were telling the truth, that their estimates were accurate for their villages, and that these estimates also hold up across the entire province (which is three times the size of France) and its 11 million Uyghurs. These are a lot of assumptions, and it leads to several important questions about this study. Why did they only interview eight people? Why only one from each village? When you interview multiple people within the same village, you get a much better estimate. This is one of the most basic rules in science. Besides, it is also quite easy to do, yet the CHRD did not. This method of relying on only eight estimates and to then generalize it over the entire province does not come close to meeting any scientific standard. And finally, in judging these estimates, you also have to assume that the CHRD — a U.S.-funded organization with a documented hatred towards the Chinese government — has conducted this research honestly. To drive

---

[293] See for example Thum, R. What Really Happens in China's 'Re-education' Camps. The New York Times, May 15, 2018.

[294] Norton, B. & Singh, A. No, the UN did not report China has 'massive internment camps' for Uighur Muslims. The Grayzone, August 23, 2018; David Ignatius, INNOCENCE ABROAD: THE NEW WORLD OF SPYLESS COUPS, Washington Post, September 22, 1991

this point home: would the Western media accept a story coming from a Russian or Chinese funded organization, one that has an anti-Western bias, which is based on little evidence and questionable methodology? Would you accept it?

The second report that formed the basis of Western media reporting on the Uyghur story comes from Adrian Zenz. A condensed version of his article — which was most frequently cited in the Western press — was published by the Jamestown Foundation, a U.S. think tank whose board is staffed by retired U.S. military generals and former U.S. government foreign policy officials.[295]

The key number of one million Uyghur detainees as determined by Zenz comes from his own speculations that, as you will see when you read his report, are based on no concrete evidence. The only source Zenz provides is a report by Istiqlal TV, which bases its estimates on a source that cannot be verified. Istiqlal TV itself is also far from neutral since its provides a platform for separatist groups who are fighting against the Chinese government for an independent Xinjiang. Finally, Zenz presents two reports with detainment estimates from Radio Free Asia — a U.S.-funded news organization originally created by the CIA to spread anti-Chinese news in Asia.[296]

Zenz himself is also far removed from being a neutral source of information. As a member of the Victims of Communism Foundation, he considers it his duty to liberate people living under communist governments. And as a Christian extremist who mixes religious ideas with political convictions, Zenz believes he is led by God on a mission to look for crimes committed by the Chinese Communist Party. Yet in the Western media, he is described as an independent researcher.[297]

An 800+ page volume written by Zenz illustrates his mixing of religious and political beliefs and his dubious research methods. In the book, which is about the End Times, he argues that with the future fall of capitalism, the anti-Christ will return. Zenz links this to the prophesied destruction of Babylon — an ancient biblical city — which he equates with a modern

---

[295] Adrian Zenz, New Evidence for China's Political Re-Education Campaign in Xinjiang. Jamestown Foundation, May 15, 2018

[296] Zenz, A. *Thoroughly Reforming Them Towards a Healthy Heart Attitude.* Central Asian Survey, September 6, 2018; Singh, A. & Blumenthal, M. China detaining millions of Uyghurs? Serious problems with claims by US-backed NGO and far-right researcher 'led by God' against Beijing. December 21, 2019. See https://thegrayzone.com/2019/12/21/china-detaining-millions-uyghurs-problems-claims-us-ngo-researcher/

[297] For the position of the Victim's of Communism foundation, see their website https://victimsofcommunism.org/about/ which states that "The real examples of socialism today are China, Cuba, Laos, North Korea, Vietnam, and now Venezuela. We must contend with these regimes and the threats they pose to free people—and we must struggle for the freedom of the more than one billion people held captive by these regimes."

financial center in today's world. To identify exactly which city this is, he ends up with two choices: New York or Tokyo. Stuck between these two, Zenz continues his research, and comes up with what he considers is the obvious solution. Since Babylon will be destroyed at the End Times, it must be a city that displeases God. New York is home to many more gay people than Tokyo, and because Satan deceived Eve into eating the apple in the Garden of Eden, the city that ushers in the return of the anti-Christ must be New York — the "Big Apple." [298]

Returning to Western media reporting on China, the above-mentioned reports come from biased and dubious sources, certainly not independent research organizations. Their work too does not meet any serious investigative reporting or scientific standards. The Western media ought to have threaded very carefully in running the "one million Uyghur detained in concentration camps" story, and they should have mentioned these shortcomings. But of course, this was not the case, and the reports were presented as fact and repeated endlessly.

Following these early reports in 2018, a second wave of articles appeared the next year. They were again based on several reports, and these took the Uyghur story to another level. Not only were there concentration camps in Xinjiang, but Uyghurs were also systematically subjected to forced labor and a process of cultural genocide.

Adrian Zenz led the charge once more. Yet when you read his 2019 work, you will find that he once again does not provide any real evidence. Even Zenz himself admits in his footnotes that the source he relies upon does not meet media reporting standards, let alone serious investigative journalism or scientific standards. It is therefore no surprise that he was unable to publish his work in a respectable journal, and instead ended up writing for the Journal of Political Risk — a journal without a scientific impact factor — whose publisher Anders Corr is a former U.S. military analyst. Corr did not bother with the lack of credible source material in Zenz's article, because he wants the United States to get tough on China. In an interview, Corr describes that he wants the West to impose economic sanctions, and kick China out of all international organizations, including the United Nations. [299]

---

[298] Zenz, A. & Sias, M. L. (2012). *Worthy to Escape.* WestBow Press. See Chapter 12.

[299] Adrian Zenz. "Brainwashing, Police Guards and Coercive Internment: Evidence from Chinese Government Documents about the Nature and Extent of Xinjiang's 'Vocational Training Internment Camps'." July 1, 2019. Journal of Political Risk 7(7); Adrian Zenz. "Break Their Roots: Evidence for China's Parent-Child Separation Campaign in Xinjiang." July 4, 2019. Journal of Political Risk 7(7); On Anders Corr, see https://www.jpolrisk.com/about/leadership/ and China Uncensored. How to Stop China From Taking Over the World | Anders Corr. December 15, 2021. https://www.youtube.com/watch?v=PnSPc6KtdvE

Zenz's work itself is also a textbook example of bad scientific practice. When you read his report, it is obvious he has already made up his mind and does not bother with evidence. When he describes actions by the Chinese government to reduce unemployment in Xinjiang, Zenz interprets this as forced labor. Government sponsored childcare facilities that help enable women to have a job — a common occurrence in Western countries — are part of a sinister Communist plot to separate women from their children and break up families. And in the poverty alleviation campaign, Zenz sees cultural genocide. Yet no evidence for any of these claims is provided.[300]

Then, starting from March 2020, a new report on alleged forced labor dominated the Western media. The report, titled "Uyghurs for Sale," comes from the Australian Strategic Policy Institute (ASPI). Although ASPI brands itself as an independent think tank, it receives its funding from the Australian Department of Defense, the U.S. Defense Department, and the U.S. State Department. Several U.S. weapon manufacturers such as Lockheed Martin and Raytheon also provide funding. According to the former Australian Minister for Foreign Affairs, ASPI pumps out a "one-sided, pro-American view of the world." Geoff Raby, the former Australian ambassador to China, explains people should see ASPI as "the architect of the China threat theory in Australia."[301]

The report by ASPI feels convincing when you read it casually. But when you go through the footnotes and start checking them one by one, you find that the conclusions drawn in the report do not match the source material. They simply do not check out. The report claims one thing, but the source that is cited does not give any supporting evidence. For example, when the report talks about the hardships that Uyghur women face when they are forced to work far away from home, the actual source that is cited as evidence describes a woman who chose to work in another province, is coping with the challenges of being a migrant worker, and decided herself to extend her contract for two extra years because she is making money to support her family. The ASPI report also relies heavily on Adrian Zenz's work and on the source that Zenz himself described does not meet media reporting standards. Overall, the ASPI report makes wild guesses and speculations without real evidence and builds its case upon misrepresentations and lies

---

[300] Adrian Zenz. "Beyond the Camps: Beijing's Long-Term Scheme of Coercive Labor, Poverty Alleviation and Social Control in Xinjiang", December 10, 2019. Journal of Political Risk 7(12)

[301] See https://www.aspi.org.au/about-aspi/funding for information on ASPI's funding. Detailed breakdowns are provided for the years 2019-2020 and 2020-2021; Myriam Robin. The think tank behind Australia's changing view of China. February 15, 2020. Australian Financial Review

about its source material. None of this was mentioned in the Western media, which again presented this report as fact.[302]

The next phase in the Uyghur news campaign was again instigated by Adrian Zenz, now promoted to the world's leading expert on what is happening in Xinjiang. In his 2020 report, Zenz takes the story to yet another level and claims the Chinese government is committing a Nazi-style genocide against Uyghurs in Xinjiang. The goal? To eliminate the Uyghurs entirely. Predictably, his conclusions dominated the headlines in the Western media. Zenz's increasingly shocking claims were, however, accompanied by a worsening quality of his research. In fact, this report, clever but hastily assembled, is based on a series of statistical manipulations and misrepresentations, cherry picking of evidence (a very bad scientific practice), and all-out fraud. But even though all of this is very easy to detect, the Western media ran with the story, presented it as fact, and repeated it endlessly.[303]

To illustrate the level of deception and fraud in Zenz's most sensational report to date, let us look at its two most important claims, namely that birth rate of Uyghurs in Xinjiang is dropping dramatically and suddenly since 2016, and that the Chinese government is carrying out mass forced IUDs (the placement of a birth control device in women to prevent pregnancy). Combined, they provide convincing evidence for genocide according to Zenz.

To start with this last point, Zenz writes in his report that in 2018, 80% of all the net added IUDs in China were performed in Xinjiang, which makes up only 1.8% of the Chinese population. It is a shocking statistic that is presented in a way to make you believe that 80% of all newly performed IUDs in China are happening in Xinjiang. But when you look at the source that Zenz cites, the 2019 China Health Statistics Yearbook, you find something vastly different. In 2018, there were 239,457 net added IUDs performed in Xinjiang, which is 8.7% of China's total for that year. It is far removed from Zenz's 80%. It thus appears that he was off by a factor of 9. So how did Zenz get his 80% number?

To turn the 8.7% into something more shocking, something that would lead people to believe a genocide is happening, Zenz came up with a clever trick — a textbook case of statistical manipulation. He calculated the difference between added IUDs and removed IUDs and expressed that as a percentage of the net total for China. When you do this, then the net added IUDs in Xinjiang are indeed 80% of the Chinese net total, and in

---

[302] Xiuzhong, V. et al. Uyghurs for sale. March 1, 2020. Australian Strategic Policy Institute; see reference 34 for the example mentioned of misrepresenting source material. Most references checked by the author suffer from similar problems.

[303] Adrian Zenz. Sterilizations, IUDs, and Mandatory Birth Control. July 2020. The Jamestown Foundation.

Henan province this is 69% (206,281 net added IUDs), and Hebei is 58%. Together these three provinces add up to a total of 207%. This confusing number only makes sense if you add in provinces that have more removals than newly added IUDs, because they get negative percentages. But there is no reason to use this type of calculation. Maybe it can serve as the basis for some sort of ranking, but even then, its use is dubious. It just happens to give Xinjiang a high percentage, although you could easily have made the case that a genocide is happening in Henan (70% of all the net added IUDs are happening in Henan, this must mean genocide!).[304]

To top it all off, Zenz also includes a chart showing that between 800 and 1,400 IUD surgeries are performed per capita every single year between 2010 and 2018. Per capita means per person, and because IUDs only apply to women, it means that every woman of childbearing age is undergoing, according to Zenz, between 1,600 and 2,800 surgeries a year, or 4 to 8 every single day. It would mean that all Uyghur women are spending the bulk of their day in the hospital to get their IUDs inserted, only to have them removed and replaced a few hours later. This obviously can never be true, and it makes no sense. Even worse, it contradicts Zenz's argument, because the chart, which is obviously wrong, shows no increasing trend over time in the number of IUD's between 2010 and 2018, yet this is precisely what Zenz is claiming.

Next, the report claims that birth rates in Xinjiang are falling and that this too is proof of genocide. Birth rates are indeed falling in Xinjiang, as they happen to be falling all throughout China. Zenz, however, does not mention this. He simply shows statistics for Xinjiang, does not comment on the obvious reasons for this decline, nor does Zenz mention other statistics that are incompatible with genocide. Interestingly, Zenz's own report gives indications to this effect. In a figure in his report that shows population growth, you can see that the Uyghur population between 2010 and 2018 grew by 16.8%, which is higher than the Han population growth of 15.3%. Despite falling birth rates, the population is growing because people in Xinjiang are living longer and healthier lives due to economic development and government healthcare programs. This has also resulted in lower infant mortality numbers for Uyghurs in Xinjiang. Obviously, these are unusual policies for a government intent on exterminating an entire people and are therefore not mentioned by Zenz.[305]

---

[304] Gareth Porter & Max Blumenthal. US State Department accusation of China 'genocide' relied on data abuse and baseless claims by far-right ideologue. The Grayzone, February 18, 2021

[305] Gareth Porter & Max Blumenthal. US State Department accusation of China 'genocide' relied on data abuse and baseless claims by far-right ideologue. The Grayzone, February

Yet Zenz is correct that the birth rate of Uyghurs is falling. In fact, as alluded to before, birth rates across China are falling. This has become a major concern for Beijing and is the reason they have abandoned the one-child policy. Why are birth rates falling? Because of the usual suspects — factors that have also determined birth rates in Western countries. An aging population, economic development, more women having a job, rising costs of living in cities etc.[306]

Finally, Zenz adds a photograph of a Xinjiang couple seeing a doctor and claims this is evidence of the Chinese government's effort of imposing birth control measures on an unwilling population. Why Zenz decided to show this particular photograph is unclear, because it shows an elderly couple of 60 or 70 years old — a couple clearly too old to have children. And the article that Zenz took this photograph from is about a Chinese government's program to provide free medical consultations. It talks about doctors measuring things like blood pressure, blood sugar, height, and weight. This elderly couple simply made use of a free medical check up.[307]

Zenz's statistical manipulations, cherry picking, and fraudulent behavior is completely ignored in Western media reporting. Instead, they focus on the 80% number and the decline in birth rates and take this report as compelling evidence that there is a genocide happening in Xinjiang.

The next major source of information that dominated much of the discussion on the alleged genocide in Xinjiang is a leak of 400 pages of internal Chinese documents. These were first reported on by the *New York Times* in November 2019. At the time of the leak, there were questions whether these documents were indeed real, but this discussion came to a quick stop when none other than Adrian Zenz confirmed they were authentic. Interestingly, when you read the documents carefully, you do indeed get the strong impression that they are real. The reason is that these documents do not support the genocide theory. Obviously, if they were fabricated by Western organizations or governments, they would include convincing evidence of genocide. The fact that they do not suggest the documents are not fabrications and therefore possibly real. So, let us take a look at what the documents

---

18, 2021

[306] Gareth Porter & Max Blumenthal. US State Department accusation of China 'genocide' relied on data abuse and baseless claims by far-right ideologue. The Grayzone, February 18, 2021

[307] See https://archive.is/F3Mp4 for the original article, and see Gareth Porter & Max Blumenthal. US State Department accusation of China 'genocide' relied on data abuse and baseless claims by far-right ideologue. The Grayzone, February 18, 2021

reveal about the Chinese government and Xinjiang, because they do give a fascinating insight into what may be going on.[308]

The general impression that you get after reading these documents is of an authoritarian state overreacting to the real threat of terrorist attacks by religious extremists in Xinjiang. The term overreacting here is key, but the Chinese overreaction to the threat of terror is quite different from the Western one. The United States' reaction to terrorism was to attack two countries and then occupy them for a combined 28 years, plus to bomb at least four other countries. The Chinese government did not overreact in this manner. What they did instead was to conduct a targeted campaign in Xinjiang that involved massive monitoring and surveillance to identify potential terrorists, followed by arrests, imprisonment, and an attempt to remove terrorist ideas and sympathies through an educational program.

To illustrate, one of the leaked documents, dated June 29, 2017, mentions that 1,869,310 Uyghurs have used the software "Kuai Ya." This clearly demonstrates the extreme extent of government surveillance that is being conducted in China. The Kuai Ya software, according to Chinese intelligence, is used by religious extremists to spread videos and audio with violent terrorist content. Of those 1.8 million Uyghurs that used Kuai Ya, the document continues, 40,557 people have watched or listened to such violent content, and that makes them suspect of harboring terrorist sympathies in the eyes of the Chinese government. Therefore, the document recommends, all 40,557 should be investigated, and if evidence of terrorist activities is found, they should be arrested and put in prison. Thus, this document shows that the Chinese government was carrying out a targeted campaign, not a general round up and imprisonment of a million people. It certainly does not suggest a genocide, yet this is how this leaked document and others like it were reported in the Western media.[309]

Several other documents explain what the prison system in Xinjiang is about. It turns out to be a two-faced system. On the one hand there is the close and complete surveillance of everyone inside. There are guards. There is a rigid schedule that tells people when to do what, where to sit, where to sleep, etc. And there is an emphasis on removing terrorist ideas and sympathies. All these things are, however, very typical of prison-like institutions. Nonetheless, it does feel quite extreme, which shows the Chinese govern-

---

[308] Austin Ramzy and Chris Buckley. 'Absolutely No Mercy': Leaked Files Expose How China Organized Mass Detentions of Muslims. The New York Times, November 16, 2019
[309] See bulletin #20 of the "China cables" translated by the International Consortium of Investigative Journalists: https://www.documentcloud.org/documents/6558508-China-Cables-IJOP-Daily-Bulletin-20-English.html

ment's overreaction to the threat of terrorism. Naturally, all these aspects dominate Western media reporting.[310]

But the news reports by outlets like the *New York Times* do not describe the other side of this two-faced prison system. These same leaked documents, for example, give clear instructions to prison management and personnel that every detainee must be able to call his or her relatives at least once a week and have a video call with them at least once a month. Another document lays out that the local government should ensure the detainee's relatives are taken care of. This is especially important when a detainee has children or is the main source of income for his or her family. The unspoken logic here is that the Chinese government does not want to unnecessarily ruin and destroy families when a family member is detained, because that would only feed terrorism against the state. Finally, the documents stress that when a person is released from prison, the local authorities must aid this person in finding a job that fits his or her ambitions and aspirations, in order to help the individual reintegrate back into society. None of this feels like genocide, and none of this is reported in the Western media.[311]

The last major piece of evidence presented in the Western media on the alleged genocide came from a study published by the Newlines Institute on March 8, 2021, titled "The Uyghur Genocide." During the weeks after the report's release, it dominated headlines across the Western media. It was presented as the final piece of evidence that once and for all proved the Chinese government was committing genocide. But when you read the report, you will find that it does not present any new information. Instead, it takes the reports discussed above and accepts them all as true. Then the authors argue this amounts to genocide. And as expected, Adrian Zenz is the most cited source in the report.[312]

So why did the Uyghur genocide get so much traction in the Western media? How come journalists and editors working for these institutions failed so badly in pointing out the flaws in the evidence, the manipulation

---

[310] See the telegram of the "China cables" translated by the International Consortium of Investigative Journalists: https://www.documentcloud.org/documents/6558510-China-Cables-Telegram-English.html

[311] See the telegram of the "China cables" translated by the International Consortium of Investigative Journalists: https://www.documentcloud.org/documents/6558510-China-Cables-Telegram-English.html; Document: What Chinese Officials Told Children Whose Families Were Put in Camps. The New York Times, November 16, 2019 https://www.nytimes.com/interactive/2019/11/16/world/asia/china-detention-directive.html

[312] The Uyghur Genocide: An Examination of China's Breaches of the 1948 Genocide Convention. Newlines Institute, March 8, 2021. https://newlinesinstitute.org/uyghurs/the-uyghur-genocide-an-examination-of-chinas-breaches-of-the-1948-genocide-convention/

and deceit in the reports, and the biased nature of the authors and institutions? Is this an example of an honest mistake, or does it highlight something else?

The answer to the first question is simple. The Uyghur genocide story received much attention in the Western media because it serves a purpose. China has been designated as the main rival (or enemy) of Western power. As such, there are many groups within the West that are calling for tough action against the Chinese. The easiest way to justify such actions and to get Western populations to support them, even welcome them, is to demonize China. The story thus serves the foreign policy goals of Western governments, and that is why influential institutions and politicians push it. The media simply parrots this narrative uncritically, as it almost always does.

This then also means that pointing out the flaws and manipulations in the evidence, and the biased nature of the sources, would obviously undermine this media campaign. Besides, once this story gets momentum, it becomes a force of its own — one that is almost impossible to stop. The whole idea of the endless repetition and the lack of any counter arguments is to turn the story into a widely held belief. When that happens, the alleged genocide becomes fact. Those who talk about concentration camps, forced labor, and forced birth control no longer need to present evidence. These things have become common knowledge that everyone accepts and believes, just like the Earth is round, the sky is blue, and the U.S. attack against Vietnam is the defense of Vietnam.

Going against this current is almost impossible. You would need at least 10 pages of arguments or a full hour of uninterrupted presentations to even begin showing people an alternative way of looking at things. And given the power dynamics that the Western media operates within, as explained in the beginning of this chapter, a media organization doing this would only risk harming itself and the careers of the journalists working for it.

To answer the last question about whether it is an honest mistake or a deliberate attempt to mislead people, nobody is going to give you a clear-cut answer. But based on the Uyghur story and others like it, it seems fair to say that journalists are generally honest and hard working. They believe in what they report and they have good intentions. In a way remarkably similar to the Communist Propaganda Department's method of selecting senior editors who know what they are supposed to say, journalists and editors working within Western media organizations are also selected on these same criteria. Consequently, what you are going to end up with are journalists who already have pro-Western and anti-China beliefs, and willingly, often enthusiastically, report in exactly this manner. They are themselves the result of the way the Western media system works, as explained in the beginning of this chapter, and produce such stories as the alleged Uyghur genocide. This then brings us to the next and last section of this chapter, which is all about shaping the entire narrative on what the U.S.–China Cold War is all about.

Democracy vs Dictatorship — Propaganda vs Reality

"The fundamental purpose of the United States," so states NSC-68, the most important Western document on the U.S.–Soviet Cold War, is to "bring about order and justice by means consistent with the principles of freedom and democracy." It is the United States, the document continues, that stands between a free world and "The Kremlin's design for world domination." Only U.S. leadership can prevent the Kremlin from doing "its evil work."[313]

NSC-68 is a remarkable piece of work. Written in the early months of 1950 by the hardliner Paul Nitze, who had replaced George F. Kennan as the director of the Policy Planning Staff, it set out how politicians and journalists ought to view the Cold War between the United States and the Soviet Union that was taking shape at that time. At the core of this narrative was the notion that the Western countries, led by Washington, are good, and that the Soviet Union, controlled by Moscow, is bad. It was as simple as that, and the entire Western mainstream media adopted it for over four decades until the "Evil Empire" was no more.

What is fascinating about the U.S.–Soviet Cold War is that the Soviets had their own version of the story, which was a perfect mirror image of the above except, of course, with the roles reversed. According to the Soviet media, the world was "divided into two hostile camps." To prevent the "American plan for the enslavement of Europe" and its aim for "strangling democracy," "the Soviet Union will continue to conduct a resolute struggle against imperialism, and firmly rebuff the evil designs and subversions of aggressors." It was the "sacred duty" of the Soviet Union to "give undeviating support to the people's struggle for democracy" and "national liberation" from Western colonialism.[314]

If you study the history of propaganda, you will quickly learn that there is nothing new about this. In fact, all empires have done the exact same

---

[313] NSC 68. April 14, 1950.

[314] Steele, J. (1985). *The Limits of Soviet Power: The Kremlin's Foreign Policy - Brezhnev to Chernenko.* Penguin Books. See p. 52; Kramer, M. & Smetana, V. (2014). *Imposing, Maintaining, and Tearing Open the Iron Curtain: The Cold War and East-Central Europe, 1945-1989.* Lexington Books. See p. 26-27, 67, 90-91; Applebaum, A. (2013). *Iron Curtain: The Crushing of Eastern Europe.* Penguin Books. See p. 235.

thing. The British, when they were colonizing the world, said they were carrying "the white man's burden." In other words, spreading civilization, defending freedom, and helping people all around the world was hard work. The French called it their "civilizing mission." The Belgians took considerable pride in their civilizing work as well, and ten million corpses in the Congo did not change their attitudes one bit. Japan too, when it colonized large parts of China, was not at all being selfish. They were simply creating an "Earthly paradise" for the Chinese to enjoy.[315]

One fascinating aspect of this is that both the political left and the right contributed to this propaganda. A notable example is John Stuart Mill — a champion of the left and a giant of Western liberalism. In fact, Mill represented the peak of intellectual and moral reasoning in 19th-century Europe. While Britain had just ruthlessly crushed an independence movement in its Indian colony, had committed a genocide in Ireland a few years earlier, and was in the middle of waging a colonial war against China by flooding the country with a deadly drug, Mill actually wrote an entire essay glorifying the British Empire.

Although all other nations seem to take advantage of the weak, Mill writes, "Not so this nation." Britain has no "aggressive designs." Its guiding principle is "to let other nations alone." Whenever Britain acts, it "is rather in the service of others than of itself." Indeed, "this nation desires no benefit to itself at the expense of others." This genuine "disinterestedness" and "self-sacrificing behavior," Mill concludes, is "a novelty in the world; so much so it would appear that many are unable to believe it when they see it."[316]

This last point is important. Every empire not only presents itself as a force for good, but it also views itself as being unique in this regard. According to British propaganda, Britain was unique in its altruism, and that set it apart from the French, the Germans, and the other colonial powers who were all selfishly seeking to shore up their power and wealth. Naturally, the French had a similar story, only with them being the good guys, and so did the Germans, the Japanese, and everyone else. Nowadays, the United States claims to be the exceptional nation that moves around the world in the defense of freedom and democracy.

It may thus come as no surprise that a similar propaganda story has been created to shape the emerging U.S.–China Cold War. *The Longer Telegram*, a

---

[315] For several good books on colonial propaganda, see Kaul, C. *Reporting the Raj: The British Press and India, c. 1880-1922*; Stanard, M. G. *Selling the Congo: A History of European Pro-Empire Propaganda and the Making of Belgian Imperialism*; Culver, A. A. *Glorify the Empire: Japanese Avant-Garde Propaganda in Manchuko*; Kushner, B. *The Thought War: Japanese Imperial Propaganda*; Aldrich, R. *Greater France: A History of French Overseas Expansion*
[316] Mill, J. S. *A Few Words on Non-Intervention*

document published in 2021, tries to mimic one of the most important U.S.–Soviet Cold War documents, warns of "the rise of an increasingly authoritarian China." Beijing is planning to "project China's authoritarian system, coercive foreign policy, and military presence... to the world at large." The goal is to destroy the American-led "open and egalitarian order" and to subject the world to "varying forms of dictatorship." The United States, of course, is the only country capable of protecting "individual freedom, fairness, and the rule of law." [317]

Meanwhile, China is sending out the exact same message, only with the roles reversed. Whereas America "seeks might by raising its fists" and is always looking for a fight, China "seeks universal peace." The United States tries to control the entire world through "hard power dominance." China, to the contrary, wants to create "a new world order that prefers peace, development, freedom, and cooperative civilization." "China is a nation that does not invade smaller or weaker nations, and does not threaten neighboring countries," so the Chinese propaganda line goes. [318]

It almost seems like every great power in history acts like a charity organization, but of course, we know that is not the case. Yet if you get all your information from the mainstream media, you will not realize that, since they have a strong tendency to parrot these messages uncritically. But what would happen if you started to question these stories? Does the emerging Cold War narrative of Western democracy vs. Eastern dictatorship hold up against the evidence? Or is this story simply yet another version of the same old propaganda game that the power elite like to play? Let us find out.

The key propaganda point to take away from the Western story on the Cold War with China is that the West believes in democracy, that this makes us the good guys, and that it justifies any action that we might take. It assumes not only that Western foreign policy is guided by democracy promotion, but that people all over the world yearn for democracy, or more specifically, Western-style democracy. This is important, because only then does it become easy to justify Western interference, manipulation of elections, the overthrow of foreign governments, and the invasion of other countries. These actions become morally just and legitimate not only because we are the good guys and everything that we do is good, but also because people in the countries that we are targeting want us to interfere or invade so they too can enjoy the blessings of Western democracy. But is Western foreign policy guided by promoting democracy? And do people around the world look at the West as the savior of democratic government?

---

[317] Anonymous. (2021). *The Longer Telegram.* Atlantic Council
[318] MingFu, L. (2015). *The China Dream.* CN Times Books, Inc.

The first question can be answered scientifically using statistical and mathematical techniques. You can do this by examining if the West prefers supporting democratic governments around the world, and if there is statistical evidence that supports this hypothesis. One fitting example has to do with weapon sales. The idea is quite simple. Dictators rule through intimidation and force. As such, they depend on strong and reliable police forces and militaries. Weapons are key, which means that selling weapons to a dictator means you are strengthening his or her grip on the country and its people. In the process, you are making it harder for a country to develop meaningful democracy. For this reason, looking at weapon sales is relevant to determine whether a country's foreign policy supports democracy or not. So let us explore this in more detail.

The SIPRI arms database has information on all major U.S. weapon sales, and there also exist useful indexes that measure the extent of democracy and dictatorship in countries all around the world. Note that these indexes focus on political participation, elections, and protection of civil liberties. They do not consider whether the government is trying to improve people's socio-economic conditions, such as by reducing poverty, stimulating employment, improving health and education, etc.

Now, when you take this data and put it into a statistical model, you get your answer: Does the United States support political democracy or not? Before looking at the results of the statistical model, let us briefly have a look at some numbers to get a general impression, because they already reveal highly interesting details.[319]

Based on the SIPRI arms database and two different democracy indexes — the Polity Democracy Score and the Democracy Dictatorship index — the United States has sold weapons to dictatorships at least 1,000 times since the year 1950. These are all deliveries of conventional weapons approved by the U.S. government. Of those, 45% went to military dictatorships, 35% to civilian, and 20% to royal dictatorships.

If you look at the major recipients of U.S. weapons, Iran ranks among the top countries. Although today Iran is presented as a major enemy and threat to the West, during the long reign of Mohammad Reza Pahlavi, also known as the Shah, the royal dictatorship of Iran was a U.S. favorite and received enormous amounts of weapons. In fact, after the United States and Britain overthrew Mossadegh in 1953, Washington quickly provided the Shah with 100 M-24 Chaffee light tanks, 100 M-8 Greyhound armored cars, and 140 M-20 armored scout cars. For the newly installed dictator, these vehicles are

---

[319] For the datasets and code of the multilevel analysis (conducted by the author), please see https://github.com/hoend008/Weapon-Sales-and-Democracy

ideal for keeping people and potential rivals under control. In the following decades, the U.S. shipped many hundreds of tanks, artillery pieces, fighter jets, guided bombs, and tens of thousands of missiles and rockets to Iran — an entire army for the pro-Western royal dictator.[320]

Another major recipient is Egypt, which received over $20 billion worth of weapons. Especially the military dictatorship of Hosni Mubarak was showered with weapons right up until 2011, when the Arab Spring movement deposed him. During his reign, Mubarak built his army based on modern U.S. weapons, including F–16 fighter jets armed with Sidewinder missiles and guided bombs, Apache AH-64A combat helicopters, hundreds of M–1A1 Abrams tanks, and many other weapon systems.[321]

Other notable mentions include figures that today are considered anathema: military dictators who ruled South Korea for much of the 1960s and into the 1980s, the Fascist dictator Franco of Spain, Saddam Hussein, Suharto who ruled Indonesia as a military dictator from 1967 to 1998, plus the royal dictatorships in the Middle East.

Several such figures, right after they rose to power, often in a military coup, received large amounts of weapons, perhaps as a gift to signal Washington's approval. Muammar al-Gaddafi of Libya received $224 million worth of arms in his first full year as the country's military dictator. In Chile, after General Augusto Pinochet seized power in a U.S. supported military coup in 1973, received vast amounts of weapons for years in a row until it peaked at $207 million in 1976. Chiang Kai-shek too, after he established his military dictatorship in Taiwan, could count on a steady flow of arms during his 25-year reign.

Washington has not only awarded long lasting military dictatorships but has also provided a steady stream of weapons to royal dictatorships like Jordan, Kuwait, Morocco, Oman and Saudi Arabia, and civilian dictatorships in Malaysia, Singapore, Mexico, and South Africa for decades. Ethiopia, which has experienced royal, military, and civilian dictatorships one after the other, each lasting for many years, received weapons during all these periods. The type of dictatorship matters little it seems, and so do other things.

Apartheid South Africa was also a recipient, and so was Portugal when its military dictatorship used its army to prevent its African colonies from gaining independence. Extreme racism and colonialism did not disrupt the flow of arms.

Dictators who were either outright fascist, like Francisco Franco of Spain, or flirted with fascism like Chiang Kai-shek of Taiwan and Phibun

---

[320] See SIPRI trade register of arms deliveries from the United States to Iran
[321] See SIPRI trade register of arms deliveries from the United States to Egypt

of Thailand, received weapons from the U.S. government, but so did several communist dictators, such as the military dictator Kim Il-sung of North Korea and the civilian dictator Deng Xiaoping of China.

What about democratic governments? Does the United States provide such governments with more weapons than it supplies dictatorships? Based on the available data, there are numerous cases in which this is not the case. Take for example the Philippines. Ferdinand Marcos ruled the island group from 1965 until 1986 as a civilian dictator. Before and after his rule, the Philippines was democratic. Two times as many weapons were provided by Washington to Marcos in his 21-year rule compared to the 38 years of democratic government. This means the dictator received on average four times as many weapons per year as his democratic counterparts.

There are also many other cases in which the type of government — dictatorial or democratic — does not make any difference. Brazil experienced democratic government followed by a series of military dictatorships from 1964 until 1985, and then again democratic governments. Over this entire period, Washington provided weapons at a steady pace.

Pakistan is another such example. The country has experienced cycles of alternating democracy and dictatorships, yet the flow of arms never stopped. Panama, Sri Lanka, Sudan, and Nigeria fit this description too. Peru and Uganda alternated between military dictatorships, civilian dictatorships, and democracy, and all of them got weapons from Washington.

But these are just examples, and while they do give a good indication where things are going, they cannot answer the question in a scientific way. You need a mathematical or statistical model to do that, which is what we will turn to now.

Based on thousands of U.S. weapons transfers all over the world over many decades, the following factors have a strong effect on whether the United States will sell weapons. First, being a NATO country increases the likelihood that a country buys weapons from the United States.

Second, (former) Soviet countries are less likely to get their weapons from the United States. This also makes sense, because they have been strongly integrated with Russia — America's favorite enemy — and that makes them far less likely to be able to buy weapons from Washington.

Third, a country that spends more on its military is also more likely to buy weapons from the United States. One would expect that countries with large military budgets are more likely to buy weapons abroad, and to look for the more sophisticated weaponry, which may bring them to the United States.

And then, finally, does the type of government matter? Is Washington more likely to sell weapons to democratic governments than dictatorships? The answer, according to the statistical model, is a definite no. Whereas all the other variables (NATO membership, former Soviet state, and military spending) are all important (or highly significant in statistical terms), the type of government does not matter. Being a dictatorship does not make a country less likely to receive weapons from the United States.

The above analysis casts serious doubts on Washington's commitment to democracy. It also goes a long way in explaining two other interesting statistics that come from other studies. American think tanks and polling agencies like Gallup Poll are always busy collecting information on what people around the world are thinking. You can use their data to answer the question whether people outside of the United States look to the U.S. as a promoter of democracy. The results are revealing.

A recent poll in 2021 assessed to what extent the United States, Russia or China are viewed by people as a threat to their country's democracy. The data comes from the world's largest study on democracy; 53,194 people from 53 different countries were asked questions about the threats to their country's democracy. Two organizations conducted this study: Lantana, a Berlin based marketing company, and the 'Alliance of Democracies', a non-profit organization founded by former NATO secretary general Anders Fogh Rasmussen. These are Western organizations and have no reason to be favorable to China.[322]

Using this data, you can easily calculate that between Russia, China, and the United States, people around the world, on average, consider Russia to be the least threatening to their country's democracy. China ended up in second place. The clear winner was the United States of America. Most countries consider the U.S. as the biggest threat to their democracy, while only a few prioritize China, and almost none Russia.

Another study, although not directly related to democracy but instead to world peace, is also highly interesting. In a 2013 Win/Gallup poll, over 100,000 people from 66 countries all over the world were asked which country is the greatest threat to world peace. As might be expected, many in the West picked Iran and North Korea. The rest of the world, however, those who are not exposed to endless Western propaganda, considered the United States to be the greatest threat to world peace. Only several countries outside of the West pointed to regional rivals instead of the U.S. (India and Pakistan for example). The fact that Barack Obama, in the middle of his

---

[322] Democracy Perception Index 2021. Alliance of Democracies. See https://www.allianceofdemocracies.org/initiatives/the-copenhagen-democracy-summit/dpi-2021/

presidency at the time, was handed a Nobel peace prize, did not ease the fear in most people around the world.[323]

The Blue Pill or the Red Pill

In the epic sci-fi movie *The Matrix*, Neo, the main character and hero of the story, has to make a choice. Neo's life has just been turned upside down. Everything he believed about the world has been challenged. Still confused, yet hungry for more knowledge, he decides not to go for the blue pill. The blue pill would certainly have been easier and more comfortable. It would have put Neo to sleep and erased his memory of recent events. He would simply wake up the next morning not remembering any of the upsetting information that had been revealed to him the previous days. Life would go on as normal, and all his beliefs about the world would remain intact.

Neo, however, decides to take the red pill. He does not want to turn back to his old beliefs. He chooses to follow a new direction and to learn things about the world that had been kept from him.

What the power elite offers us is the blue pill, a continuation of the same old story about noble intentions to spread democracy, defend freedom and human rights, and uphold the rule of law. In fact, in many foreign policy documents, U.S. government officials and other Western intellectuals are encouraging Western governments to carry out "education campaigns" to teach people in Europe and America that China is evil and that Beijing poses a threat to our Western way of life. They also encourage governments to monitor social media platforms for so-called disinformation — which refers to information that contradicts the pro-Western story. Ideally such information, the experts continue, should be banned to prevent people (especially in the West) from getting exposed to any alternative way of looking at the world.[324]

There are calls to set up centralized government agencies that will monitor and control information. The U.S. Information Agency that was disbanded in 1999, after the U.S.–Soviet Cold War nominally ended, may indeed make a comeback if it has not already done so. Children should again be taught in school who the enemy is and who the good guys are. Instilling such beliefs from a young age is an effective means of making sure that future

---

[323] Win/Gallup International Global End of Year survey, 2013, https://web.archive.org/web/20170516104629/http://www.wingia.com/web/files/services/33/file/33.pdf?1464661002; For the map see https://brilliantmaps.com/threat-to-peace/ and the creator, Joe Hammer, who has the Joe Hammer YouTube channel where you can find many interesting maps, each of them telling a different story.
[324] Paul, C. et al. (2021). *A Guide to Extreme Competition with China*. RAND Corporation.

generations will obediently and enthusiastically rally behind their country's flag and cheer for whatever steps their leaders take to uphold Western global dominance and to contain and combat China, whether it is in Taiwan, the South China Sea, or anywhere else in the world.[325]

At the same time, the Chinese government looks at this, learns, and copies the same techniques. China too is building up its media systems and seeks to increase its reach to countries around the world. If a U.S.–China Cold War takes hold, the information war will be intense. Western power elites, and the media systems they own and control, will work overtime to present us with one message, a single point of view, one truth. Meanwhile, contradictory information and voices will be condemned, maybe even punished and outlawed. As difficult as it is already to inform people on what is really happening, and to inspire people to stand up to their leaders to stop them from pushing us into another war, hot or cold, it will be many times more difficult once the information war has gone into full swing. If there ever is a time to try and make your voice heard, it is now.

---

[325] Paul, C. et al. (2021). *A Guide to Extreme Competition with China*. RAND Corporation.

CHAPTER 6: WASHINGTON'S ENDGAME

There are people who accuse Washington of not having an endgame. According to these critics, the strategy that U.S. administrations use to counter or combat China lacks a clearly defined objective. When exactly do U.S. officials declare victory? What does victory even look like? These are valid questions. The critics, however, are wrong. When you listen carefully to what U.S. politicians are saying, it becomes clear that there is in fact a well-defined objective. Indeed, Washington knows exactly what it wants to achieve. The problem is that its endgame is a fantasy. And unfortunately, this makes it extremely dangerous.

What does Washington hope to achieve? As we have seen in the previous chapters, U.S. officials are making extensive plans to counter, undermine, and wage war against China. They are spending enormous resources in the process. There are numerous strategies, ranging from containment and military buildups to blockades, sanctions, color revolutions, and information warfare. But at what point does Washington declare victory?

You can get an idea of what Washington's endgame is by listening to what leading U.S. foreign policy officials are saying. Take, for example, the U.S. Secretary of State Anthony Blinken. On May 26, 2022, at the George Washington University, Blinken laid out the U.S. foreign policy approach towards the People's Republic of China. In his speech, Blinken makes two interesting statements that define the U.S. endgame.[326]

First, the Secretary of State makes the point that Washington is not seeking war. "We are not looking for conflict or a new Cold War. To the

---

[326] Anthony J. Blinken. The Administration's Approach to the People's Republic of China. Washington, D.C. May 26, 2022. See https://www.state.gov/the-administrations-approach-to-the-peoples-republic-of-china/

contrary, we're determined to avoid both." Blinken then goes on to say the following: "We don't seek to block China from its role as a major power, nor to stop China — or any other country, for that matter — from growing their economy or advancing the interests of their people." So, the United States does not want war, and has no issue in China becoming stronger. But then, what does Washington want?

Blinken lays out Washington's objective. It is, unsurprisingly, shrouded in propaganda, but when you strip away all the fancy phrases, you do end up with something very real. In fact, Blinken talked about "the rules-based international order — the system of laws, agreements, principles, and institutions that the world came together to build after two world wars to manage relations between states, to prevent conflict, to uphold the rights of all people." The United States, the U.S. Secretary of State continued, has led this system after World War II and by doing so has brought freedom, security, and progress to people all around the world. But now, Blinken concludes, this system is under threat.

According to him, "the foundations of the international order are under serious and sustained challenge." This challenge comes from China. "China is the only country with both the intent to reshape the international order and, increasingly, the economic, diplomatic, military, and technological power to do it." "Beijing's vision would move us away from the universal values that have sustained so much of the world's progress over the past 75 years."

Blinken then makes an important statement on what this means in practice. The United States "cannot rely on Beijing to change its trajectory. So we will shape the strategic environment around Beijing to advance our vision for an open, inclusive international system."

Now, with this much propaganda, it is likely that the real U.S. objective may still elude you. In fact, hidden behind such wonderful words lies a simple but ruthless geopolitical agenda. Interestingly, Biden's National Security Strategy makes this abundantly clear.

In this important document, which was released on October 12, 2022, President Biden and Vice President Harris state that the United States is "in the midst of a strategic competition to shape the future of the international order." Biden and Harris identify the same threat as Blinken. "The People's Republic of China harbors the intention and, increasingly, the capacity to reshape the international order in favor of one that tilts the global playing field to its benefit." China, they continue, feels that the current international order stifles their ambitions, and therefore Beijing is intent to reshape or remake it and "to become the world's leading power."[327]

[327] The White House. National Security Strategy, October 2022

184

In other words, and now we are going to leave all the propaganda out, there exists a world order. Washington calls it the "rules-based international order" to make it sound benign, even good. In reality, however, it means a U.S.-dominated world system created and led from Washington. It is a system that gives the United States an advantage over everyone else. Countries are encouraged to integrate themselves into this system. They are even allowed to develop their economies and grow — but only if they do not challenge U.S. supremacy. Beijing, however, not only has realized that this system is designed to benefit primarily the United States of America, but China has also become so strong that it is increasingly able to challenge this U.S.-dominated world system. And that brings us to what Washington really wants.

U.S. politicians know they cannot defeat and occupy China militarily, like they did for example in Iraq. Once upon a time during the Century of Humiliation, this may have been possible, but today, it is simply beyond U.S. capabilities. Washington even states that it prefers to avoid war. But, and this is the key point, there is one thing that the U.S. does want from China. What the United States wants, what the endgame really is, is for China to return to the 1980s and 1990s. During those years, China was too weak to seriously challenge the United States. China was a place of cheap labor and vast markets for U.S. businesses to make money. And, most importantly, Beijing accepted its subordinate place within a U.S.-dominated world system. Washington wants to have China return to that position once again. If Beijing does so, it is a "responsible power." But if the Chinese do not accept a subordinate position — as Blinken expects they will not — U.S. foreign policy is designed to force them to accept it. The containment, the barrage of sanctions, the ways to counter the Belt and Road Initiative, and everything else is supposed to achieve that objective.

Nothing, however, seems to indicate that it will work. In fact, this kind of endgame is a fantasy, one that U.S. politicians, who are so used to being the world's dominant superpower, cling on to. In their minds, for the United States to be reduced to the number two position is utterly unacceptable, and they will do anything to prevent that from happening. As such, U.S. leaders may say they do not want war, and they may even mean it, but at the same time they have set a condition that will never be met, except through military conflict (if then). Indeed, Washington's endgame makes war a highly likely outcome.

Interestingly, the notion of keeping countries in their subordinate position within a U.S.-dominated world system is the single most important U.S. foreign policy goal ever since this world order was created. During this whole period, it has always been about ensuring that countries and governments obey Washington and do not act too independently.

In the next section, we will look at this history. Then, Beijing's 'disobedience' will be described in detail, which refers to a range of Chinese policies that in Washington's eyes undermine U.S. dominance. This includes initiatives like the Belt and Road, BRICS, independent Chinese diplomacy, and many more.

The chapter, and this book, will then conclude by laying out the dangerous attitude that has taken hold in Washington in response to Beijing's challenge. It has resulted in a two-faced nature of U.S. foreign policy and diplomacy. This then has led to a severe lack of trust among the Chinese. Finally, a way to prevent a new Cold War is presented. But first, let us explore how Washington likes to deal with disobedient governments.

A History of Disobedience

Inside the luxurious Waldorf Astoria hotel in New York, an anonymous CIA agent passed a box of cigars to New York City's chief inspector Michael J. Murphy. This is the device, he explained. You only need to put it near the target. It is really not a difficult job, the CIA agent continued, and you will be doing your country a great service. Washington wants this communist killed, and you can make that happen.

It seemed like the perfect plan. The new Cuban leader loved his cigars. It is one of the trademarks of his country. And now, with Fidel Castro visiting New York in the flesh, it handed the U.S. government the perfect opportunity. Of course, these were not ordinary cigars. The Agency carefully designed them. Anyone who lit one of these bad boys was in for a nasty surprise.

The CIA agents involved in the operation could already imagine the result. While on an official visit to the United Nations in New York to speak in front of the General Assembly, Castro would sit down to relax in the hotel lounge. While enjoying a moment of peace and quiet, he would open the box, put one of the cigars in his mouth, and light it. Then, to the horror of the other guests in the lounge but to the CIA's satisfaction, Castro's head would be blown right off in a sudden explosion. At the footsteps of the United Nations and in a fountain of blood, pieces of this foreign leader's skull and brain tissue would be splattered all over the hotel's lounge floor — a fitting testament to Washington's commitment to the rules-based international order.[328]

---

[328] Maier, T. (2019). *Mafia Spies.* Skyhorse Publishing. See p. 40 eBook.

Unfortunately for the CIA, the New York chief inspector — a man who took the rule of law seriously — was appalled by the idea and flatly refused. History would have played out differently if he had not. It was 1960, only one year after Fidel Castro had overthrown Fulgencio Batista, the U.S. supported dictator of Cuba. For this act of disobedience, Washington already wanted him dead.

Although the United Nations assassination attempt had not gotten off the ground, the U.S. government was not about to give up. While upholding its so-called international order with its left hand, Washington's right hand delved deep into the American underworld until it reached America's most notorious criminals. Perhaps they would accept what the New York police officer had not. Washington shook hands with Sam Giancana, boss of Chicago's Mafia organization and arguably the most powerful criminal in the world at that time, and his long-time friend and fellow mobster Johnny Roselli. Together these two ruled the largest Mafia empire in American criminal history. With vast experience in violence and assassinations, they seemed perfect for the job.[329]

Sam Giancana started his criminal career as a driver for "Machine gun Jack" McGurn, a notorious criminal and associate of the legendary Al Capone. Because U.S. army doctors had rejected Sam from the draft to serve in World War II after they diagnosed him as a "constitutional psychopath," he spent his time in the 1940s to climb, or butcher, his way to the top. Being prone to extreme violence and with a hair-trigger temper, he earned himself the nickname "Mooney" — meaning crazy — which Sam came to like because it intimidated others. Finally, in 1956, Sam reached his goal and became the boss of the Chicago Mafia organization.[330]

Over a thousand henchmen worked for Sam Giancana's billion-dollar crime empire. They earned their fortunes through bribes, threats, killings, robberies, extortions, drugs, prostitution, and casinos.

Sam's most trusted partner in crime was Johnny Roselli, a handsome smooth-talking fixer. Always dressed in the finest clothes, typically accompanied by a young and beautiful woman at his arm or on his lap, there was no problem he could not solve. Roselli, although that was not his real name, was contacted first by the CIA in 1960. Being a man with as many secrets and identities as the Agency itself, perhaps this was only fitting.

Roselli liked the idea of "whacking" Castro, and so did Sam after Roselli informed him the U.S. government wanted Fidel dead. The Mafia had a score to settle with the Cuban leader after Castro had closed all the casinos in

---

[329] Maier, T. (2019). *Mafia Spies*. Skyhorse Publishing.
[330] Maier, T. (2019). *Mafia Spies*. Skyhorse Publishing. See chapter 6.

Cuba and kicked out the Mafia. "I can't wait to kill the xxx," Sam had said about Castro. And now none other than the CIA offered them a chance.[331]

During a meeting in the iconic luxury Fontainebleau Hotel at Miami Beach, the CIA's representative explained to the two mobsters that the Agency liked a bloody assassination, preferably in public. Maybe Castro could be gunned down in a classic Hollywood style drive by shooting. Sam, however, disagreed. No assassin in his right mind would agree to this kind of suicide mission. Besides, killing was an art, and there were cleaner alternatives. A poisonous pill would be better, Sam and Roselli explained. It would make it seem like Castro died of natural causes, thereby preventing a witch hunt to find the perpetrator. And because the Mafia had many connections to the anti-Castro opposition within Cuba, the CIA would only have to hand them the pills and Sam and Roselli would arrange Castro's death.

The Agency quickly agreed. The method did not matter to them, as long as Castro ended up dead. The design of the poison pill was put in the hands of Dr. Gottlieb, the CIA's top expert, a man who took it as a hobby to invent new methods to assassinate America's enemies. Six months and a lot of dead monkeys later, the pills were ready. It was March 1961, and with a little bit of luck, Fidel Castro would be dead within weeks. Unfortunately for Washington, it was not meant to be.

During the following years the CIA, in close cooperation with the Mafia, would try everything to kill the Cuban leader. Poison pills, bazooka teams, and rifle squads were thrown into the mix to get the job done. President Lyndon Johnson later commented that under John F. Kennedy the CIA was "operating a damned Murder Inc. in the Caribbean." Nothing, however, worked. A combination of great counterintelligence and a good dose of luck enabled Castro to survive. Even the world's largest international terrorist operation to date — Operation Mongoose — launched by the CIA against Cuba from Florida with the blessings of the Kennedys, failed. And so did the barrage of economic sanctions in its attempt to cause the overthrow of the Cuban government. All of this begs the question: Why did Washington want to get rid of Castro? What did this man do to become America's number one enemy?[332]

The answer is surprisingly simple. Under the pro-U.S. dictator Batista, Cuba had done everything the United States government wanted. Castro, however, was different. He followed his own economic policies, however misguided they may have been. Castro also pursued his own foreign policy

---

[331] Maier, T. (2019). *Mafia Spies.* Skyhorse Publishing. See p. 87 eBook.

[332] Maier, T. (2019). *Mafia Spies.* Skyhorse Publishing; See also Rabe, S. G. (2012). *The Killing Zone.* Oxford University Press, chapter 4.

and chose his own allies, even if these contradicted Washington's plans for Cuba, the Caribbean, and Latin America as a whole. By doing so, in the words of U.S. officials, Fidel Castro was "successfully defying the United States" — an extremely dangerous crime to commit, indeed. [333]

Washington also realized that this could inspire other nations in the region — the so-called Domino effect. U.S. officials feared "the spread of the Castro idea of taking matters into one's own hands." As every Mafia boss immediately understands, this kind of disobedience has to be punished. You cannot allow people to think they can do whatever they want. If you tolerate one case of independence and disobedience — also when it is just a small island nation — it can inspire others to do the same. And when that happens, before you know it, the whole U.S. dominated world order may unravel. As such, you must kill these things in their infancy. Indeed, Castro had to die. [334]

The case of Cuba is a prime example of what U.S. officials call "independent nationalism." It refers to countries, governments, and their people pursuing their own economic, political, and social policies. Typically, the main aim of independent nationalism, as stated by the U.S. State Department, is that "the main beneficiaries of the development of a country's resources should be the people of that country." Now, if you remember the Grand Area as discussed in chapter 1, you quickly realize this is a problem.

The Grand Area was the world order that the United States created following World War II. Countries all over the world were given a function. For Latin America, including Cuba, this meant being a source of raw materials, markets, and profits for U.S. businesses. As such, the first beneficiary of the resources of these regions was supposed to be the United States. Therefore, independent nationalism, sometimes also referred to as economic nationalism, was an obstacle that Washington needed to overcome. As such, already in 1945, the U.S. government declared the "New Economic Charter of the Americas." In the charter, the stated U.S. goal was the "elimination of economic nationalism in all its forms." In other words, people like Castro who act independently from U.S. designs, must be eliminated in order for the Grand Area to survive and flourish. [335]

This threat of independent nationalism is why the United States has been so active in its foreign policy all over the world. It included the overthrow

---

[333] Chomsky, N. (2000). Cuba and U.S. Government. Excerpted from Rogue States. See https://chomsky.info/roguestates03/; see also Rabe, S. G. (2012). The Killing Zone. Oxford University Press, chapter 4.

[334] Chomsky, N. (2000). Cuba and U.S. Government. Excerpted from Rogue States. See https://chomsky.info/roguestates03/; see also Rabe, S. G. (2012). The Killing Zone. Oxford University Press, chapter 4.

[335] Economic Charter of the Americas. February 26, 1945. See http://www.ibiblio.org/pha/policy/1945/450226a.html; Chomsky, N. (2015). Year 501. Pluto Press. See p. 47.

of governments in Guatemala (1954), Brazil (1964), and Chile (1973); the invasion of Cuba (1961) and the Dominican Republic (1965); and savage wars in Guatemala, El Salvador, and Nicaragua, among others. All these countries, at one point in time, had governments that were too independent, and as such, they had to go.

The threat of independent nationalism also brought the United States to the Middle East. It was nationalism, not communism, that "was always a greater danger in the Arab world," according to George McGhee, one of the key architects of U.S. Middle East policy. Consequently, Washington intervened in Iran (1953), Jordan (1956–57), Syria (1957), Lebanon (1958), and several other places.[336]

Asia too, did not escape, as the Indochina wars highlight the threat of too much independence once again. Indeed, if you need to boil down U.S. foreign policy to one thing, one goal, one endgame, then this is it. And as we will see, today nothing has changed.

Before discussing the case of China and its greatest sin of being too independent, it is useful to briefly look at three other recent cases that illustrate that Washington is still driven by the same obsession. Ask yourself the question: who has Washington consistently designated as being so-called 'rogue nations' in the past few decades? The answer is Venezuela, Iran, and North Korea. And what have these countries all in common? They all have successfully defied the United States.

In the case of Venezuela, the election of Hugo Chavez in 1998 marked the beginning of troubled U.S.–Venezuela relations. Chavez's biggest crime was that he and his country served as a model of independence. He strongly opposed Washington's Neoliberal agenda while presenting an alternative which he called 21st century socialism. Chavez countered Washington's plans to integrate the America's within the context of U.S. hegemony (FTAA), and instead he pushed for the integrating of Latin America without the United States (e.g., ALBA). He also condemned the U.S. invasions of Afghanistan and Iraq. No wonder Washington tried to overthrow the Venezuelan government in a violent coup in 2002, followed by economic warfare, a Color Revolution starting in 2019, and again much more economic warfare. Iran and North Korea too, for opposing U.S. foreign policy, have suffered endless economic warfare, military threats, and, in the case of Iran, the occasional military attack, the latest of which took out Qasem Soleimani,

---

[336] See for example La Feber, W. (1993). *Inevitable Revolutions.* W. W. Norton & Company; Rabe, S. G. (2012). *The Killing Zone.* Oxford University Press; Yaqub, S. (2004). *Containing Arab Nationalism.* The University of North Carolina Press.

a popular figure and the second most powerful man in the country, in a U.S. drone attack in January 2020.[337]

Naturally, Washington has presented its opposition to Venezuela, Iran, and North Korea in terms of democracy and human rights concerns, but it is not difficult to see through this propaganda. As discussed in the previous chapter, Washington supports dictatorships all around the world, and in Venezuela's case, during Chavez's presidency the country has ranked among the top of Latin American countries in people's satisfaction with democracy — a fact conveniently ignored by the West. No, it is too much independence that makes you a target, and China has now been added to that list. In fact, it may even top that list, as we will see in the next section.[338]

China's Sins

History was made in Beijing on March 10, 2023. It was a special moment for China, for Saudi Arabia and Iran, and for the world. It was not, however, a good day for Washington. Four days earlier on March 6, representatives from Saudi Arabia and Iran had started discussions in the hopes to normalize relations. Their countries had been at odds with each other for far too long. Both sides trusted Xi Jinping and allowed him to mediate the negotiations. In the historical agreement, U.S. officials were nowhere to be found.

"It was not supposed to be this way," reported Foreign Affairs, the leading Western foreign policy magazine. Washington's goal in the Middle East was to contain Iran, and Biden had just pressured Saudi Arabia and other Gulf States to help him do just that. The United States wanted, even needed, Saudi Arabia and Iran to be rivals and enemies. Only then could Washington use one against the other. The two countries, however, were intent on making peace. Consequently, they decided to ignore the West, which stood in their way, and shift their attention East, until an agreement to normalize relations was signed in Beijing. Next, Iran, Saudi Arabia, and other Arab states may even begin discussions on a new regional security framework, with China in an ideal position to help mediate, and influence, all of these steps, Foreign Affairs concludes.[339]

Just a few years ago, something like this would have been utterly unthinkable. The United States has been the dominant power in the Middle East for decades. Governments in the region needed Washington's blessings before

---

[337] On Venezuela and Chavez, see Hugo Chavez and the Bolivarian Revolution

[338] See reports by the Chilean polling agency Latino Barometro: http://www.latinobarometro.org/latContents.jsp

[339] Maria Fantappie & Vali Nasr. A New Order in the Middle East? *Foreign Affairs.* March 22, 2023. See https://www.foreignaffairs.com/china/iran-saudi-arabia-middle-east-relations

they could make big decisions like this one. Normalizing relations, a new Middle East security framework — these decisions used to be made with U.S. officials actively involved, perhaps even in the lead. But no more. As a result of China's rise, countries all around the world have a choice. They can ask the United States for support, or they can turn to China. If one will not help, then the other might be willing. In this case, Beijing got a big diplomatic win that caught headlines everywhere.

For Washington, it meant a big setback in its foreign policy in a region it used to dominate. The China-brokered Iran-Saudi Arabia deal is yet another crack in the U.S. dominated world order. In fact, China, through its actions, has been chipping away steadily, and each time it does so, U.S. officials grow angrier and more frustrated. Indeed, China, like Cuba and other so-called rogue nations, is successfully defying the United States. And the list of examples is already growing very long.

Another example of successful defiance is the Shanghai Cooperation Organization (SCO). The SCO was founded in 2001 and includes a range of Central Asian states. From its inception, security cooperation has been its focus point. For China and Russia, one of the major goals was to prevent U.S. and NATO encroachment into Central Asia. Remember, in the late 1990s and early 2000s, NATO was beginning to expand, and the United States and Europe were instigating Color Revolutions throughout the former Soviet states. In other words, Beijing's foreign policy through the SCO was designed to counter Washington's. This is also exactly how U.S. officials interpreted it. In a U.S. Army War College study, the authors write that China can use the SCO to "counter U.S. and Western activity in Central Asia." They refer to the SCO as "a coalition of anti-U.S. sentiment" and recommend that Washington should seek to "exploit" some of the mistrust that SCO members have towards each other to weaken and perhaps even break up the organization. In other words, U.S. officials are not happy with this development, and see it as a threat to their dominance.[340]

Over time, the SCO shifted its focus also towards a full range of other issues, including political and economic cooperation, cultural exchange, energy and scientific partnerships, and immigration. Beijing also started using

---

[340] Marochkin, S. & Bezborodov. Y. (2022). The Shanghai Cooperation Organization. Routledge. See p. 46, 229; Henry Plater-Zyberk and Andrew Monaghan, Strategic Implications of the Evolving Shanghai Cooperation Organization (US Army War College Press, 2014), https://press.armywarcollege.edu/monographs/486. See p. v, x, 33.

the SCO as a vehicle to promote another project that defies Washington, namely the Belt and Road Initiative.[341]

Contrary to the SCO, the Belt and Road Initiative (BRI) stretches out all over the globe. Most countries in Southeast Asia, Central Asia, the Middle East, and Africa have signed up. More shockingly, even most countries in Eastern Europe are part of the BRI. And most humiliating from a U.S. point of view, in more recent years some Latin American countries have also joined — in blatant defiance of Washington's "Monroe Doctrine." Beijing, through the BRI, has now moved into what America arrogantly calls its own "backyard."[342]

Interestingly, besides offering countries around the world a non-Western source of finance and infrastructure development, which already undermines several pillars of Washington's international order, China also uses the BRI to spread its economic model. No longer has the West a monopoly on ideas about economic development. For decades, Western politicians and their institutions have pushed, sometimes forced, countries in the world to adopt neoliberal economic policies. The "Washington's Consensus," as it is often called, told countries how they should run their economies, supposedly for their own benefit, but very often the first beneficiaries were Western corporations and investors. China's rise, however, has enabled Beijing to spread another economic development model, one that contradicts and thus undermines the Washington Consensus — yet another example of how China is successfully defying the United States.[343]

Another and particularly important addition to the list is BRICS. Each of the letters of this acronym stand for a major economy in the non-Western world, namely Brazil, Russia, India, China, and South Africa. Together, the BRICS focuses on trade, finance, economic development, and political and security matters. In Western circles, BRICS is often presented as the counterpart to the G7. In this way, BRICS groups together major non-Western economies, the biggest one being China, and the G7 includes the Western economies, the biggest one being the United States. What this means is that China has helped create a parallel system of states that exists next to the Western one. To Beijing, this is important, because BRICS enables Beijing to socialize with other countries to offset a hostile United States and its

[341] Marochkin, S. & Bezborodov. Y. (2022). *The Shanghai Cooperation Organization*. Routledge. See p. 3, 229-230

[342] For an overview of BRI countries see David Sacks. Countries in China's Belt and Road Initiative: Who's In And Who's Out. March 23, 2021. https://www.cfr.org/blog/countries-chinas-belt-and-road-initiative-whos-and-whos-out

[343] For an introduction into neoliberalism, see Harvey, D. (2007). *A Brief History of Neoliberalism*. Oxford University Press.

Western partners that are trying to contain China. But BRICS does not stop there.[344]

For years, non-Western countries have expressed their dissatisfaction with the international financial institutions, especially the World Bank and the International Monetary Fund (IMF). Both are dominated by Western countries. Not only do they have their headquarters in Washington, and not only do they always have a U.S. and European president, but the way power is distributed within these institutions among their member states is tilted in favor of the Western powers. The most famous example is that of the IMF. As it turns out, a big decision can only be made within the IMF when at least 85% of the votes are in favor. And the United States alone holds 16.5% of the vote. This means that when Washington says 'no', it does not happen. Washington is the only member who has this kind of veto-power. China, the 2nd biggest economy, has only 6% of the votes within the IMF voting system. The BRICS countries together hold 14.15%, which is still less than the United States and not enough for a veto. Note that the BRICS countries together have a higher GDP than the United States, and almost 10 times the population (330 million vs. over 3.2 billion). Yet the U.S. holds more voting power within the IMF. As a result of the lopsided pro-Western nature of these institutions together with Washington's unwillingness to reform them in a meaningful way, China, together with its BRICS partners, have set out to create an alternative system.[345]

In 2014, the BRICS countries announced the creation of the New Development Bank, which was officially opened in Shanghai the next year. They also created the Contingent Reserve Arrangement. These can develop into powerful alternatives to the Western-dominated international financial institutions, and as a result, take away Washington's monopoly. BRICS thus weakens the U.S. dominated international order in several ways, which obviously does not sit well with U.S. officials. It is yet another example of successful defiance.[346]

Note that China has also helped set up other international financial institutions that serve as an alternative to Western dominance. The Asian Infrastructure Investment Bank (AIIB) is one example, and with 26% of the vote, China holds veto power over important decisions — a move that mirrors

[344] Kumar, R. et al. (2023). *Locating BRICS in the Global Order*. Routledge. See p. 4. and chapter 13-14.

[345] Kumar, R. et al. (2023). *Locating BRICS in the Global Order*. Routledge. See p. 1. For IMF voting quotas, see the website, accessed 18-05-2022. https://www.imf.org/en/About/executive-board/members-quotas; See World Bank GDP statistics, accessed 18-05-2023. https://data.worldbank.org/indicator/NY.GDP.MKTP.CD; See World Bank population statistics, accessed 18-05-2023. https://data.worldbank.org/indicator/SP.POP.TOTL

[346] Kumar, R. et al. (2023). *Locating BRICS in the Global Order*. Routledge. See chapter 2-3.

Washington's IMF designs. The AIIB is a direct competitor of the U.S. and Japan-dominated Asian Development Bank and is also seen as a rival of the World Bank and IMF. In other words, more successful defiance.[347]

And the lists go on. For example, China is slowly but steadily positioning its own currency as an alternative to the dollar. Beijing is increasing its footprint in regions all over the world. They are creating alternative institutions, building foreign military bases, are catching up technologically, economically, and militarily with the United States, and so forth and so on. Indeed, the Chinese government is busy creating its own version of the Grand Area, or the rules-based international order as Western leaders like to call it. It is the ultimate challenge to Washington's global dominance, and as such, has driven U.S. officials to dangerous levels of anger, frustration, and recklessness, as we will see in the next section.

Washington's Anger

The Grand Area is shrinking. The era of the unipolar world, with America as its lonely superpower, is ending. On all fronts, whether it is diplomatic, economic, financial, or military, Washington's power and influence are in decline relative to the rising power of the People's Republic of China. This has made U.S. officials terribly angry, similarly to a spoiled child who no longer gets everything his way. But there is something else happening. A strange and reckless mindset has taken hold in U.S. foreign policy and military circles. One that could doom us all.

On April 18, 2023, the U.S. Senate Armed Service Committee held a full hearing on how to deal with a rising China. Three distinguished guests joined them. From behind a long table facing the senators sat Mr. Jedidiah P. Royal, the Principal Deputy Assistant Secretary of Defense for Indo-Pacific Security Affairs of the Department of Defense; Admiral John C. Aquilino, the Commander of the U.S. Indo-Pacific Command; and General Paul J. LaCamera, the Commander of U.S. Forces Korea. In a grueling three-hour session, they delved deep into the strategy to counter a rising China. It is a fascinating hearing, not only for what was said, but especially for what was not.[348]

---

[347] See the websites of the institutions for a layout of their voting share, for the AIIB this is https://www.aiib.org/en/about-aiib/governance/members-of-bank/index.html and for the ADB this is https://www.adb.org/work-with-us/investors/credit-fundamentals

[348] Full Committee Hearing: U.S. Military Posture and National Security Challenges in the Indo-Pacific Region. April 18, 2023. See https://armedservices.house.gov/hearings/full-committee-hearing-us-military-posture-and-national-security-challenges-indo-pacific

During those three hours, Admiral John Aquilino, technically the commander of all U.S. forces aimed against China, stressed repeatedly that he does not want to start a war. In fact, all his actions are aimed to prevent one. According to the Admiral, he is simply defending the rules-based international order. And he is defending it right at China's borders in and around South Korea, Japan, the Philippines, Malaysia, Thailand, Australia, Guam, and anywhere else in the Indo–Pacific. As such, the many hundreds of military bases surrounding China in a "noose," are all just purely defensive. And so is sending military advisors to Taiwan, selling billions of dollars worth of weapons to U.S. clients in the region that includes nuclear-powered attack submarines to Australia, and conducting frequent military exercises to practice cutting off China's economic lifelines. This then brings us to what was not being said.

In all the statements from the Admiral, the General, the Defense Department representative, and the Senators, with just one exception, nobody showed any concern for how Chinese leaders perceive this military buildup all along their borders. It is stunning to see this attitude or mindset that has taken hold among U.S. officials. They simply do not care.

They not only feel that the United States owns the world, but they feel that they have the right to own it. Consequently, every challenge to U.S. dominance is perceived as an act of aggression that needs to be combatted, even if it is many thousands of miles away from U.S. territory. U.S. officials are simply going to do whatever they want, and Beijing must accept it. Why? Because we are the good guys, and they are bad. And in case Chinese leaders do not play along, then, as the Admiral repeatedly stated, his forces are ready to fight.

The result is that Washington has set itself on a dangerous and confrontational course vis-a-vis China. And it has had its effect on Chinese leaders. They see the vast resources that Washington is investing in undermining China's development. They see the hundreds of military bases all around them. They know about the weapons and military hardware Washington has brought to bear against them. And they listen to what U.S. officials say. Would you expect them to believe all this talk that comes out of the Pentagon, the State Department, and the White House about trying to prevent war and maintain peace? No, Beijing seems fed up with this two-faced nature of American diplomacy and military posture.

Beijing's Mistrust

In November 2022, President Joe Biden and President Xi Jinping met in Bali, Indonesia, during the G20 summit. They shook hands like old friends and smiled in front of the cameras. Then they started serious discussions on U.S.–China relations, and trouble quickly arose.

The key point to take away from their meeting was the same one that Xi made in an earlier phone call with Biden in July of 2022. That time, however, Xi had chosen his words very tactfully. Now, during the G20 meeting, the Chinese President was no longer that subtle. In fact, he dropped a diplomatic bombshell. "We hope that the U.S. side will match its words with action," Xi stated, reflecting the lack of trust that dominates in Beijing. And then, in response to Biden's pledge to not provoke a conflict over Taiwan, Xi said "We hope that the U.S. side will act on this assurance to real effect." In other words, Xi twice told Biden to his face that he does not trust him. In fact, Xi pointed out a nasty habit that U.S. officials have of saying one thing and then doing the opposite. And Chinese leaders have had about as much of this as they could take.[349]

Now, how did Biden respond to this? Well, very much as you would expect. During the G20 meeting with Xi, Biden repeated the usual words and phrases. The United States does not seek conflict with China. Biden's government does not seek a new Cold War, nor does it want to contain China. The U.S. also has no intention of trying to halt China's economic development. Instead, they want peace and stability in the Taiwan Strait, and good relations with China in general. It sounds wonderful, but as Xi points out, these promises must be matched with actions. The answer came quickly enough.

After Biden's meeting with Xi ended and the G20 came to a close, the U.S. President and his team returned to Washington. Two months later in January 2023, Biden announced that he decided to block the sales of all computer chips, including the less advanced ones, to the Chinese tech

---

[349] For China's transcript of the G20 Xi-Biden meeting, see President Xi Jinping Meets with U.S. President Joe Biden in Bali. Ministry of Foreign Affairs of the People's Republic of China. November 14, 2022. See https://www.fmprc.gov.cn/mfa_eng/zxxx_662805/202211/t20221114_10974686.html; For the White House's transcript, see Readout of President Joe Biden's Meeting with President Xi Jinping of the People's Republic of China. The White House Briefing Room. November 14, 2022. See https://www.whitehouse.gov/briefing-room/statements-releases/2022/11/14/readout-of-president-joe-bidens-meeting-with-president-xi-jinping-of-the-peoples-republic-of-china/; For the earlier phone call between Biden and Xi, see President Xi Jinping Speaks with US President Joe Biden on the Phone. Ministry of Foreign Affairs of the People's Republic of China, July 29, 2022. See https://www.fmprc.gov.cn/eng/zxxx_662805/202207/t20220729_10729593.html

giant Huawei to bankrupt China's most prestigious company. That same month Biden also successfully pressured the Netherlands and Japan to stop selling chip-manufacturing tools to China to halt Chinese technological and economic development.[350]

A few weeks later, in late February 2023, the White House announced it was sending 100–200 military advisors to Taiwan to train its military. In March, Washington approved $619 million of weapons sales to the island. Next, in April, the U.S. Defense Department announced it had acquired four new military bases in the Philippines. And the list goes on.[351]

No wonder Xi and the rest of the Chinese leadership have little to no trust in Joe Biden, his team, and Washington in general. And this is not only expressed at the highest levels in president-to-president meetings, but you also see it everywhere in the Chinese media and in government circles.

Following the Xi–Biden summit, for example, Chinese Foreign Minister Wang Yi said to the U.S. Secretary of State Anthony Blinken, as reported by Xinhua News Agency, that "the United States should not engage in dialogue and containment at the same time, neither should it talk cooperation but stab China simultaneously.... This is not reasonable competition, but irrational suppression. It is not meant to properly manage disputes, but to intensify conflicts."[352]

Chinese foreign policy specialists working within think tanks and universities have come to this same conclusion. Referring to U.S. actions towards Taiwan, a Chinese scholar states that "It is as if the United States removed the Buddha statues from the temple, leaving only an empty structure, and then claimed that the temple was still there." In other words, as long as say they do not want war, do U.S. officials really believe they can do whatever they want, hollow out all the important U.S.–China agreements

---

[350] Freifeld, K., Alper, A. & Nellis, S. U.S. stops granting export licenses for China's Huawei - sources, Reuters, January 31, 2023. https://www.reuters.com/technology/us-stops-provision-licences-export-chinas-huawei-ft-2023-01-30; Sevastopulo, D. & Fleming, S. Netherlands and Japan join US in restricting chip exports to China, Financial Times, January 28, 2023. https://www.ft.com/content/baa27f42-0557-4377-839b-a4f4524cfa20

[351] Nancy A. Youssef & Gordon Lubold. U.S. to Expand Troop Presence in Taiwan for Training Against China Threat. The Wall Street Journal. February 23, 2023. See https://www.wsj.com/articles/u-s-to-expand-troop-presence-in-taiwan-for-training-against-china-threat-62198a83; Ben Blanchard. Taiwan military to get $619 million U.S. arms boost as China keeps up pressure. Reuters, March 2, 2023. See https://www.reuters.com/world/asia-pacific/taiwan-reports-21-chinese-air-force-planes-entered-its-air-defence-zone-2023-03-02/; David Vergun. New EDCA Sites Named in the Philippines. DOD News. See https://www.defense.gov/News/News-Stories/Article/Article/3350297/new-edca-sites-named-in-the-philippines/

[352] Xinhua. Chinese FM holds phone talks with U.S. secretary of state on bilateral ties. December 23, 2022. see https://english.news.cn/20221223/6840ecfd6f65452b9a57b586074f60f8/c.html

and promises to the point that they are completely meaningless, and expect to be held innocent when war does break out?[353]

Chinese news organizations also constantly point out the "two faced" or "double faced" nature of U.S. foreign policy. In doing so, they emphasize yet again that U.S.–China relations cannot be improved or fixed if Washington says one thing, and then does something else. If you make a promise or commitment, you keep it. Otherwise, there can be no trust between us. This is Beijing's position. Nothing indicates that the Chinese will change this, and there is no sign that Washington's anger will subside any time soon. It seems something has to give. But what? Fortunately, the solution could be surprisingly simple.[354]

Stopping a New Cold War

The late Howard Zinn wrote a most remarkable book. Its title is *A People's History of the United States*, and it is a fascinating read. Zinn treats history differently than virtually all other historians do. The average history book tells the stories of kings, emperors, presidents, and generals. We learn about their successes and failures, and how their actions have shaped events and impacted populations, countries, and even the entire world. Zinn, however, does not. He puts people, ordinary people, at the center. History is made by them, by us, far more often than you may think.[355]

The point here is not to completely downplay the significance of those leaders whose names and faces cover our history books. But it would be a mistake to overstate their importance. As Zinn shows, great moments of historical change have their roots below. Indeed, "the countless small actions of unknown people" have transformed societies and shaped the turn of events far more so than the decrees of kings and presidents. In fact, the power elite often only manage to stand in the way.[356]

What typically happens is that when populations have legitimate grievances, they start to demand change. A long and often difficult struggle then ensues between the people below against the resistance of the power elite at the top. From popular demands for more equality, more democracy, freedom

[353] Da Wei. *How Can We Achieve New Stability on the Taiwan Issue - Dialogue, Crisis, or War?* China Foundation for International Studies. August 22, 2022. English translation made available by CSIS, Interpret: China, p. 4.

[354] Global Times. US cannot be 'double-faced' if it really wants to fix China ties: Global Times editorial. December 13, 2022. See https://www.globaltimes.cn/page/202212/1281727.shtml

[355] Zinn. H. (2015). *A People's History of the United States.* HarperCollins Publishers Inc.

[356] Chomsky. N. Remembering Howard Zinn. Resist newsletter, March/April 2010. See https://chomsky.info/201002__/

of speech, and ending wars, these have all been resisted by those in power until the very end. Sometimes, the struggle was successful and society changed for the better and lives were saved. Other times, however, the power elite prevailed, and democracy, freedom, and peace suffered as a result.

This then begs the question: what can we do? How do we put an end to the developing U.S.–China Cold War? And is this even possible?

At the moment of this writing, the world is moving towards World War III. Where, when, and how it will begin, nobody knows. But our own leaders are determined to see it through to the end. They will destroy the world before recognizing China as an equal and treating it as such.

The only ones who can put a stop to it are us. Resistance from the mass of the population, whether organized or spontaneous, is our only hope. When you decide to join this struggle, you will not only be helping to create a better world and safer lives, but you will also be among those who helped stop two superpowers from destroying the world. And who wouldn't want to be a part of that?

Printed in the United States
by Baker & Taylor Publisher Services